Tuning Out Blackness

Tuning Out

Console-ing Passions

Television and Cultural Power

Edited by LYNN SPIGEL

Blackness

YEIDY M. RIVERO

RACE & NATION IN THE

HISTORY OF PUERTO RICAN

TELEVISION

DUKE UNIVERSITY PRESS

Durham and London 2005

© 2005 Duke University Press

Printed in the United States of America on acid-free paper ∞

Typeset in Minion by Tseng Information Systems, Inc.

Library of Congress Cataloging-in-Publication Data appear

on the last printed page of this book.

To my theater friends
and to my parents,
Agustín Rivero Quintero
and Iris Vázquez Merced

Contents

Acknowledgments

Anyone who performs studies on television knows that access is essential. In the case of Puerto Rico, where there is a vacuum of research in the area of media studies and where most documents and visual materials are in the hands of private corporations and individuals, the issue of access is even more relevant. That is precisely why this study would have been impossible without the unconditional support of my theater friends.

I cannot recount how many times I heard the comforting words (in Spanish) "do not worry, I will get the tape for you" (or whatever I was desperately looking for), or "so and so is expecting your call." These friends never let me down. What is more, throughout the seven years of sporadic phone calls and visits to Puerto Rico and New York City, these *teatreros* (theater people) served as personal cheerleaders in addition to offering something that I really miss from my theater years: relaxing, unpretentious, and witty conversations filled with laughter.

Two of these ex-colleagues, Judith Pizarro and Deborah Carthy-Deu, played a crucial role in various stages of my research. Judith opened the doors to Telemundo-Puerto Rico and Paquito Cordero Teleproducciones. Also, thanks to Judith, *Mi familia*'s creative personnel welcomed me as another "player on the team." Deborah coordinated interviews with several media professionals and used her universal Puerto Rico power to get me tapes from shows and contacts inside Puerto Rico's modeling world. Deborah also took time from her extremely busy schedule to dig up information and last minute material unavailable in the United States. I never heard a "no" from Judith Pizarro or Deborah Carthy-Deu. That is why no words can express my immense gratitude.

Pablo Cabrera, Tony Chiroldes-Carbia, and Radamés Vega also contributed to the hunting and research process. Pablo not only offered valuable firsthand information about television but he also connected me with a network of television professionals. Tony confirmed my worst fears that Leopoldo Fernández's documents might be in a garbage can somewhere in Hialeah. However, thanks to Tony, I was able to contact individuals who have impressive private collections of Puerto Rican popular culture. Finally, Radamés provided the highly guarded—and thus not publishable—Mediafax numbers (which means the reader has to trust me when I write "a highly rated show"). Thanks to these friends, other contacts emerged from a snow-ball sampling.

This project also benefited immensely from the "kindness of strangers," some of who are not strangers anymore. I am extremely grateful to Alicia Bibiloni and José Orbi who lent me all of Ramón Rivero's scripts and pho-tos and who welcomed me into their home (primo Puerto Rican coffee in-cluded). Mayra Montero and Olga Montero allowed me to borrow Manuel Montero's scripts for an "indefinite period of time." Javier Santiago and Dr. Carmen S. Ortega supplied key documents from *La Fundación Nacional para la Cultura Popular*. In addition, Javier shared his private Luz Ester Benítez (Lucecita) and Wilnelia Merced collections and provided many of the photos included in this book. I am indebted to the openness, goodwill, and trust of these individuals.

Several media professionals offered important information on Puerto Rico's commercial television in particular and media and popular culture in general. Thanks to William Agosto, Amaury Ayala, Carlos Camuñas, Berta Cordero, Jorge Cordero, Paquito Cordero and Paquito Cordero Teleproduc-ciones, Magdalis Cruz, Malín Falú, Brunilda García, Flavia García, William García, Lillian Hurst, Felipe Jiménez, Victor Montilla, Tommy Muñiz, the late and enormously influential yet sadly forgotten *telenovela* director Raúl Nacer, Vilma Reyes, Angel F. Rivera, Gilo Rivera, Luis Antonio Rivera, Ray Rodríguez, Felipe San Pedro, Telemundo–Puerto Rico executives, sales rep-resentatives, and technical personnel, and Otilio Warrington. Thanks also to Ramón Luis Brenes-Berríos at *Teve Guía* magazine, Gabriel Suau, Mayra Cue-Sierra—my Cuban contact in Cuba—the staff of the Cuban Heritage Col-lection at the University of Miami, Nélida Pérez at Hunter College's Center for Puerto Rican Studies Library, and the librarians and staff of *La colección puertorriqueña* at the University of Puerto Rico, Río Piedras campus.

Many of the ideas presented in this book began to develop during my years in the Radio, Television, and Film Department at the University of Texas, Austin. Here I had the privilege of studying with fine scholars and teachers. While not directly involved in my dissertation, Federico Subervi and Karin Wilkins were (and still are) great supporters of my scholarship. Dana Cloud and América Rodríguez offered invaluable comments during the dissertation process. Horace Newcomb, Cesar Salgado, and John Downing began as my professors and became my mentors. Newcomb shared his contagious passion for television and taught me to love the medium while maintaining a critical eye. Salgado, who as I am, is fascinated with the Spanish Caribbean, provided challenging questions about the relationship between Puerto Rico and Cuba. And of course, a key member of the team was the remarkable John Downing (i.e., J.D.-JDito—the Renaissance man). Only those who have had the privilege of working with J.D. truly know how caring he is. As a first-class educator, J.D. guides his students without threatening them with his broad and well-rounded knowledge. Simply put, J.D. is an impressive scholar and a great human being, the latter which, at least for me, is far more important. Last, I want to thank Trudy's Restaurant for its Mexican martinis and mango margaritas, which offered Cesar Salgado, Sonia Labrador, and me an extra incentive to talk for hours and even philosophize (mostly Cesar, of course!) about what Cesar categorized as the CubaRican space.

Throughout the years, I have shared my ideas with other colleagues who, in return, engaged in fascinating dialogues and motivated me to continue this research. I am grateful to Nancy Morris who provided eminently useful feedback during various stages of this project. Susana Kaiser, Clemencia Rodríguez, and Naomi Warren have provided friendship and sensitive ears during moments of academic frustration. Eva Cherniavsky, my colleague at Indiana University, Bloomington, expressed immediate interest in my project. Even though—like most academics—Eva did not have a lot of time to spare, she willingly read parts of the manuscript and offered thoughtful suggestions. Additionally, this research benefited from questions from anonymous reviewers at two International Communication Association conferences, the *Centro Journal*, and *Media, Culture, and Society*.

I am also grateful to Chon Noriega for inviting me to participate in the "Race and Independent Media Project" and for welcoming me into the Chicano Studies Research Center (CSRC) during the 2003–2004 academic year. Chon and the CSRC team received this *boricua* with open arms. Furthermore, the research, writing, and publishing of this book enjoyed financial support from the Ford Foundation Post-Doctoral Fellowship Program, Indiana University's Research Leave Supplement, the Office of the Vice President for Research, and the Department of Communication and Culture.

I want to thank all my colleagues at Indiana University, Bloomington, Department of Communication and Culture, Latino Studies, Latin American and Caribbean Studies, and American Studies. Special thanks to Christopher Anderson, Richard Bauman, Nicky Evans, Jane Goodman, Joan Hawkins,

Roopali Mukherjee, Beverly Stoeltje, and Robert Terrill for their mentorship. Thanks also to Patricia Andrews, Carolyn Calloway-Thomas, Jorge Chapas, Sam Cronk, Arlene Díaz, Tom Foster, Jeffrey Gould, Robert Ivy, Daniel James, Candida Jaquez, Barbara Klinger, John Lucaites, James Naremore, Phaedra Pezzullo, Darlene J. Sadlier, and Gregory A. Waller for their support. I am also grateful to Darrel Enck-Wanzer for sharing his passion for the Young Lords, and to Bonnie Clendening, Amy Cornell, Sonja Rasmussen, and Sabrina Walker for their never-ending assistance.

From the first day that I met Ken Wissoker, I knew that he was the right editor for this project. Not only was he engaged with the topic but I was pleasantly surprised to discover that he was also familiar with many of the issues that I address in this book. Ken, Christine Dahlin, Courtney Berger, and Pam Morrison at Duke University Press were extremely helpful in the birth of this book.

This work matured, directly and indirectly, from the steady phone calls and e-mail interventions of a close network of friends and family. Ramón Albino, Axel Cintrón, Harry Nadal, Shirley Santos, Rochelly Serrano, and Eva Cristina Vázques have helped me keep in touch with reality. My dearest friend Gilberto Blasini asked stimulating questions throughout the entire writing process and provided constant encouragement. Who would have thought that two people who became friends in seventh grade were going to continue a personal and professional relationship for so many years? My parents, Agustín Rivero Quintero and Iris Vázquez Merced, have always been present, offering their emotional and, in some cases, financial backing. As dedicated parents, they have provided their unconditional love. And not to be undervalued, thanks to my parents I was able to consume daily doses of Puerto Rican coffee.

Finally, the research and writing of this book would have been an incredibly lonely and arduous enterprise without my partner Stephen Berrey. Stephen has been my main reader and academic supporter. He read several drafts of this book and, as an intelligent historian, he constantly asked me thought-provoking questions. Stephen has also helped me keep things in perspective during moments of professional crisis. His love, trust, and wittiness have been my emotional antibiotics for the superciliousness of some members of this profession. Indeed, Stephen has helped me regain part of my personality that I thought I had lost: my sense of humor. For all of these things and many others, I simply say, *mil gracias.*

Translating Televisual "Blackness"

It was a time when we were islanders, and the sea, on every side the sea, was our only frontier. We lived surrounded by water and submerged in family tradition. And we have always been good, my brother and I. We ran in the solitude of our house, playing with American toy soldiers, Spanish decks of cards, and with dreams of leaving forever. We were growing up in the brightness of Puerto Rican mornings and in the shadow of the trees that shaded houses full of shadows in the stupor of identical and tranquil afternoons of Santurce in the fifties.

   Magali García Ramis, *Happy Days Uncle Sergio*

And in this warehouse that Pedro borrowed and that has an interior, I mean, an inside part, his best friends are waiting for him, I mean, Lindbergh, Moncho Tarralla, Glostora, Chan el Cabro and Jalisco. . . . Jalisco is the artist who came from abroad, so we can sell the *telenovela* abroad. . . . You know how it is!

   El lince de la barandilla in Pablo Cabrera's 1980 play
   La verdadera historia de Pedro Navaja

Ok, and now you are going to look at the camera and you are going to say these very simple lines: "bunga, bunga, water." Remember the character . . . give me more flavor . . . more . . . it is the Caribbean, more . . . rhythm.

   Javier Cardona's 1997 performance piece *You Don't Look Like*

On September 14, 1994, after forty years of local programming Telemundo's network affiliate in Puerto Rico (wkaq–channel 2) began to broadcast *Mi familia* (My Family), the first locally produced situation comedy in the history of Puerto Rico's commercial television featuring a fictional "black" family. According to one of *Mi familia*'s production members, the show's idea originated after witnessing the commercial success of U.S. "black"-oriented situation comedies such as *The Jeffersons* and *The Cosby Show*. However, the media professional noted that contrary to these U.S. programs, in *Mi familia* "there is no color, there is nothing established. The show is about a Puerto Rican family, period."[1]

In contrast, on January 17, 2000, the Ramón Rivero Foundation announced the possibility of reviving Ramón Rivero's character Diplo, the most famous "black" voice and blackface character in Puerto Rico. According to the president of the foundation, "the people longed for that figure who made them laugh for many years and who had become part of the people's consciousness."[2] Although the foundation's plans have not yet become a reality, a plethora of blackface *negrito* and *negra* characters performed by "white" actors and actresses have intermittently surfaced on the island's commercial television since its beginning in 1954.

The transformation from U.S. televisual "blackness" to a "colorless" *Puerto Ricanness* expressed by a *Mi familia* production member and the ongoing use of blackface hint at the differences between U.S. and Puerto Rican racial ideologies and cultures. In addition, while seemingly not interconnected, "colorless" and blackface bring to light the U.S.-P.R. cultural, political, and social tensions on the island and the ongoing debates regarding the distinctions between these two nations. Within these discourses of difference, "race" and "race" relations in Puerto Rico are generally located as distinctly superior antitheses to U.S. racial practices.

This study examines the ways in which "blackness" has been represented and discussed in Puerto Rico's commercial media entertainment programming. By focusing on "black" voice and blackface characters that became popular media icons, locally produced radio and television shows, and particular racialized TV events, this book disentangles the ways in which Puerto Rico's racial discourses and cultural, political, and social practices have permeated the island's mediated "blackness." I do not aim to deconstruct every single "black" character or locally produced show with "black" performers who have been part of Puerto Rico's commercial television. Rather, this study considers the translations and significations of the media's racial representations during particular historical periods and the ways in which the island's racial ideologies, together with specific political, economic, and sociocultural conditions influenced these constructions.

In exploring how race was constructed within Puerto Rican television and media, the concept of translating blackness is a useful analytical tool. Translating blackness refers to a multiplicity of meanings that relate not only to the appropriation and adaptation of a particular foreign theater genre, character, or television show but also to the media professionals' and audiences' negotiations of race, politics, culture, and socioeconomic shifts during formative historical moments. From Ramón Rivero's 1940s black voice radio era to the 1990s situation comedy *Mi familia*, the island's media constructions and discussions of blackness functioned through historically specific ideological processes that fostered a variety of racial, political, cultural, and social meanings. These diverse manifestations of mediated blackness were largely informed by four primary discursive *translations*: the articulation of Puerto Rico's *mestizaje* and racial democracy discourses; debates regarding U.S. colonial control and cultural influences on the island; the conciliation of "local" and "foreign" alternative political, cultural, and social movements; and the sociocultural responses and contentions associated with the post-1959 Cuban migration to Puerto Rico. In other words, embodiments of "blackness" within Puerto Rico's entertainment programming were connected not only to the nation's racial discourses but also to the relations between Cuba and Puerto Rico before 1959, the Cuban post-Revolution migration, and Puerto Rican-U.S. colonial relations.

Puerto Rico's hegemonic national culture and its ideology of a racially integrated (*mestiza*) and raceless "ethnic family" were defining elements in the translations of blackness in Puerto Rico's media from the late 1940s to the 1990s. The ongoing rearticulation of discourses of Puerto Ricanness that mark the boundaries of "family" membership circumscribed portrayals of "blackness" and their significations. Who was (and still is) deemed a member of the Puerto Rican ethnic family, the member's position within the family's racial and cultural hierarchical structures, as well as the "outside" (ethnic) members' historically ingrained connections, racial mobility, and power to negotiate their inclusion into the family were fundamental ideological factors in the representations and interpretations of mediated blackness in Puerto Rico.

Whereas this project primarily focuses on the discursive realms of signification that specific media artifacts, dialogues, and televisual events conveyed in relation to "family," racial ideologies, and "blackness," more generally this study also addresses the academically unexamined and thus uncertain location of Puerto Rico's commercial television. The relationship between Puerto Rico and the United States is pivotal in this research, not only to understand some racial translations, political discussions, and familial marginalizations but equally important, to comprehend the cultural, legal, and economic position of the island's commercial media. Culturally, to delve into Puerto Rico's commercial local programming is to map routes through moments in history and observe the ways in which some producers, scriptwriters, and performers utilized the medium to discuss, reproduce, and sometimes even radically challenge dominant social, political, and racial discourses. To explore locally produced programs is also to discover multiple crossroads that directly and indirectly linked Puerto Rico to the United States, the Spanish Caribbean, and Latin America. Legally and economically, to broach the subject of Puerto Rico's commercial media one should consider its unique position within the U.S. broadcasting system.

Even though since its inception the island's commercial medium has been interconnected to both the United States and Latin America, television in Puerto Rico has been largely erased from these regions' media histories. In terms of U.S. studies, the island's complex, unresolved, and even confounding political situation might have accounted for this academic exclusion. Simply put, the fact that Puerto Rico is defined as a Commonwealth, a political status that nationally situates the island as autonomous within the United States, even while it is completely beholden to it in practice, might have influenced the academic invisibility. However, given that in 1898 Puerto Rico became a U.S. colony, that in 1917 Puerto Ricans obtained U.S. citizenship, and that the Federal Communications Commission (FCC) controls the island's media, Puerto Rico's commercial television is U.S. Spanish-language television.

From a strict political and legal perspective then, the first U.S. Spanish-language television stations were on the island.[3] Therefore, while some scholars locate the first station in San Antonio, Texas (KCOR-TV, 1955), and others situate the 1961 KMEX (Los Angeles) and KWEX (San Antonio) as the first two Spanish-language television stations, in reality, those stations emerged after Puerto Rico's WKAQ-Telemundo, channel 2 (March 1954) and WAPA-TV, channel 4 (May 1954).[4] My aim in including this basic chronological information is not to question research on U.S. Spanish-language media or the significance of exploring these early groundbreaking stations. Instead, I cite these examples to illustrate the absence of Puerto Rico in U.S. television scholarship.

Although most television scholars completely ignore Puerto Rico, some of the few who include it often focus exclusively on the island's colonial position to the United States, rendering indigenous elements and discussions of the national invisible.[5] In other words, these scholars' analyses are overdetermined by the cultural imperialism paradigm. True, if one considers that the

Commonwealth government has no legal control over its communication systems and that currently all commercial television stations are part of U.S. and multinational conglomerates, Puerto Rico might be characterized as the epitome of media imperialism. These political, legal, and economic conditions might explain why, according to some scholars, U.S. colonial power has precluded the possibilities of any debates in the local televisual landscape. This position is clearly laid out by Roberta Astroff:

> Because of the economic, political, and social constraints and motivations that shape television in Puerto Rico, there cannot even be discussion on the possible uses of broadcasting as a forum for questions of national concern. The questions of political status, of the use and quality of Spanish on the island, of solutions to social and economic problems, and of national culture are excluded by both the economic system of broadcasting, i.e. the "logic" for the industry, and by the decision makers in the industry who have no interest in creating a public forum for questions they would rather see disappear. There is considerable question as to whether television can be that forum under any circumstances.[6]

Throughout this book it will become evident that Astroff's analysis is indeed misleading. Puerto Rico's locally produced shows have in fact created various sites for discussions of social, cultural, and political issues. What is more, media and television professionals' (or "cultural *bricoleurs*") identities have been significant in the representation of particular political and social themes in media texts.[7] Privileging television's economic and legal components without performing close analyses of texts and of the diverse creative individuals involved in the production of televisual cultural artifacts risks overgeneralization by classifying locally produced programs as examples of U.S. cultural imperialism.

On the other hand, with rare exceptions, studies on Latin American television have also neglected Puerto Rico.[8] Considering the multiple exchanges between television professionals among Puerto Rico and countries such as Cuba (before 1959), Peru, Venezuela, and Mexico, one might expect Latin American scholars to be fully aware of the island's commercial medium. Yet, research on Latin American television has largely focused on telenovelas or on the major players (Mexico and Brazil) that since the 1980s have dominated the regional and global exportation of this cultural product. To be sure, these studies are valuable because they demonstrate that exchanges in the region transcend the predominance of U.S. commercial television. Still, there seems to be a research fixation on powerful media conglomerates. Not surprisingly, a small television market such as Puerto Rico, which for the most part remained "local," has been ignored. In addition, the island's Commonwealth status and FCC regulation may also be responsible for Puerto Rico's exclusion from Latin American television histories.

Similar to the cultural imperialist approach, Latin American scholars may tend to see Puerto Rico's commercial television as lacking cultural autonomy from the United States. However, this silence implies either that Puerto Rican television is insignificant because of its minor influence outside the island or that because of its colonial status, the island's television is not a site of local cultural agency. In the process, academics have silenced the voices of those on the island who have been producing, writing, directing, and performing on television. Through large-scale political economy interpretations, scholars have obfuscated the cultural, social, and political debates that have been part of Puerto Rico's locally produced programs since 1954.

The value of examining local television, its cultural elements, creative interactions, and production processes brings us to a vast and critical group of individuals—media and television professionals. In Puerto Rico, television professionals include station executives (station director, programmer, sales director, and sales representatives, among others), station technical staff, independent production teams (producer, assistant producer, scriptwriter, director, and so forth), and *talento* (talent) (such as actors, masters of ceremony, models, singers, and bands). Based on my formal and informal conversations with members of these distinct subgroups, it is clear that media and television professionals in Puerto Rico are fully aware of the Commonwealth government's lack of control. The selling of local stations that first began in the mid-1970s and then intensified in the 1980s and the drop in local programming that accelerated in the 1990s have directly affected the lives of technical staff, independent producers, scriptwriters, directors, and performers. Actually, at the end of the 1980s when telenovelas ceased to be produced by the two most successful stations in Puerto Rico (WKAQ-Telemundo, channel 2 and WAPA-TV Televicentro, channel 4), several unemployed actors migrated to Miami, New York City, and Los Angeles. Despite disparate legal, political, and economic conditions, members of media and television's diverse subgroups still categorized locally produced shows as "Puerto Rican."

This mediatic Puerto Ricanness alludes to the cultural, social, and political ideological discourses associated with Puerto Rico's national and vernacular cultures that have been repackaged and represented in local texts. This Puerto Ricanness also implies the multiple mediations of the local where through accents, embodiments, performances, and commentaries, televisual shows have operated as *acts of transfer* "transmitting social knowledge, memory, and a sense of identity."[9] In sum, the media and television professionals' description of locally produced programs as Puerto Rican refers to the island's distinct culture and identity based on a common heritage and history, a culture that makes it both Caribbean and Latin American.[10]

Puerto Rican also describes the ethnicity of the audience-consumers that are sold to advertisers in the U.S. dollar-run local television world. For programming, production, advertising, and rating purposes, television audiences in Puerto Rico are categorized by age and gender. Although social class is not part of the audience ratings classification, commercial stations tailor their programs to the lower-middle-class segment of the population.[11] Thus, the programming broadcast on commercial stations is designed and scheduled to sell and appeal to the majority of Puerto Ricans.

Implicitly, the media and television professionals' description of local shows as Puerto Rican brings to the forefront not only the local but also the regional (Spanish Caribbean and Latin American) and U.S. influences that have informed locally produced programs. Since 1954 many shows produced in Puerto Rico have borrowed genres, concepts, ideas, and scripts especially from the United States but also from pre-revolutionary Cuba and Latin American commercial television. Nonetheless, despite these "foreign" mediations, Puerto Rico's locally produced programs have functioned through what Milly Buonanno calls "the paradigm of indigenization." Buonanno contends that even though local television around the world is influenced by foreign (mostly American) forms, concepts, or genres, these local productions "give rise to new forms and products which are hybrid, original, and unmistakably domestic."[12] In the case of Puerto Rico's entertainment programming, these productions have created media artifacts that contain the cultural meanings associated with Puerto Rico's social spaces, even though, in some cases, the "original" idea was "borrowed" from a "foreign" place.

Bearing in mind the U.S. and Latin American intersections that have been part of Puerto Rico's commercial television since its inception, I locate the island's medium in an in-between cultural space. In fact, commercial television has functioned as a mediatic bridge. While maintaining a local perspective in terms of production, cultural representations, and inter-actions with audiences, it has also been connected with and influenced by these diverse regions. In terms of the Spanish Caribbean and Latin Ameri-can dynamic, the main associations have been present in the exchanges of creative people, the incorporation of performers and musicians in locally produced programs, the purchasing of scripts (particularly from Cuba be-fore 1959), and the importation of programming (first Mexican movies, but then also movies produced, for example, in Argentina, and Latin American telenovelas).

In the case of U.S. mainstream commercial television, the cultural influ-ences have been more prevalent in relation to television genres and pro-gram ideas and concepts. Whereas U.S. mainstream television programs and movies (dubbed in Spanish) have aired in Puerto Rico since 1954 and English-language cable television has been available in Puerto Rico since 1970, these cultural artifacts, at least until the late 1990s, were not widely consumed by local audiences.[13] It appears that audiences in Puerto Rico, as Joseph Straub-haar has argued in relation to Latin American television audiences, prefer to watch locally produced programs or shows that are "culturally similar" to their own experiences.[14]

However, while this mediatic bridge has linked the people on the island to Latin America and the United States, the results of contemporary global-ization processes have been detrimental to local programming. For example, consider Elizabeth Fox and Silvio Waisbord's observation regarding the 1990s revisionist research on media imperialism and the contemporary television globalization process:

> When revisionist studies first appeared, Brazilian and Mexican program-ming was flooding television screens in Latin America, Spanish-language networks in the United States, and newly opened markets in Europe. Perhaps it is necessary to take this revisionism a step further and ana-lyze television programming flows inside one region. Television in Latin America suggests that analysis of flows inside regional/linguistic markets also needs to discriminate among complex inflows and outflows.[15]

In the case of Puerto Rico, the main problem is not U.S. mainstream tele-vision programs. The principal menace comes from powerful Latin America media conglomerates such as Televisa and Venevision and from the U.S. Spanish-language networks, particularly the new (2001) player in Puerto

Rico: Univision.[16] One must remember that Puerto Rico's commercial television is legally and economically entrenched in the U.S. broadcasting system. Therefore, while television, as Thomas Streeter contends, "is something people do," the legal and economic ramifications of U.S. corporate liberalism "doings" have had a direct impact in Puerto Rico.[17] Given that the Commonwealth government has no way of controlling the ownership of local stations and the importation of programming, the FCC deregulations that have taken place in the United States have affected the people who work on and culturally "do" television.

Until the early 1980s, four principal commercial stations operated on the island: WKAQ-TV, WAPA-TV, WKBM-TV (channel 11), and WLUZ-TV (channel 7).[18] Although all of these stations combined local and imported programming, prime time (6:00 P.M.–10:30 P.M.) was dominated by locally produced shows. Additionally, even though producers have tested a wide variety of program formats in prime-time television, the genres that dominated prime-time until the 1980s for the most part included locally produced telenovelas, situation comedies, comedies, variety shows, music shows, game shows, and news magazine shows. Throughout the 1980s, as I previously mentioned, all stations became part of U.S. and multinational conglomerates and the production of local programming has gradually decreased. Although, according to some television professionals, local business groups were interested in buying either WKAQ or WAPA (the most profitable stations in Puerto Rico), these stations were sold at "exorbitantly high" prices and local groups "could not compete with the offers made by U.S. media conglomerates."[19]

Presently, three major commercial stations operate in Puerto Rico: WKAQ-Telemundo (channel 2) — part of Telemundo's network, which is owned by NBC; WAPA-TV Televicentro (channel 4) — owned by LIN Television; and WLII-TV (channel 11) — bought by Univision's network in 2001.[20] Before the arrival of Univision, all of these stations functioned as semi-independent entities. They established commercial autonomy through business arrangements with independent producers, programming selection, audience viewing measurements, and sponsors. Yet, this semi-independent business practice is being transformed by Univision. The Univision-Puerto Rico station (contrary to the Telemundo-Puerto Rico station and Televicentro) operates as a network — a totally new business entity in Puerto Rico's television market.

It is difficult to predict the future of Puerto Rico's commercial television.

Nonetheless, based on recent changes, the island seems to be rapidly moving toward becoming part of the U.S. Hispanic television market. For example, performers who formerly worked in Puerto Rican telenovelas were recruited to be part of Univision's "pan-ethnic" morning program produced in Miami. Some Puerto Rican comedians were hired to participate in Univision's Miami-based productions but were then required to eliminate vernacular Puerto Rican phrases and words from their acts in order to appeal to the U.S. Mexican majority that comprise the Hispanic television market.[21] A token Puerto Rican actress was hired by Televisa to participate in their telenovelas (which were then broadcast on Univision) and she substituted her Puerto Rican accent for a Mexican one. Miami, as John Sinclair writes regarding U.S. Spanish-language television, is the place "of exchanges between American continents," a space "of production, as well as distribution, and distribution of programs as well as of signals."[22] However, through the Univision-Miami signal, prime-time Hispanic television is dominated by Mexican imports.[23]

The in-between cultural space that has characterized Puerto Rico's commercial television could be transformed into a cultural place where the local may cease to exist. If Puerto Rico's television professionals are able to travel on what would become a new and exclusively one-way mediatic bridge, they would have to produce, write, direct, and perform television artifacts with generic (pan-ethnic) phrases and de-centered social, political, cultural, gendered, and racial meanings disconnected from the local. What is more, if Puerto Rico becomes Hispanic, audiences will consume a predominantly white televisual world. Yet, this U.S. Hispanic television whiteness does not correspond to the U.S. black and white racial ideologies and practices. Instead, its whiteness comes from the Latin American televisual invisibility of blacks, mulattos, and indigenous-looking people.[24] Thus, all the struggles that black Puerto Rican performers endured to have a place for translating blackness in the local televisual landscape might soon become anecdotes from the past. I therefore hope that the research presented throughout these pages will open dialogues not only about the absence of black and indigenous citizens in Latin America's commercial televisual world but equally important, about the relevance of maintaining local television sites of production and consumption.

Given that this project examines local media and audience translations of blackness, I would like to clarify my own position as a cultural translator. I was born and raised in Puerto Rico, which situates me as part of the constructed "ethnic family." I grew up watching Puerto Rico's commercial television and was an avid fan of some of the shows and characters discussed in this research. I donned blackface for my second grade talent show and became a miniature version of the hugely popular 1970s Puerto Rican blackface character Chianita. In the Catholic school where I studied, none of the Spanish nuns or Puerto Rican and Cuban teachers seemed to have a problem with my performance. All of us sang and danced to Chianita's hit song *Chianita gobernadora* (Chianita for governor).

For many years I was oblivious to the racial hierarchies and racist practices that affected the daily life of the black and mulatto islanders. Like many Puerto Ricans, I had been taught that racism was not part of the culture despite the fact that I had grown up listening to derogatory remarks about black and mulatto people. It was not until I began my studies at the University of Puerto Rico (UPR) Drama Department that my privileged middle-class and "white" (I am considered white in Puerto Rico and the Spanish Caribbean) perceptions crumbled and my process of *conscientização* (consciousness raising) began.[25] It did not matter how hard my black and *trigueño/a* (mulatto) colleagues worked for a college play audition or how talented they were or how elegantly they dressed for a commercial casting call, they were nearly always dismissed. Indeed, few of these former colleagues were able to enter Puerto Rico's commercial television. Still, some of the people I met during my theater years, following the long established tradition of negrito characters, have performed in blackface.

The connections and friendships that I established while studying and performing in college and commercial theater productions in Puerto Rico and in New York City (Spanish-language theater) facilitated my access to various sources of information that are not generally available to the public. Also, while I cannot provide any concrete evidence, I assume that because of my race, class, and education, some of the media and television professionals interviewed for this research were more open than they might have otherwise been about their understanding of blackness and race relations in Puerto Rico. Along with my associations with the less powerful individuals in Puerto Rico's commercial television (the actors) and my Puerto Rican and Spanish Caribbean whiteness, the respect that I have for television's creative community established an ambiance of camaraderie between me and this study's participants. In their view (and mine, too), they are important agents in the production of culture and they understand that because of the elitism (i.e., high versus low culture hierarchies) that characterizes some academic circles in Puerto Rico, their contributions are frequently devalued.

Nonetheless, throughout this book, I am critical of television characters, performers, producers, writers, journalists, and the industry. It is not my intention to characterize media and television professionals as insensitive and bigoted individuals. It is counterproductive to blame media and television professionals because, as Stuart Hall argues, ideologies are part of a larger system of meanings located in specific social formations.[26] Instead of focusing on the often prejudiced actions and views of media and television creators, journalists, and audiences, a far more valuable endeavor is to examine these performances and opinions within the context of Puerto Rican culture, society, and historical processes. Consequently, to understand Puerto Rico's commercial media and audiences' translations of blackness, one first needs to consider the formation of *la gran familia puertorriqueña* (the wide Puerto Rican family) discourse.

Puerto Rico: A Mestiza "Family"

Since 1898 and as a result of the Spanish American War, Puerto Rico has been defined as a territory that "legally belongs to but is not part of the United States."[27] Whereas Puerto Rico is not sovereign, this Spanish Caribbean island is, as Nancy Morris contends, a nation, "a self-defined community of people who share a sense of solidarity based on a belief in a common heritage and who claim political rights that may include self-determination."[28] Despite constant and multidimensional efforts by the U.S. government to Americanize the islanders and the existence of three political parties largely differentiated by their stance on the island's status (pro-statehood, pro-commonwealth, and pro-independence), many Puerto Ricans do not feel culturally attached to the United States.[29] The direct and indirect U.S. colonial, legal, economic, political, and cultural presence along with the island's complex status has actually "strengthened the sense of peoplehood among Puerto Ricans."[30]

Although the levels of cultural nationalism in Puerto Rico might fluctuate according to political preferences, there has been an ongoing official discourse regarding Puerto Rican national "authenticity" and ethnic unity vis-à-vis the U.S. cultural, political, and economic influences.[31] Several scholars have argued that the core of Puerto Rico's national culture and identity discourses emerged during the 1930s.[32] The intellectual discussions of this era crystallized the location of blackness within the island's national culture and the formation of the ideologies of racial and cultural mestizaje that inform Puerto Rico's identity.

During the economic and political transformations generated by the island's annexation to the United States, several intellectuals questioned the essence of its culture and identity.[33] La gran familia puertorriqueña, an ideological discourse developed by nineteenth-century Puerto Rican *hacendados* (landowners) to forge class and racial solidarity against the Spanish colonial government, was rearticulated to affirm Puerto Rico's national unity against the new colonial regime. Throughout this period of identity formation, "race" and "blackness" became integral elements in the discussion of the spirit of Puerto Rico's people and culture. Although it is difficult to summarize the 1930s debate, particularly because intellectuals presented numerous perspectives in terms of Puerto Rico's historical, social, economic, political, cultural, and gender dynamics, one can map distinctive discursive formations of race.

Some intellectuals, influenced by the Eurocentric biological paradigm of race, assigned specific moral, cultural, and psychological attributes to white, black, and mulatto populations, while concomitantly situating the white race as intellectually and morally superior.[34] Others focused on the distinctions between the U.S. and Puerto Rican (Spanish) slavery institutions and race relations, describing the island's culture as nonracist and mestiza (mixed), but primarily occidental (Spanish), thus positioning African elements and people as moderate influences within the island's cultural and social terrains.[35] A final group "celebrated" the African elements of the culture through the *cultura negroide* movement.[36] These writers' cultural productions located blackness as a key component of Puerto Rico's identity, and more broadly, as the unifying cultural and racial symbol of a transnational *Caribbeanness*. Although the 1930s debates depicted complex and even contradictory postures regarding race and blackness, the core of Puerto Rico's hegemonic identity was defined as racially and culturally mestiza yet as a predominantly white (European or Spanish) family.

In Puerto Rico, as in many Latin American and Spanish Caribbean nations, mestizaje, or racial mixing, is a key factor in the construction of a racially integrated society, because everyone, regardless of skin color, is racially mixed and hence, an equal member within the nation.[37] However, behind the comforting screen of racial mestizaje lies the racist ideology and process of *blanqueamiento* (whitening) where racial mixing with white (European) people makes populations whiter, thereby improving on or lessening the supposedly inferior black or Indian racial traits. Conversely, this racial mixing is sometimes constrained by class. For example, mixing among lower-class segments of the population was commonly practiced during the Spanish colonial period in Puerto Rico and in the Spanish Caribbean.[38] Also, while some mixing may occur among upper classes in Puerto Rico and other Latin American and Spanish Caribbean nations, the practice is more common among lower classes who might see it as a path to material gain and social status.[39]

Mestizaje not only delimits sexual mixing between distinct sectors of the population, it also permeates the ways in which gendered racial bodies are socially constructed. In Puerto Rico, as in other Latin American countries, the Eurocentric-patriarchal gaze has informed discourses of beauty and sexuality, situating whiteness as the epitome of elegance for the female body. From beauty pageants to televisual representations, the beautiful body embodies "the mythical norms of [a] Eurocentric esthetic."[40] Conversely, in Puerto Rico and Cuba, black and *mulata* women have been socially constructed as hypersexual and sensual bodies. In addition, the mulata has also been positioned as a socially permissible outlet for white males' sexual desire, and as a result, an acceptable avenue for racial mixing.[41]

On the cultural terrain, mestizaje highlights the egalitarian fusion of European, African, and indigenous cultures and traits, constructing a nationally mixed culture and identity. In Puerto Rico, cultural mestizaje represents the amalgamation of *Taíno* (indigenous), African, and Spanish elements. Within this cultural formation, black and mulatto contributions (for example, musical styles such as *Bomba* and *Plena*) are part of the national culture.[42] Nonetheless, the primary symbols of Puerto Ricanness are the *jíbaro* (white mountain peasant) and jíbaro music. An iconic figure created by the nineteenth-century hacendados, the jíbaro represents Puerto Rico's authentic culture and identity, a symbol that reaffirms racial and class hierarchies among white, black, and mulatto Puerto Ricans.[43] Furthermore, within this hegemonic negotiation of Puerto Ricanness, "whiteness" is defined as the central component of the national culture, while Spain is situated as the motherland in historic and contemporary public discourses.

La gran familia puertorriqueña discourse, the ideology of an integrated

mestiza culture and identity, and contentions on the island between Puerto
Rico and the United States informed locally produced programs' black representations, racialized debates, and discussions of the national from the 1940s
to the 1990s. From Ramón Rivero's complex use of blackface and black voice
to criticize class stratification and colonial subjugation in the 1940s and 1950s,
to the 1970s battle between black actors and television industry officials over
blackface and antiblack racism, to the 1990s creation of a situation comedy
with a black family that was "Puerto Rican, period," la gran familia puertorriqueña played a prominent role in the media's and audiences' translations of
blackness. In sum, the social and historical construction of the Puerto Rican
national culture and identity that emerged in the 1930s, but that has been
constantly rearticulated through the decades, has functioned as a symbolic
shield against the United States. By creating an imaginary island-based unified cultural space that can counteract U.S. influences and Americanization,
discussions of race and racism are generally evaded because problematizing
the national culture can result in the division of a unified collective identity. However, although la gran familia puertorriqueña discourse creates and
promotes a color-blind and culturally mixed sociocultural space, a series of
racial categorizations and cultural practices that comprise the vernacular ex-
poses the myth of racial equality.

"Race" and Racial Categories in Puerto Rico

"Race" in Puerto Rico, the Spanish Caribbean, and Latin America can
be understood as a social construction influenced by Western (colonial and
racial) ideologies but which manifests itself in particular cultural practices.
In other words, even though there might be similarities regarding race and
racial constructions throughout the (Western) world in general and the
Spanish Caribbean and Latin America in particular, race responds to specific
"colonial/racial formations" based on distinct social, historical, political, and
cultural contexts.[44] In Puerto Rico, as previously discussed, the established
polarity between Puerto Rican and U.S. cultures and racial ideologies has
produced a dominant misconception that prejudice is effectively nonexistent
on the island.

Despite the widespread prevalence of the ideology of an egalitarian national space, the island is not a racially harmonious society. This is clearly
seen in the ongoing racial prejudice against Puerto Rican blacks in general, and, more recently, against Dominican immigrants. These immigrants,

who are primarily mulattos and blacks, have been cast as scapegoats for the island's economic and social problems.[45] Furthermore, according to the 2000 Census, 10.8 percent of the island's population defined themselves as "black," while 84 percent categorized themselves as "white."[46] It seems that, as one writer has remarked, Puerto Ricans opted to become "Nordic."[47] Certainly, one of the reasons for this outcome was that the census used in Puerto Rico followed U.S. black-white categorizations. However, these classifications do not tell the whole story.

Similar to other Latin American and Spanish Caribbean nations, racial categories in Puerto Rico are most clearly associated with physical appearance and in some cases social status but not the specifics of biological descent.[48] The range of racial classifications includes *negro, moreno, prieto, trigueño, indio, jabao,* and *blanco.* It is extremely difficult to translate these terms because they are rooted in the island's vernacular language. However, in general, negro, moreno, and prieto mean black; trigueño is a shade of brown and can be categorized as mulatto; indio means Taíno (indigenous) looking; jabao refers to a person whose skin color is white but who has features commonly associated with black people; and blanco means white. In addition, like some of the previous categorizations (trigueño and prieto), *gente de color* (colored people) and negrito have been used in Puerto Rico and in some Latin American societies to avoid using the term *negro* (black).[49]

Negrito/a (diminutive for black) is currently used in Cuba and Puerto Rico and is sometimes employed as a derogatory reference to black people. Although *negrito/a* and *negro/a* may be used in reference to blacks, in Puerto Rico it has also been adopted as a term of affection, regardless of race. A person may be called negrito/a or negro/a despite the fact that this individual may have white skin. Likewise, a series of phrases rooted in racial stereotyping inform the vernacular and espouse a problematic construction of blackness. For example, the expression *mejorar la raza* (improve the race) codes the belief that black and mulatto people should marry white individuals to improve or *blanquear* (whiten) their race. Conversely, the socially constructed and derogatory phrase *tiene raja* or *se le ve la raja* means that a person has visible black features (nose, hair, or lips) even though her or his skin is white.

The issue of racial consciousness and the historically and culturally ingrained ideology of a nonracist society permeate the recurrent use of the aforementioned socially and culturally normalized proverbs. Puerto Rico, contrary to the United States, South Africa, and Brazil (*Movimiento negro*), has never witnessed any large-scale political and social mobilization against racism. Newspaper articles, local organizations, individuals, and performers have certainly criticized the island's closeted racism.[50] Still, many of these discussions have occurred on special occasions such as the discovery of the Americas, the emancipation of slavery, or more recently, the anniversary of Dr. Martin Luther King Jr.'s birthday. Furthermore, as Miriam Jiménez-Román contends, those who have protested against racism on the island "have been labeled overly sensitive, as suffering from an inferiority complex, or as unwitting victims of an imported, i.e. alien racial ideology."[51] Protests against racism generally reactivate the U.S.-Puerto Rico cultural debates and the historical differences between the two nations' racial discourses.

Through these racial categorizations, cultural discourses, and historical processes, Puerto Rico's commercial media representations of and discussions on blackness functioned within the theatricality of nationalism embedded in la gran familia puertorriqueña discourse. The theatricality of nationalism to which I refer relates to the ways in which public performances and discourses (or to use James C. Scott's theoretical concept, *public transcripts*) across historical periods have operated as theatrical, staged, or scripted discursive representations to create "scenarios" of racial equality.[52] These scenarios of mestizaje, racial fairness, and ethnic unity have been performed in an ongoing juxtaposition to the also locally and theatrically scripted scenarios of U.S. racial segregation, racial discrimination, and national fragmentation. In other words, since the 1930s these discursive and scripted formations have been theatrically represented on the national stage as a way of maintaining the unity within the ethnic family.

What is more, these scenarios have been frozen in time. Regardless of the transformations of racial discourses in the United States after the civil rights and black power movements or the fact that U.S. political, social, popular, and mediatic cultural elements have infiltrated the nation, the scenarios have been recreated in the island's public spheres as unchangeable, memorized, and hegemonically scripted representations. Indeed, despite their recurrent reenactment, the fragmentations within the nation are never really dissolved. However, when social actors (which in the case of this research mostly refers to television's mimetic actors and performers) have tried to incorporate a new ideological performance on the national stage that rearticulates the marginalization of blackness or have attempted to transform the discourse of la gran familia puertorriqueña, their Puerto Ricanness (i.e., family authenticity and membership) has been questioned.[53] When social performers have publicly denounced racial prejudice in Puerto Rico, the national audience (which obviously comprises other social actors) has delivered (like a Greek chorus) the scripted lines, "Puerto Rico is not like the U.S. There is no racism in Puerto Rico. We are all equal regardless of race." In short, the theatricality of nationalism embedded in la gran familia puertorriqueña discourse has been staged across historical periods to achieve a national or familial consensus that ultimately reinforces the racial and cultural mestizaje.

The use of the term *theatricality* is not meant to imply that Puerto Ricans do not experience or feel a strong nationalistic sentiment. The cultural artifacts and debates analyzed throughout this book will illustrate the ways in which Puerto Rico's cultural nationalism was used, in some instances, as a symbolic weapon to counteract U.S. colonial exploitation (for example, the 1930s persecution of nationalist sympathizers, the 1940s–1950s massive consignment of Puerto Ricans to the United States for cheap labor, and the process of economic modernization and development). Furthermore, through multiple performances in radio and on television, media creators spawned "forums" wherein U.S. imperialistic practices and abuses of power by the local government were challenged.[54] Actually, one of the television shows examined in this study directly and indirectly attacked Puerto Rico's cultural nationalism and Puerto Ricans' prejudices against particular immigrant communities on the island. Still, in the national imaginary, either in times of pride or crisis (real or fabricated), the nationalism embedded in la gran familia puertorriqueña has functioned as a hegemonic strategy to break down the internal divisions within the nation.

Puerto Rico's ideologies of cultural and racial mestizaje, racial categorizations, and the conflicts regarding U.S. colonial influences were key elements in the local media constructions and discussions of blackness from the 1940s to the 1990s. In addition, and intertwined with Puerto Rico's cultural nationalism, the binary ideological constructions of us versus them, wherein "us" is defined not only around nationality but also around territorial space (the island), permeated local television dialogues on blackness.[55] Nonetheless, the U.S. presence was highly influential not only concerning the adaptation of black-oriented programming, but more importantly, in terms of alternative racial, sexual, and gender mobilizations. A significant factor in these U.S. alternative influences in Puerto Rico was the circular migrations that characterize Puerto Rican movements from the island to the United States.[56] The "here" (Puerto Rico) and "there" (the United States) have marked the boundaries of "a transient and pendulous flow, rather than a permanent, irrevocable, one-way relocation of people."[57] Therefore, the 1960s–1970s New York City and Chicago African-American–Puerto Rican–Afro Puerto Rican coalitions that were formed during the civil rights and black power movements and the process of (partial) desegregation that took place in U.S. commercial television had an impact on the island's commercial medium during the 1970s.

Consequently, in this research I call attention not only to the ways in which foreign television ideas or formats have at times influenced indigenous productions and created spaces for marginalized communities, identities, and cultures but also to how the flows of people (or what Arjun Appadurai defines as "ethnoscape") have permeated the local.[58] In the case of Puerto Rico's television, media cultures, and representations of and dialogues on blackness, one needs to examine the U.S.-Puerto Rico multiple flows and intersections along with the close relationship between Puerto Rico and Cuba before the 1959 Cuban Revolution and the colliding tensions that emerged after the post-1959 massive migrations of Cubans to Puerto Rico.

In sum, the local aspect of television in Puerto Rico has been hybrid in nature because, as Nancy Morris argues, "identity and the practices and symbols that express it are never pure and 'uncorrupted,' symbols and traditions —whether invented, imposed, emergent, constructed, begged, borrowed, or stolen—change all the time."[59] Even though la gran familia puertorriqueña hegemonic discourse constructs a unified and impermeable culture and identity, the migrations of various ethnic groups to the island (particularly Cubans, but also, and more recently, Dominicans), the circular migration of Puerto Ricans from the island to the mainland and vice versa, and the political and cultural connections with the United States have influenced the local cultural elements of Puerto Rico's television. Despite the fact that some of the identities submerged within Puerto Rico's societal and cultural terrains have been marginalized, the multiple levels or stories that inform the nation will become evident through my analyses in ensuing chapters.[60]

Interpreting Race in Puerto Rico's Entertainment Programming

Throughout the following chapters I use *negro*, *trigueño/a*, *mulata* and *mulato*, and *blanco* as intertwined socially and ideologically constructed racial categorizations and cultural signifiers when addressing particular characters, shows, and cultural elements. These labels are somewhat problematic given their connection to a biological paradigm of race and the fact that the racialization of various groups transcends skin color. Nevertheless, in the case of the cultural artifacts and events examined in this book, specific cultural practices and racialized discourses are associated with *lo negro*, *lo mulato*, and *lo blanco*, which cannot be grasped without these racial and cultural categorizations.

The book is organized chronologically. Chapter 1, "Caribbean Negritos: Ramón Rivero, Blackface, and Black Voice in Puerto Rico," focuses on Ramón Rivero (Diplo), the most famous blackface and black voice actor in Puerto Rico. Examined through Cesar Salgado's theoretical concept of *anastomosis* and the creation of the CubaRican space, the first representations of blackness in Puerto Rico's commercial media were a product of the exchanges between Cuba and Puerto Rico and the translations of Cuba's *Bufo* theater tradition and its *negrito catedrático* type to Puerto Rico's culture.[61] By considering the economic and political conditions that informed Puerto Rican society during the 1930s, 1940s, and 1950s, I maintain that Rivero's "Caribbean" blackface and black voice characters' criticism of the island's colonial conditions and the subjugation of the working class, together with his charismatic public persona, normalized blackface as a symbol for the marginal sectors of the Puerto Rican population.

Chapter 2, "Bringing the Soul: Afros, Black Empowerment, and the Resurgent Popularity of Blackface," analyzes the 1970s and explores the debates surrounding a television performer who wore an Afro, programs that directly and indirectly dealt with blackness, the resurgent popularity of blackface, black actors and actresses' protests against racism, and the selection of a mulata as Miss World–Puerto Rico. Although initially the translations of alternative political, social, and cultural movements and practices and the indigenization of U.S. black-oriented programming concepts destabilized the whiteness that characterized local television, blackface was ultimately reinstated as a protected masquerade for social criticism. Furthermore, the emerging prejudices against the Cuban community in Puerto Rico following the post-1959 migration were crucial to the 1970s ethnic transformation of Caribbean blackface to a Puerto Rican jíbara version.

The participation of Cubans in Puerto Rico's commercial television production processes, their predominance in the area of scriptwriting, and the construction of Cubans in locally produced entertainment programming are the subject of chapter 3, "The CubaRican Space Revisited." As seen through the 1980s locally produced situation comedy *Los suegros* (The In-Laws) and the narrative's rearticulation of Puerto Rican–Cuban tensions after the 1959 migration, by the 1980s Cubans were televisually portrayed as ambivalently welcome members in Puerto Rican society and family. This representation of Puerto Ricans and Cubans as family members reasserted the alleged whiteness of these two ethnic groups and discursively transferred the undesirable blackness to the new immigrant group in Puerto Rico: Dominicans.

Chapter 4, "*Mi familia*: A Black Puerto Rican Televisual Family," examines the incorporation of black Puerto Ricans into the previously predominantly white situation comedy genre. Since the initial conceptualization of *Mi familia*, the media professionals involved in the production processes downplayed the fictional family's blackness. Although *Mi familia*'s text rearticulated ideologies of racial and cultural mestizaje and never problematized the island's racist ideologies, this cultural product reconfigured the local television family sitcom genre, creating a space that reinstated black and mulatto members as part of the Puerto Rican and televisual ethnic family.

The concluding chapter, "Translating and Representing Blackness," locates performers, producers, and the television industry as the primary translators of blackness in Puerto Rico's commercial media. Whereas these translations of blackness contained a variety of meanings, and while journalists and audiences produced diverse interpretations, the ideology of ethnic unity that informs la gran familia puertorriqueña discourse permeated the translating processes and in some cases the erasure of blackness. Moreover, even though Puerto Rico's commercial television has the potential for more complicated representations of racial ideologies and culture, recent changes in the local television landscape might impede not only the production of more shows with black performers but could also eliminate the possibilities of exploring the problem of racism in Puerto Rico or anywhere else in the Spanish Caribbean.

Caribbean Negritos Ramón Rivero, Blackface, and Black Voice in Puerto Rico

Diplo was the sentimental negrito who possessed the "Cuban wit" and used his ingenuity for personal gain.
  Julio Cordero-Avila, *El Mundo*, May 6, 1973

From the late 1930s through the 1950s, Puerto Rico's media representations of blackness were located in an ambiguous geographical space. While some blackface and black voice characters addressed local political, cultural, and social issues, negritos and negras were mostly described as *caribeños/as* (Caribbean), not as Puerto Ricans. This black Caribbeanness can be traced to Puerto Rican and Cuban cultural, social, and business relations.[1] The influence of Cuba's Bufo theater tradition and its negrito characters as well as the pattern of buying radio scripts from Cuba were key in Puerto Rico's media translations of a Caribbean negritud. In addition to these dynamic exchanges, one should also consider the location of blackness on both islands.

Similar to Puerto Rico's 1930s ideological reconceptualization of la gran familia puertorriqueña, Cuba's postindependence nation-building stages created a discourse of *cubanidad* (Cubanness) that, through the mestizaje ideology, merged African and Spanish cultural elements. Although this ideological conceptualization of the Cuban identity redefined and integrated some Afro-Cuban traditions, it also positioned the Spanish culture and whiteness at the top of the racial and cultural hierarchy.[2] Therefore, Puerto Rico's media representations of blackness articulated hegemonic racial discourses, which situated negros and negras as marginal gendered Others within and across both Puerto Rico's and Cuba's colonized and neocolonized sociocultural spaces.

While locally produced radio and television shows in Puerto Rico during the 1940s and 1950s depicted black voice and blackface Caribbean negra characters, these earliest racialized representations — unlike the negritos — did not become iconic cultural symbols of Puerto Ricanness. Certainly, the suffering, dedicated, and submissive black voice and blackface negra servants such as mamá Dolores in the Puerto Rican adaptation of the Cuban radio-novela and subsequent telenovela *El derecho de nacer*, and la negra Balbina in the local adaptation of the Cuban radionovela *Sierra negra* were highly popular characters in Puerto Rico during the duration of these programs.[3] However, in contrast to the locally written and locally produced comedy shows that depicted black voice and blackface Caribbean negritos, these radio-novelas and telenovelas did not address Puerto Rico's political, cultural, and social conditions, and more importantly, they did not criticize the island's political and class systems. For example, Nora Mazziotti notes that during the early stages of radionovela and telenovela production in Latin America and the Spanish Caribbean, nearly identical scripts were produced in various countries.[4] Although radionovelas and telenovelas and their negra characters were not exclusively Caribbean cultural products (after all, *El derecho de nacer* was produced in countries such as Mexico, Brazil, and Argentina), they probably became popular in Puerto Rico for a number of reasons.[5]

First, the negra characters were part of successful radionovelas or tele-novelas. As several scholars have argued, from the early stages of commercial radio and television in Latin America and the Spanish Caribbean, radionovelas and telenovelas became some of the most culturally and commercially appealing media artifacts in the region.[6] These cultural products, as well as Mexican movies and musical expressions such as mambo, bolero, and tango, surpassed the local significations and created what Jesús Martín-Barbero refers to as "a process of sentimental integration" that generated a transnational Latin American and Spanish Caribbean cultural space of production and consumption.[7]

Second, in Puerto Rico the radionovela and telenovela scripts (all of which were purchased in Cuba before the 1959 Revolution) underwent some linguistic transformations to accommodate Puerto Rico's vernacular language and geographical locations while maintaining the story line of the original text.[8] Third, the black voice and blackface Caribbean negra characters such as mamá Dolores and la negra Balbina were performed by a well-respected and locally famous white Puerto Rican radio and theater actress (Mona Marti). Finally, in terms of racial signification, these scripts positioned black women as content with their class and racial position in the telenovela's fictional social space. Although the negra characters seemed to be integral to the narrative and were constructed as sacrificing heroines, they never challenged their racialized, gendered, or class status. What is more, these characters apparently never faced any form of systemic racial oppression. Instead, it appears that the source of subjugation for the negras was never the system, but rather the actions of an immoral individual.[9] Considering this racialized construction in the context of Puerto Rico in particular and Latin America in general, the Caribbean negras could be read as a reaffirmation of the ideology of racial democracy that informs the mestizaje discourse. In other words, racism was located as a personality or a moral trait instead of as an intertwined and endemic cultural, political, social, and economic practice.

As I explain in chapter 2, these racialized and gendered constructions, and the use of white actresses in blackface to represent black maids in telenovelas continued until the late 1970s in Puerto Rico. However, what emerged in the late 1930s and remains part of Puerto Rico's contemporary televisual culture is the blackface and the black voice negrito character. The negritos, and specifically Ramón Rivero's characters Diplomacia and Calderón, embodied a Caribbean mediated blackness and became an ambivalent symbol of the oppressed sectors of the population.

From the late 1930s until his death in 1956, Ramón Rivero's blackface and black voice negrito characters, Diplomacia and Calderón, became one in Puerto Rico's popular culture, merging the actor's creations and his public and private personae into a single signifier: Diplo. With Rivero, blackface and black voice in Puerto Rico became synonymous with the voice of the marginal sectors of the population. It was a symbiotic relationship: Rivero symbolized *el pueblo* (the people) and el pueblo venerated Rivero.

Ramón Rivero (Diplo) is considered one of the most important media professionals in the history of Puerto Rico. As a theater, radio, film, and television actor, producer, scriptwriter, songwriter, and director, he has become a legend. From the early stages of his theater and radio career to contemporary newspaper stories, radio, and television shows, Rivero has been characterized as a "very talented and highly professional actor," a "Divo," "a great colleague and human being," a "symbol of the Puerto Rican people," and a "true Puerto Rican who loved his island deeply."[10] A self-identified *nacionalista* (nationalist) and, later, an *independentista* (pro-independence advocate) during a transitional political period when, as I will further explain, U.S. and local law enforcement officials prosecuted any mobilization against the U.S. colonial power, Ramón Rivero was beloved by audiences, respected by intellectuals, and admired by the media professionals of his time.

One important element of Rivero's public persona was his use of star status and economic power for humanitarian efforts. He raised money for cancer research, financially assisted his unemployed theater colleagues, and reportedly drove around poor barrios in Puerto Rico giving away food to impoverished children and the elderly. In addition, Rivero was one of the first actors to perform in New York City for the Puerto Rican community, and during World War II he was invited by the U.S. State Department to present his act for the Puerto Rican soldiers stationed overseas. In terms of political activism, Rivero was a key figure in the 1951 *El gremio de prensa, radio y teatro* (the Newspaper, Radio, and Theater Union) labor strike against Angel Ramos, the owner of WKAQ radio (the radio station where Rivero did most of his professional work).[11] Moreover, despite the threat of possible censorship or the potential of becoming an outcast, Rivero was open about his political ideology, declaring, "I believe in the independence of Puerto Rico as I believe in God."[12]

When analyzing the celebrity status of Ramón Rivero one needs to consider not only his public and private personae, but also the discourses that have constructed Puerto Rico's cultural nationalism. In the descriptions of Rivero, particularly after his death in 1956, his blackface and black voice negrito characters are submerged in discourses of Puerto Ricanness. The nation becomes the center of these narrations, creating a nostalgic feeling not only about the untimely death of Rivero but, more broadly, about Puerto Rico's past. Regardless of the stereotypical representations of blackness that are never problematized, the narrations focus on a time when comedy did not rely on sexual innuendos. What is more, they also center on the fact that Ramón Rivero made people laugh during the difficult economic and political transitional periods of the 1940s and 1950s.

As Eliseo Colón-Zayas notes, Ramón Rivero and his comedy re-created "the popular and the grotesque," incorporating the body of el pueblo into political, social, and cultural discourses.[13] Nonetheless, Colón-Zayas's analysis of Rivero downplays the colonial, "complex, ambivalent, and contradictory mode of representations."[14] More than simply the body of the people, Rivero's negritos are complicated and multilayered symbols. Through his theater troupe (*La Farándula Bohemia*), plays, vaudeville acts, radio and television shows, blackface and black voice became protected political masquerades for criticizing U.S. colonialism, the Puerto Rican government, and the oppression of the working class. With Rivero's characters, negritos were depicted as the anti-heroes, as illiterate and lazy and yet street smart, conniving,

Diplo, singer and composer Myrta Silva, and Puerto Rican soldiers
stationed in Panamá, 1944. Courtesy of Fundación Ramón Rivero.

and sometimes endowed with class or political consciousness as Caribbean or Puerto Rican citizens who, by way of their cleverness, were able to trick everyone — especially those who possessed cultural, economic, political, and symbolic power.

In the following pages I argue that Rivero's popularity as a blackface and black voice performer operated within three intertwined discursive spaces: the translation of Cuba's *Bufo negrito catedrático* (a blackface character, pretentious) type as a symbol of anticolonialism and political satire, the actor's left-wing nationalistic political persona and social activism, and the re-articulation of la gran familia puertorriqueña hegemonic discourse. I suggest that these interlaced political, social, cultural, and racial significations regularized the performance of blackface in Puerto Rico's televisual space. Indeed, Rivero's complex constructions of blackface blackness have been transformed over the decades. Yet his mythical position in the national imaginary, his construction of blackface as a safe space for satire, and Puerto Rico's discourse of a racially democratic nation have been used as points of reference for the ongoing representation of blackface in local programming.

To trace the emergence of blackface and black voice in Puerto Rico, I first present a historical background of Cuba and Puerto Rico's cultural, political, and business connections. Using Cesar Salgado's concept of cultural anastomosis, I position mediated blackness in Puerto Rico as part of the Cuba-Rican socio-cultural space.[15] Following this historical overview, I focus on Cuba's Bufo theater and the 1868 *bufomanía*, the adaptation of this genre by nineteenth-century Puerto Rican playwrights, and Rivero's revision of Bufo's negrito catedrático type. I pay special attention to Rivero's radio show *El tremendo hotel*, that served as the basis for his television shows *La taberna India* and *La farándula Corona*.[16]

In this chapter I contend that although Rivero's performances created a space for criticizing Puerto Rico's colonialism and the oppression of the working class, his representations of "blackness" became racial signifiers that normalized "whiteness" in Puerto Rico's radio and televisual spaces. Consequently, after Rivero's death in 1956, the Caribbean negritos became buffoonish, racialized figures who reaffirmed the hegemonic whiteness not only of the Puerto Rican nation but also of the emerging post-1959 Cuban migrant community in Puerto Rico.

Last, I am directly and indirectly foregrounding the pressing need for historical and cultural contextualization of the performances of black voice and blackface across multiple national contexts. Although one can trace similarities among, for example, black voice and blackface in Puerto Rico, Cuba, and the United States, the ideological meanings inscribed on these cultural artifacts responded to specific discursive formations. Simply put, one cannot generalize about black voice and blackface in Puerto Rico (or, for that matter, in other parts of the world) and categorize these racial constructions as mere copycat versions of U.S. minstrelsy. Rather, it is imperative to perform in-depth analyses of the multiple cultural exchanges, performers, and political, national, and racial ideologies that informed local and global black voice and blackface "blackness." Only in this way can one begin to understand the ways in which mediated cultures reproduced, challenged, or complicated the positionality of black citizens across various national scenes and moments in history.

The CubaRican Space

In reference to Puerto Rico and Cuba's combined and ongoing struggles to obtain their independence from Spain, the Puerto Rican poet Lola Rodríguez de Tio wrote in 1893 that "Cuba and Puerto Rico are the two wings of a single bird." Rodríguez de Tio's verse epitomizes the interconnections of these two nations not only in terms of their colonial pasts but also in terms of contemporary invasions of their cultural and social arenas. A revision of these transcultural flows and the creation of what Cesar Salgado calls the CubaRican space crystallizes the construction of Caribbean blackness that informed Puerto Rico's media from the late 1930s to the 1950s.[17]

Salgado uses the analogy of the heart's circulation in the human body to map the colonial relationships among Spain and the United States and Cuba and Puerto Rico. By locating the heart as the colonial metropolis, he argues that we can distinguish three sanguineous circulations between and across the colonial hearts and the continental body: the arterial flow, the venous flow, and the anastomosis flow. The arterial flow relates to political infusions of ideologies and the mobilization of armies and colonizers into the continental body. The venous flow conveys the economic exploitation of territorial resources, people, and the ongoing migrations of colonized or neocolonized subjects to the metropolis. Finally, there is the circulatory process of anastomosis, which relates to the lateral, capillary, and semi-independent streams across the continental body parts.[18]

Salgado employs the process of anastomosis to locate the ongoing cultural, social, economic, and political influxes between Puerto Rico and Cuba that are interconnected to each other and to Spain and the United States. By categorizing this relationship as CubaRican, he positions Puerto Rico and Cuba as a third cultural region that is influenced by colonial or imperial powers but that maintains a distinctive cultural enclave. This symbolic third cultural space is presented in "discourses, populations, words, nightmares, utopias, gestures, movements, ornaments, and rhythms."[19] The anastomosis flows and the CubaRican space are important elements for understanding the Cuban influences in Puerto Rico's commercial media and the performance of blackface.

Several factors explain Cuba and Puerto Rico's close economic, political, and cultural connections. First, although not culturally identical, these two islands share similar traits in language, traditions, religion, and vernacular Spanish language use patterns. The origins of these similarities can be traced to their shared colonial histories and their nation building processes. As previously observed, both islands (similar to other Latin American nations) incorporated the mestizaje ideology as a fundamental element of their identity formation. However, alongside the comparable racialized and hierarchical locations of their white, mulatto, and black citizens and cultural artifacts, Cuba and Puerto Rico's associations can be observed in both islands' fight for independence. During the late nineteenth century, Puerto Ricans and Cubans formed political alliances to fight against the Spanish colonial regime. New York City became an effervescent cultural and political center where Puerto Rican and Cuban political refugees built coalitions and founded a series of cultural organizations to raise funds for their respective independence movements.[20]

Intellectuals from both countries expressed their desire to form an "Antilles Confederation" whereby Puerto Rico, Cuba, and the Dominican Republic would create a combined "national" project for the Caribbean.[21] This collective project can be seen in Puerto Rico's and Cuba's pro-independence uprisings. On September 23, 1868, a group of Puerto Ricans staged the unsuccessful insurrection of *El grito de Lares* (the uprising of Lares). Similarly, on October 10, 1868, Cubans began their fight for independence through *El grito de Yara* (the uprising of Yara), which initiated the Ten Year War (1868–1878), the Little War (1879–1880), and finally, the War for Independence (1895). Although the independence of Puerto Rico never became a reality, several Puerto Ricans were actively involved in Cuba's fight for political freedom.[22]

Cuba and Puerto Rico were also linked through their trade connections with the United States. By 1830, in New York City, merchants from both islands had established *La sociedad benéfica cubana y puertorriqueña*, a business organization that created a triangular economic relationship among the three nations.[23] These business relationships continued after 1898, despite (or as a product of) the changes in the colonial regimes occasioned by the Spanish-American War. As a result of the war and the Platt Amendment, the United States controlled most of Cuba's economic and political structures.[24] Because Puerto Rico had become a United States colony in 1898, it was easy to establish business relations between the two Caribbean islands before 1959.

In terms of culture, several scholars claim that what unifies these territories is their "blackness," their language, and their rhythms, which are vividly present in the literature, music, and cuisine of the region. Cultural elements such as Afro-Spanish Caribbean music, typical dishes, and vernacular language position lo negro as a fundamental element of the islands' vernacular cultures. As I discussed in the introduction, during the 1930s Puerto Rican intellectuals celebrated the island's African elements through the cultura negroide movement. Puerto Rican and Cuban literary figures such as Luis Palés Matos (Puerto Rican) and Nicolás Guillén (Cuban) created numerous poems mapping la negritud as the axis of a trans-Caribbean borderless identity. Although each nation's cultural production relates to specific historical, political, and economic conditions, these various trajectories merge within the African diaspora, a pivotal element in the cultural enclave.[25]

Regarding media exchanges, the Cuban–Puerto Rican connection can be traced to the beginning of commercial radio. From the anecdotal story about the ship with all the radio equipment that was supposed to travel from the United States to Puerto Rico but that instead arrived in Cuba (due to weather conditions), to the actual owners of the first radio stations on both islands, one can observe the anastomosis flows. The first radio station in Cuba (PWX) began broadcasting during October 1922, while the first station in Puerto Rico (WKAQ) began operations two months later.[26] Both radio stations were owned by Hernam and Sosthenes Behn who also owned Cuba's and Puerto Rico's telephone companies.[27]

Throughout the 1940s and 1950s there were ongoing exchanges of bands and singers between Cuba and Puerto Rico. Puerto Rican singers and composers such as Daniel Santos, Bobby Capó, Rafael Hernández, and Ruth Fernández visited Cuba, while Cuban bands and singers such as Rafael Pérez

Prado, La Sonora Matancera, El Trio Matamoros, Xiomara Alfaro, and El trovador Portabales performed on radio shows and in nightclubs in Puerto Rico.
Certainly, both Puerto Rican and Cuban musicians traveled across Latin
America becoming part of multiple and interconnected trans-Spanish Carib-
bean and Latin American performative, cultural, and mediatic spaces.[28] Yet,
in Puerto Rico, the Cuban–Puerto Rican cultural exchanges were so prevalent
that they led to some confusion regarding the ethnicity of several performers.
For example, from talking with friends about the Cuban influences in Puerto
Rico's commercial television, I discovered that many of them thought that
Myrta Silva, a Puerto Rican who was the lead singer of the Cuban band La
Sonora Matancera until 1950, was Cuban. Besides being a generational misunderstanding, this *Cubanization* of Puerto Rican performers might be related to the fact that several Puerto Rican musicians (similar to other parts
of Latin America) played Cuban musical styles.[29] As I previously observed,
Cuban music (for example, mambo) became highly popular cultural artifacts
in Latin America; thus, Puerto Rican performers were likely influenced by
this transnational popularity.

Finally, and key to the creation of Caribbean and mediated blackness in
Puerto Rico, although Puerto Ricans wrote radio comedy shows during the
1920s and 1930s, an ongoing pattern of buying Cuban comedy and particularly radionovela scripts emerged. This Cubanization occurred across the
Latin American region largely because U.S. advertising agencies made Cuba
the center of radionovela production and exportation.[30] In Puerto Rico, besides the dominant influence of U.S. advertising agencies, cost was also an
issue. Cuban scripts were so inexpensive that the adage *compralos por libra*
(buy them by the pound) was coined. However, in addition to economic factors, it seems that many media professionals in Puerto Rico (as well as in
other Latin American nations) admired the quality of both Cuban scripts and
commercial radio (and later television) modes of production.

For example, by the mid-1940s to early 1950s, Cuban adventure radio
shows such as *Tamakún* and *Los tres Villalobos* and radionovelas such as *Lo
que pasa en el mundo*, *La mentira*, *El enemigo*, *Yo no creo en los hombres*,
and *El dolor de ser pobre* were highly successful programs in Puerto Rico, the
Dominican Republic, Colombia, and Venezuela.[31] Therefore, whereas Mexican cinema dominated the movie screens across Latin America, Cuban radio
shows conquered the Latin American and Spanish Caribbean airwaves during the 1940s and early 1950s. And based on this historical and commercial

reality, I would argue that if there had been no revolution in Cuba, its commercial television would probably be one of the dominant forces in today's Latin American televisual world, given that many successful telenovelas produced, for instance, in Mexico and Venezuela during the 1970s and 1980s were in fact scripts either written for Cuban radio or authored by post-1959 Cuban exiles (such as Caridad Bravo Adams, Delia Fiallo, and Armando Couto). Indeed, Cuba is the forgotten yet extremely important link in Latin American and Spanish Caribbean media histories.

Clearly, Cuba, like Puerto Rico and other Latin American nations, incorporated the U.S. model of commercial radio and television production not only in terms of sponsors but also in terms of specific genres and programming. Still, at least in Puerto Rico, alongside this U.S. influence, there was a desire to emulate the success of the Cuban media. Although the U.S. modes of production and genres were part of the success formula, some Puerto Rican media professionals believed that the Cuban programs were "better" because they had a "Latin flavor."[32] For instance, in my conversations with directors, producers, actors, and technical personnel who worked in Puerto Rico's commercial radio and television during the 1940s and 1950s, many of them praised the quality of Cuban programming.[33]

All the aforementioned factors, in addition to Cuba and Puerto Rico's location of black citizens at the bottom of their cultural and racial hierarchies were pivotal in the construction of Caribbean black voice and blackface negras and negritos in Puerto Rico. However, before black voices invaded Puerto Rico's radio airwaves, the Cuban Bufo theatrical tradition had already made a significant impact on Puerto Rico's nineteenth-century *teatro costumbrista*'s (theater of manners) constructions of blackness and Ramón Rivero's appropriation of blackface.

Cuban Bufo Theater and the Negrito Catedrático

The first constructions of blackface negritos appeared on Cuba's stages in 1812. These racial representations articulated the colonial, Eurocentric, racist, and oppressive conditions ingrained in the institution of slavery.[34] Cuban theater historian Rine Leal observes that, "if Afro-Cuban expressions 'represent' the black man gazed through the black pupil, acting his own language, for black audiences, and offering a theatrical image of his culture and identity, white authors began to create their antipodal in the *negrito*. This means in the black character performed by white actors, for the white audience, acting in Spanish or in *bozal* (parody of black speech), and of course, showing the point of view of the slave culture."[35]

Although there is limited research regarding the sporadic representations of negrito characters on Cuba's stages, negritos were part of Cuban theater from 1847 to 1864.[36] Most of these early performances were written and portrayed by Spaniards or "white" Cubans for elite Spanish and Cuban audiences. Furthermore, at least in the written texts, the first negrito characters spoke "in *bozal*," which, as Jill Lane notes, was a belittling way of describing the Spanish spoken by African slaves.[37] This fact notwithstanding, it was not until the late 1860s that negritos and the Bufo comedy genre became highly popular cultural artifacts in Cuban society.

Even though Cuban Bufo's origins are traceable to France and Spain, some scholars have suggested that U.S. minstrel shows may have influenced Cuba's Bufo theater.[38] However, no one has examined the potential connections between U.S. minstrelsy and Cuba's Bufo, despite the fact that minstrel companies visited Cuba between 1860 and 1865.[39] Furthermore, due to political persecution and censorship during Cuba's Ten Year War, Bufo groups were banned from Cuban stages; thus, various theater companies performed in Europe and the United States.[40] Therefore, it is quite possible that minstrel groups and Cuban Bufo companies were representing the stereotypical black dances and black dialect (in English and Spanish) on the same night for diverse ethnic audiences in New York City. Although both types of representations perpetuated nineteenth-century racial ideologies of black moral and intellectual inferiority and primitivism, U.S. minstrelsy and Cuban Bufo were imbued with culturally and politically distinct meanings.

United States' scholars have situated minstrelsy and blackface as white working-class vernacular theater that embodied racial hatred and fears, cross-dressing and sexualized desires, interracial or class solidarities, and grotesque racial constructions of the black Other.[41] Minstrelsy represented "the emergent historical break between high and low culture" and served as a symbolic whitening–melting pot space for Irish and Jewish immigrants in the nineteenth and twentieth centuries.[42] Minstrelsy was a product of an independent nation-state that redefined ethnic, class, racial, and gendered citizens and provided an avenue for certain groups to become "American."[43] On the other hand, Bufo was a product of Cuba's colonial period and became a symbol of the anti-Spanish colonial sentiment that characterized the island's tumultuous political climate during the late 1860s.

The 1868 bufomanía, similar to U.S. minstrelsy, represented a detachment from bourgeoisie high culture theatrical genres such as Italian opera and melodrama. Moreover, in Bufo companies, most of the performers came from marginal sectors of the population (poor white and mulatto Cubans), and the audience comprised members from various classes.[44] However, in contrast to U.S. minstrelsy, Bufo, and more specifically, lo negro — expressed in blackface and with Afro-Cuban music — created political icons representative of an emerging Cuban identity and culture.[45] Bufo developed into the first Cuban vernacular theater and, as Rine Leal argues, this genre epitomized the birth of racial marginality on Cuba's stage.[46]

Through political satire, Bufo theater companies and performances became emblems of the fight for independence. Due to their political innuendos, indirect criticisms of colonial authorities, and the popularity of Bufo companies, the Spanish colonial government banned Bufo theater from 1869 to 1878. After 1878, Bufo theater companies continued to perform in Cuba until the late 1930s. Although the political connotation of Bufo was transformed after Cuba gained independence in 1902, what remained popular in the island's public sphere were Bufo's traditional characters: *el negrito, la mulata* (sexualized figure), and *el gallego* (a Galician business man). Originally, the stock characters in Bufo's plays were the aforementioned trio. However, other characters such as the Chinese immigrant, the black asexual older "witch" woman, and the "loud and intrusive American" were added to the repertoire.[47] Additionally, it is important to mention that while in early Bufo plays el gallego was situated in a superior social, cultural, and racial position in comparison to la mulata and el negrito, following Cuba's independence the three characters became symbols of the socially constructed mestiza Cuban identity. In several Bufo plays, el negrito, la mulata, and el gallego were represented as cultural and political allies who satirized the new source of imperial domination: the United States.[48] Still, the emblems of Bufo theater and what served as a major influence in Puerto Rico's theater were the negrito characters, and specifically, the negrito catedrático.[49]

According to Laurie Aleen Frederik, the negrito catedrático was constructed as an arrogant black man who tried unsuccessfully to use "bourgeois intellectual vocabulary" as a way of placing himself within Cuban white society.[50] Although the performances created a hierarchical structure between various negrito characters, the comical element associated with the negrito catedrático was his inability to learn and speak proper and sophisticated Spanish. In some ways, the negrito catedrático can be compared to the U.S. Zip Coon urban dandy stereotype, a representation and mockery of blacks imitating whites. Nonetheless, in several Bufo plays, the negrito catedrático became the most astute of the traditional Bufo characters. The negritos rearticulated an anticolonial political and cultural ideology, first against the Spanish government and later, after 1895, against U.S. interventions in Cuba.[51] It is precisely this anticolonial ideological construction of "blackness" that created a space for political and contradictory negritos in Puerto Rico during the late nineteenth century and then later in the 1930s, 1940s, and 1950s.

The Bufo comedies were first performed on Puerto Rico's stages in 1873. According to Angelina Morfi, the negritos Bufo first appeared in the local productions of the Cuban scriptwriter Francisco Fernández's plays *Los negros catedráticos*, *Un negro bueno*, and *Los negros espiritistas*.[52] In addition, Cuban Bufo theater companies' participation in Puerto Rico's cultural environment can be traced to 1879. Following this theatrical form, several nineteenth-century Puerto Rican theater writers incorporated the stereotypical negrito into their creative work and adapted it to the Puerto Rican political and economic conditions of the period.[53] Puerto Rican playwrights localized the negritos, representing them as jíbaros (Puerto Rican peasants), while also integrating what would become the national emblem of Puerto Rico's identity for the years to come: the white jíbaro.

As Lillian Guerra suggests, the nineteenth-century literature of manners' constructions of white jíbaros represented both the "legitimization of the elite self as well as the reliance on the 'Other.' "[54] This racial and class construction of Puerto Ricanness should be contextualized through the formation of la gran familia puertorriqueña discourse. Although la gran familia puertorriqueña embodied an anticolonial ideology of ethnic solidarity against the Spanish colonial regime, it also reflected the paternalistic, class, and racial (white) position of the Puerto Rican hacendados.[55] Thus, these intertwined racial, class, and gendered ideological significations permeated the construction of negritos in nineteenth-century Puerto Rican theater.

Even though Puerto Rican playwrights represented both white and black jíbaros as underclass, poor, and illiterate citizens, the negritos were located in a subordinate position in comparison to the white jíbaros. Through their race, class, and *catedratismo* (affectation in their speech), negritos were an object of mockery for the white jíbaro and the hacendado characters.[56] Whereas some of the plays were political satires that criticized the island's colonial and social conditions, and a few theatrical texts during this period actually condemned Puerto Rican and Latin American racist practices, it was not until the 1930s, and through Rivero's characters, that the stereotypical negritos became racially and politically complex icons of Puerto Ricanness.[57]

1930s–1950s Puerto Rico, La Farándula Bohemia, and Ramón Rivero's Blackface

In the half century following the 1898 Spanish-American War and Puerto Rico's transition from a Spanish to a U.S. colonial possession, the traditional agrarian economy that characterized the island during the nineteenth century was turned into "a model of capitalistic production and economic dependence."[58] United States corporations gained control of most of the sugar industry on the island while concomitantly diminishing the production of coffee and the power of the Puerto Rican hacendados. According to Angel Quintero Rivera, the new modes of production debilitated the hacendados' hegemonic control and created a new working class and bourgeoisie class that rejected the ideological discourse of la gran familia puertorriqueña and supported Puerto Rico's annexation to the United States. Nonetheless, although during the early-twentieth-century political coalitions in Puerto Rico had formed around class-based identity politics, these associations where transformed during the 1930s.[59]

The 1930s was a period of political, economic, and social instability in Puerto Rico. The U.S. economic depression, the subsequent decline of the sugar industry, and impoverished conditions on the island nurtured pro-independence sentiments across diverse sectors of the population. Segments of the working class joined individuals from the Puerto Rican elite (sons and daughters of the hacendados class) who developed a radical nationalistic political ideology. This radical nationalism constructed "the family, religion (Catholic), culture, language (Spanish), and history" as sites of resistance against U.S. colonial authorities.[60] Ongoing disputes and divisions among local political parties regarding the island's colonial status, labor strikes, and political repression by U.S. authorities against sympathizers and leaders of the nationalistic movement permeated the 1930s and 1940s.

Two prominent episodes of political repression were the 1936 arrest of Pedro Albizu Campos (the president of Puerto Rico's Nationalist Party) and the 1937 police assault of a peaceful Nationalist Party protest in Ponce, Puerto

Rico.[61] Furthermore, since the early 1940s, U.S. authorities had associated Puerto Rico's nationalist and pro-independence movements with communism, keeping a watchful eye on the "subversive and terrorist agitators" in both Puerto Rico and New York City.[62] This connection between Puerto Rico's nationalistic movement and communism was not wholly unfounded given that in the early 1940s Albizu Campos (while in prison) created coalitions with the Communist Party of the United States which in turn financially supported Puerto Rico's nationalist movement in New York City.[63] However, in addition to the containment of nationalist leaders both on the island and in New York City, the U.S. political domination in Puerto Rico was legalized in 1948 through Law 53, which criminalized any mobilization that threatened the colonial establishment.

Another important social transformation during the mid-1940s to the early 1950s was the massive migration of Puerto Ricans to the United States, particularly to the East Coast. Although Puerto Ricans began to migrate from the rural parts of the island to the cities and then to the United States during the first decades of the twentieth century, the post–World War II economic boom precipitated a dramatic increase in migratory influxes to the mainland.[64] Closely interconnected to this massive migration was the modernization process officially designated as Operation Bootstrap, a social and economic development plan aimed at changing Puerto Rico's economy from an agricultural to an industrial base. To attract U.S. corporations, the government offered incentives such as a cheap labor force, special tax exemptions for a maximum period of thirty years, and tariff benefits to industries willing to invest in the "new market."[65]

The final drastic "reconstruction" in Puerto Rico occurred during the late 1940s. After experiencing years of U.S. military and civil governors, in 1948 Puerto Ricans elected their first governor, Luis Muñoz Marín, founder and head of the Popular Democratic Party (PDP, pro-commonwealth ideology). Despite the fact that in 1938, when Muñoz Marín founded the PDP, the party's political platform favored Puerto Rican independence, the charismatic leader transformed the party's political ideology into one that accommodated a relationship with the United States. Muñoz Marín embraced Puerto Rico's cultural nationalism while concomitantly reassuring his supporters that the island's unique culture was compatible with commonwealth status.[66] In 1952 Puerto Rico's constitution was approved, establishing the *Estado Libre Asociado* (ELA, Free Associated State, Commonwealth). All the aforementioned social, political, and economic conditions and transformations from the 1930s through the 1950s directly and indirectly influenced Ramón Rivero and informed his vernacular theater group's plays, his radio shows, and his construction of blackface.

Rivero began performing in theater during 1933 while working as a physical education teacher in Cayey (a small town in the eastern part of the island). With the assistance of two high school students (José Luis Torregrosa and Guillermo Bauzá), he created *La Farándula Bohemia* (The Bohemian Troup), which was characterized as a politico-burlesque theater troupe. Initially, La Farándula Bohemia performed primarily in Cayey. However, two years after the company was established, the trio traveled around the island presenting their plays in various theaters immediately preceding movie screenings.

In 1935 Rivero decided to don blackface after seeing the Cuban comedian Leopoldo Fernández and his Bufo theater company in San Juan. Rivero performed his first blackface character in the Bufo-style play *El chico mambí* (The Mambí Boy). The play, written by Torregrosa (La Farándula Bohemia's playwright), centered on a "negrito who stole chickens."[67] Although the only available information regarding *El chico mambí* is a flyer advertising the play and newspaper stories, which document that this was Ramón Rivero's first blackface performance, the title and subject of the play reveal interconnections to two racially and politically distinct levels of Cuban blackness: Bufo's embodiment of blackness and the historical accounts of the mambí army.

In Cuba, *mambí* is a term that refers to the individuals (many of them black and mulatto) who participated in Cuba's war of independence and who contested Spanish colonialism and Cuban racial inequalities. Although the term *mambí* originally embodied a negative connotation describing the slaves who joined Cuba's Ten Year War, members of the multiracial Liberation Army "appropriated the name [*mambí*] to proudly refer to themselves."[68] Considering the historical, political, racial, and cultural significance of the term *mambí* in Cuba, one could say that in the process of translating the Bufo genre, Torregrosa and Rivero de-politicized the term and merged it into Bufo's stereotypes of blackness, thus constructing a morally dubious black character. Based on the title, one might also say that with *El chico mambí* Torregrosa and Rivero began to create a trans-Spanish Caribbean or Cuba-Rican embodiment of blackness.

As I will further discuss, multiple elements connect Rivero's blackface to Cuba's Bufo blackness. For example, in Rivero's radio show *El tremendo hotel*,

A La Farándula Bohemia flyer advertising a comedy ("Pedro Montaña vs. Frankie Wallie"), 1937. Courtesy of Fundación Ramón Rivero.

his negrito characterizations contained elements of the Cuban Bufo catedra-
tismo, and the texts presented character types germane to the Bufo genre.
However, after *El chico mambí*, Torregrosa and Rivero re-conceptualized the
Cuban Bufo negritos by constructing them as vehicles for representing Puerto
Rico's 1930s political environment.

During the 1930s, most of La Farándula Bohemia's plays narrated the
internal conflicts within political parties on the island, which revolved primarily around the issue of independence versus U.S. colonialism.[69] Conversely, according to Torregrosa, the text that represented the group's political position was the 1936 piece *Como no será y como será nuestra república*
(How our republic would and would not be).[70] In this play, Rivero's blackface character Alma Negra (Black Soul) was characterized as a narrator who
guided the audience through the various stages of Puerto Rico's political history. The play's resolution positioned independence as the only way to solve
the island's economic and social problems. Based on these accounts of the
early stages of La Farándula Bohemia, it seems that Rivero's blackface — similar to the 1868 bufomanía — was used as a symbolic, visually distinctive, and
racially complex masquerade to criticize Puerto Rico's political, social, and
economic conditions.

During this time Rivero created the negrito character that would make
him a legend in Puerto Rico: Diplomacia/Diplo. He based his portrayal on
an "eloquent and politically informed poor black man" who played a gui-
tar on the streets of Old San Juan and diplomatically begged for money.[71]
From this point forward, most of Rivero's characterizations in blackface and
black voice were performed through Diplomacia. In 1937 he introduced this
black voice character to a wider audience in the radio show *Los embajadores
del buen humor*.[72] For the next nineteen years Rivero (as Diplo) continued to
portray various black voice characters in his radio comedy shows such as *El
colegio del amor*, *La vida en broma*, *La farándula bohemia*, *El tremendo hotel*,
Viernes social, *Los jíbaros de la radio*, and in his and Torregrosa's adaptations
of Castor Vispo's *La tremenda corte* scripts, which had been bought in Cuba.
In addition, Rivero (through his character Diplo) maintained his blackface
theater career by acting in plays such as *Los mil y un días*, *A mi me matan
pero yo gozo*, *Hay que defenderse*, and the theatrical adaptation of his radio
show *El tremendo hotel*. Although some theater critics decried that Rivero's
plays lacked dramatic structure and character development, his farces were
huge commercial successes.[73]

By the 1950s Rivero was a rising star in the Spanish Caribbean and Latin America. He sold his radio show *El tremendo hotel* to Radio Caracas where "the best Venezuelan comedians would perform Rivero's scripts."[74] In addition to his radio and theater performances, Rivero participated in the locally produced film *Los peloteros* (1951), playing a dramatic role and a nonblackface character. However, with the arrival of television in March 1954, Rivero (as Diplo) resumed his blackface career, performing the character Calderón in the comedy sketches of his locally produced variety show *La taberna India*.[75] As I previously mentioned, the comedy segment included in the variety show was a spin-off of Rivero's radio program *El tremendo hotel*.[76] *La taberna India* became the most popular program during Telemundo's first year.[77] According to Gladys Jiménez-Muñoz's recollection of Rivero's televisual blackface character, he was one of the most memorable figures during the early years of Puerto Rican television.[78]

In 1955 Rivero participated in the Cuban film *Una gallega en la Habana* where he performed in blackface.[79] Rivero also produced several commercials in Cuba and Puerto Rico, and through his production company (Rivero, Inc.), he made plans to produce short films on "Caribbean music — *plena*, *danzón*, *merengue*, *danza*, and other popular dance music."[80] Finally, in 1956 he produced the show *La farándula Corona* for Telemundo and signed a contract with Columbia Pictures to participate in the movie entitled *Wherever You Go*.[81] In sum, Rivero was one of the most powerful media professionals in Puerto Rico during the 1940s and 1950s.

The early stages of La Farándula Bohemia and Rivero's subsequent radio and television shows are differentiated by their political focus. Although Rivero's radio scripts included political satire, the pro-independence and nationalistic ideology that permeated the theatrical texts was submerged into more general socially satiric references. One can map two interconnected reasons for this transformation. First, the repression of individuals connected with Puerto Rico's radical nationalism and the independence movements is significant. As I previously observed, local and U.S. authorities on the island targeted sympathizers of the nationalistic movement during the 1930s and 1940s. Therefore, although both Rivero and Torregrosa "had coffee" with important leaders of the nationalistic movement (for example, Pedro Albizu Campos) during the early days of La Farándula Bohemia, it seems that the repressive political environment limited their inclusion of pro-independence themes.[82]

A second reason for the transformation can be traced to the political censorship that emerged from the U.S. involvement in World War II and, later, the Korean War. All of Rivero's *La vida en broma* (1943) scripts were screened by Sterling Products International, the show's sponsor. Although Rivero's radio scripts for *El tremendo hotel* (1948, sponsored by Sello Rojo) and his television scripts for *La taberna India* (1954, sponsored by India Corporation) and *La farándula Corona* (1956, sponsored by Corona Corporation) did not have any stamp or visible indication of censorship, he probably knew that it was not politically and financially savvy to include direct references to pro-independence in his radio and television scripts. According to Rivero's widow, despite the fact that Rivero was a nacionalista, he did not mix politics with his artistic work.[83] Regardless, political and social commentaries were directly and indirectly present in Rivero's radio show *El tremendo hotel*.

Embodying Blackness and Whiteness: Satire and Stereotypes in *El tremendo hotel*

El tremendo hotel (The Tremendous Hotel) was a fifteen-minute comedy that aired Monday to Friday on WKAQ radio (1948–1956).[84] From 12:45 P.M. to 1:00 P.M. the negrito Calderón, Doña Polita (the hotel owner, a Puerto Rican woman), Don Nepo (guest, a Spanish businessman), Tranquilino (Doña Polita's husband, an old retired Puerto Rican man), and other sporadic visitors performed their daily routine in a third-class hotel located in a rundown San Juan barrio.[85] Usually following an accumulative narrative structure, the episodes presented Calderón as a young troublemaking black man who was always trying to mislead the owner and guests of the hotel. None of the characters of *El tremendo hotel* were financially affluent; in reality, they were working-class individuals. The process of modernization that was taking place in Puerto Rico during the late 1940s and early 1950s never made it to the San Juan barrio, and none of its inhabitants benefited from the economic and social transformations. Still, Doña Polita, Don Nepo, Tranquilino, and the other guests were in a better economic, social, and racial (white) position than Calderón who was (primarily) the hotel's errand boy.

For the most part, the show's narrative revolved around Calderón's constant efforts to obtain money without performing any labor. In addition to being lazy, what defined Calderón was his cleverness and wit. His misdeeds included stealing chickens from a neighbor, avoiding work by convincing the other characters that he was dying, selling the tires of a doctor's automobile

The characters of *El tremendo hotel*:
(from left to right) Don Nepo, Calderón, actress/singer/dancer Mapy Cortés,
Doña Polita, and Tranquilino. Courtesy of Fundación Ramón Rivero.

that he was supposed to be guarding, and persuading an American visitor to buy a horse that could read. Regardless of Calderón's errant actions, he gracefully tried to convince other characters of his innocence and usually achieved his goal. Although he was fired on multiple occasions, Calderón always stayed around the hotel doing other jobs until Doña Polita rehired him. In any case, if something bad happened, it was not because of Calderón but rather because the other characters were not smart enough to prevent a misfortune or a trick.

Like Bufo's negrito catedrático type, Calderón made up words and phrases that sounded sophisticated or used urbane words out of context to present himself as a refined man. Nevertheless, more than portraying himself as articulate, Calderón used his verbal skillfulness to confuse or convince others of his virtuousness. None of the other characters actually knew whether the words and phrases were correct and they always asked him: "where did you get those terms?" Calderón usually replied, "from Spain. You can buy a dozen for a dollar there," thus satirizing people who wanted to present themselves as intellectually superior and showing the Eurocentric and class-based divisions between high and low cultures.

In addition to mocking cultural hierarchies, *El tremendo hotel* also parodied distinctions between the Puerto Rican characters and Don Nepo (the Spaniard). For example, Don Nepo continually referred to his aristocratic Spanish background by using all of his last names when introducing himself (Don Nepomuceno Algarín de la Alcachofa) and characterized himself as a "refined Spanish gentleman." Don Nepo was the only member of the hotel who placed importance on his lineage while the other characters never mentioned their last names. In addition to Don Nepo's ongoing pronouncements of his last names, the selection of names was designed to ridicule socially constructed notions of Spanish nobility. For instance, the first last name (Algarín) is not a common name in Puerto Rico (as is Pérez, García, or Rivera, which in the U.S. context would be comparable to Smith or Johnson). However, the second last name (Alcachofa) means artichoke. Yet, when mentioned together, the last names *sound* aristocratic. In other words, it is not the same to be named Don Nepomuceno Pérez Rivera (two common last names) as it is to be called Don Nepomuceno Algarín de la Alcachofa.

Nonetheless, regardless of Don Nepo's alleged ties to landed gentry, nobody paid attention to his snobbish persona because the other hotel members knew he was a "poor devil." More important, he was constructed as part of the hotel family, indirectly hinting at the Spanish element of the ethnic (Puerto Rican) family. Although the inclusion of Don Nepo's character articulated a Eurocentric racialized and cultural discourse that through ethnic accents created a distinction between Puerto Rican and Spanish whiteness, he possessed less financial power than the Puerto Rican white characters (Doña Polita and Tranquilino). Therefore, although the constructed Spanish element was an integral part of this community (and thus, the nation), the hotel was in the hands of white *criollos* (Puerto Ricans).

It is probably no coincidence that the jíbaro, a key cultural icon in the nineteenth-century literature of manners and in the Puerto Rican playwrights' adaptations of Bufo comedy, was not part of *El tremendo hotel*'s family. This absence was likely related to the new political signification of the jíbaro during the 1940s and 1950s. Although the jíbaro remained a major cultural symbol of Puerto Ricanness in the late 1940s, this figure was also beginning to be associated with the Popular Democratic Party (pro-commonwealth status). The party's flag incorporated a silhouette of a jíbaro and underneath it the slogan, "Pan, Tierra, y Libertad" (bread, land, and freedom).[86] Accordingly, the jíbaro came to represent an ideology in opposition to Rivero's own nationalist and pro-independence beliefs.

Furthermore, *El tremendo hotel*'s fictional family erased any traces of the racially sexualized mestizaje.[87] The mulata character that was emblematic of Bufo comedy and also — albeit culturally and politically distinct — of the 1930s Puerto Rican–Cuban cultura negroide movement was lost in the translation. The *El tremendo hotel* community comprised black and white Puerto Ricans and Spaniards.[88] Consequently, Bufo's ideology of Cuba as a mestiza nation that was exemplified through la mulata, but also via the relationship among el negrito, la mulata, and el gallego, was altered in *El tremendo hotel*.

Instead of focusing on the racialized mixing that informed ideologies of Puerto Ricanness and mestizaje, *El tremendo hotel*'s narrative portrayed the hotel as a nonracist social space. As I discussed in the introduction, the ideology of mestizaje constructs the nation as racially integrated and void of racism because everybody, regardless of skin color, is mixed and thus an equal member in society. Accordingly, this discursive signification of a nonracist nation was represented in the daily interactions among Doña Polita, Tranquilino, Don Nepo, and Calderón, and through the sometimes complicated mother-son-like relationship between Doña Polita and Calderón. Still, even though none of the local characters rejected Calderón based on his race, the fact that el negrito was at the bottom of the hotel's social and economic environment articulated the fissures in Puerto Rican discourses of racial equality. Through stereotypical and contradictory racialized constructions, *El tremendo hotel*'s narrative was both inclusive and indirectly critical of Puerto Rico's ideology of a racially democratic society. After all, only Calderón and apparently his countryside blood family members worked as servants in the houses of financially solvent Puerto Ricans.

According to general references included in the narrative, Calderón had family members in his hometown (Naguabo, Ramón Rivero's hometown), and he sometimes received visits from his aunt mamá Yoyo; however, Doña Polita was portrayed as his mother figure.[89] Doña Polita was Calderón's *madrina* (godmother), a woman who, regardless of Calderón's mischievous actions and laziness, always tried to provide him with some type of job. Furthermore, the other local hotel members were portrayed as Calderón's city family. In other words, the hotel was not only the location where Puerto Rico's ethnic, racial, class, and political relations were articulated but it also represented an intermediary migratory space. Whereas Calderón was the only character who exemplified the country-to-city migration that took place in Puerto Rico, his move to the city symbolized the next migratory step to the United States. Without Doña Polita's support, and without Calderón's own survival skills, he presumably would have had to migrate to the United States.

Migration to the United States was portrayed in *El tremendo hotel* as a last resort for the individual and as a process that was ultimately detrimental to the nation and to the island's people. Based on *El tremendo hotel*'s narrative, to endure Puerto Rico's route to modernization, which encompassed the massive migration to the United States of jobless working-class individuals, the marginal groups needed to take advantage of any situation to improve their economic status and avoid the exodus. Additionally, the most financially solvent individuals were responsible for keeping the hotel (and nation) functioning and assisting even the "undesirable" members of the family.

In *El tremendo hotel*, Doña Polita was the character who maintained the order and boundaries within the hotel. Actually, after Calderón, Doña Polita was the most astute individual in this community. She was portrayed as a strong, hard-working, savvy, and skillful woman who did not need the assistance of any men (or anybody) to keep the business running. However, it should be clear that, contrary to late-nineteenth- and early-twentieth-century literary texts and music lyrics in Puerto Rico and Latin America that intertwined ideologies of womanhood, nationhood, and race, Doña Polita was not in charge of preserving the alleged whiteness of the nation.[90] Besides the fact that Doña Polita and the other white characters were middle-aged individuals, none of the members of this community were interested in sexual pleasures or were constructed as hypersexual. Instead, money (i.e., class) and local politics dominated the day-to-day lives of Doña Polita, Don Nepo, Tranquilino, and obviously, Calderón. These family concerns about money, politics, and financial stability acquired various levels of signification with the sporadic appearances of the American characters Mr. Sandwich and Ruth, *la americana* (the American woman).

The two Americans were constructed and perceived differently from the typical local guests and visitors of the hotel. Although, as previously observed, hotel members adhered to a social code informed by hierarchical structures that established the social position of each character, the Americans were represented as part of a higher economic strata. Their economic solvency was sometimes intertwined with ideologies of cultural superiority. For example, Ruth described Doña Polita and her guests as "uncultured and uncivilized" and expressed her intention to open another hotel that would "wipe them out of business." On the other hand, Mr. Sandwich was not fluent in Spanish and constantly made mistakes when he spoke. Nonetheless, he was a stubborn man who never paid attention to Doña Polita or Don Nepo's corrections because he apparently did not trust their intellectual ability even when it concerned their native language.

Although the American characters were part of *El tremendo hotel*'s cultural and social environment (which was obviously a direct correlation to the U.S. presence in Puerto Rico), they were nevertheless outside the fictional and symbolic (national-ethnic) family structure. Although they visited the hotel, they never stayed in it. These characters represented a particular imperialistic discourse that destabilized the hotel's racialized, class, cultural, and familial normalcy. Whereas, at the surface level, the American characters served foremost as the target of jokes for the local hotel guests and obviously, for Calderón (who was the only bilingual individual in this community), these characters articulated the ongoing destructive possibilities of fragmenting the hotel, family, and nation construct. This potential disruption of the hotel family became more prevalent through the brief romantic relationship between Calderón and Ruth.

Calderón decided to pursue Ruth primarily because she was a financially

solvent woman who could provide him with enough money to avoid working at the hotel. A crucial aspect of this affair was that whereas Ruth constantly treated the hotel workers and guests condescendingly (and allegorically, the Puerto Rican constructed family), she seemingly transcended her
class, whiteness, and presumably her U.S. segregationist ideology to pursue
a romance with a black and poor Puerto Rican man.[91] Through Rivero's narrative translation of U.S. gendered whiteness, a white American woman socially, and probably sexually, interacted with the ethnic and racial Other.

El tremendo hotel's romantic relationship across color lines marked a drastic ideological distance from the portrayals of race relations in U.S. commercial radio entertainment programming. As Michele Hilmes argues, during
the 1920s, 1930s, and 1940s "national narratives" in U.S. radio positioned
blacks and whites in separate cultural and racial spaces, thereby rearticulating U.S. dominant discourses of whiteness and segregation.[92] On the other
hand, in *El tremendo hotel*, a white American woman seemed to appropriate
Puerto Rico's racial democracy and mestizaje discourses and dated a black
man. Yet, despite those outward appearances, this racially progressive romance was in fact complicated by Ruth's use of U.S. racial and racist epithets
when addressing Calderón.

For instance, local hotel guests addressed Calderón by his name and sometimes by calling him el negrito or *el trigueño* (mulatto), a re-appropriation
of Puerto Rico's racial and racist categorizations.[93] Conversely, Ruth always
referred to Calderón as "blackie." Consequently, in the few episodes in which
Ruth appeared in *El tremendo hotel*, the narrative and characters embodied
not only Puerto Rico's racial ideologies but also indirectly, the U.S. 1940s
and 1950s stereotypes of blackness and the racialization of Puerto Ricans,
Mexicans, and other nonwhite groups in the United States.

In their propaganda in defense of Jim Crow, U.S. segregationists utilized the modality of race via the "bad Negro" label to position all ethnic
Others outside what Stephen Berrey categorizes as "the imagined community of whiteness."[94] That is, in justifying racial domination, southern officials
sought nonsouthern support for segregation by likening the South's "bad
Negroes" (criminal, immoral) to nonwhite groups in other regions: Puerto
Ricans in the East, the "Asiatics" in the West, and the Mexicans in the South-
west.[95] Similarly, Ruth, as a "typical" American, utilized a racist caricature
("blackie") that suggested that in the eyes of white Americans, Puerto Ricans
were a racial Other.

The American characters embodied a third level of whiteness that can be distinguished from a Puerto Rican or a Spanish whiteness. American whiteness obscured the racial and class distinctions among the local members of the hotel by positioning local whites in a subordinate and similar location to el negrito, Calderón. One could say that the inclusion of Ruth in *El tremendo hotel* served as a vehicle for exposing the U.S. dominant ideology of white racial and cultural supremacy while concomitantly (yet indirectly) comparing U.S. Jim Crow segregation laws to Puerto Rico's mestizaje discourse. In other words, through the romance between Ruth and Calderón, the narrative juxtaposed 1940s and 1950s U.S. racial ideologies (racial purity, antimiscegenation laws, and segregation) with Puerto Rico's hegemonic discourse of a racially mixed, equal, and thus nonracist society. Furthermore, based on *El tremendo hotel*, regardless of the island's political associations with the U.S., Puerto Ricans could never obtain equal membership in the American family or first-class citizenship given the U.S. historically fixed and politically, socially, and culturally contained positionalities of whiteness and blackness.

Still, it should be emphasized that more than articulating U.S. racial ideologies, American whiteness signified U.S. capitalist accumulation and expansion — a new "matrix of power" that created and operated within distinct racialized, class, and cultural discourses.[96] This third level of whiteness represented the U.S. imperialistic power structure in Puerto Rico and the U.S. investments that were taking place on the island during the 1940s and 1950s. Based on *El tremendo hotel*'s narrative, these foreign investments had the potential to destroy the hotel as well as the financial future and stability of Puerto Ricans because, as I previously observed, Ruth's main objective was to "wipe out" Doña Polita's business. As a result, in the episodes where Ruth and Calderón had a romantic relationship, the narrative positioned Calderón as the only individual who (through shady actions) could force Ruth out of the neighborhood.

When Calderón briefly abandoned Doña Polita and ran away with his girlfriend Ruth, he soon drained Ruth financially. As expected, Ruth "dumped him" and returned to the United States. Certainly, in this case, Calderón's actions did not articulate a class-based political empowerment. Nor did he purposely join the local hotel members to fight the foreign intrusion. Then again, Calderón was fully aware of his subordinate position and the fact that, regardless of who ran the hotel, he was always viewed as the Other in this community. However, even though these episodes did not function through

Ramón Rivero in blackface, most likely as the character Calderón.
Courtesy of Fundación Ramón Rivero.

a direct nationalistic political posture, their narratives depicted Calderón as being more comfortable with Doña Polita as the hotel owner. Calderón knew that no matter what he did, phrases such as "I am sorry madrina," or "madrina, you know that I love you very much," would convince Doña Polita to accept him again. Simply put, despite Calderón's dubious actions, he was part of the hotel family.

Besides being a lazy and opportunistic young man, Calderón sometimes demonstrated a class-based social consciousness that transcended his questionable ethics and self-centered survival tactics. In the January–March 1951 episodes entitled *Elección de alcalde* (Mayor's election), Ramón Rivero created a political campaign in which Calderón, Don Nepo, Tranquilino, and Doña Polita ran for mayor of Mirafanguito. Although Mirafanguito was a fictitious place, it directly referenced *Miramar*, an upper-class neighborhood, and *El fanguito*, a San Juan slum. After a series of political debates, the radio audience was asked to select the mayor by sending their votes to WKAQ radio. As was expected, the audience elected Calderón by an overwhelming majority.[97]

One might assume that Calderón won the election because of the character's popularity with the audience. However, in addition to being the protagonist and the more astute character in the show, Calderón was the only one of the four candidates who in his campaign embodied the voice of the working-class, while the others were depicted as being more interested in money and power. For example, in one episode, Calderón condemned the government's abuse of lower-paid public officials, noting that, "While one señor earns thirty thousand dollars, a policeman with four children earns more or less thirty dollars. And then this policeman has to look for Correa Cotto! Of course, Correa would kill this policeman and the widow would receive forty dollars each month. In the meantime, el señor keeps earning thirty thousand dollars annually. Isn't this funny?"[98]

Furthermore, through direct criticism of Doña Polita and Don Nepo (who were political allies at the beginning of the *Elección de alcalde* series and who were identified as offering "Pan, Tierra, y Libertad," which was the official slogan of the pro-Commonwealth Party), Calderón denounced the candidates' and government's excesses at the expense of the taxpayers, remarking that, "Pueblo . . . Don Nepo is not the mayor yet, nor Doña Polita, and they are already asking for cars and windowed balconies. Cars, many cars. . . . Cars that stop in front of the people's residences, people who supposedly use

Calderón's victory parade as mayor of Mirafanguito.
Courtesy of Fundación Ramón Rivero.

them for the so called official duties. Then these cars are rotted by mold. Who pays for those cars? Don Nepo, Doña Pola? Cayayo? Lechuga? No, el pueblo pays for them!"

In another episode, Calderón condemned the government's lack of support for the arts and countered by promising free theater to local producers. If he were elected mayor, Puerto Rico would be "a beautiful country, a country where the artist has free theater . . . where theater is encouraged." Finally, in a number of episodes, Calderón saluted the Puerto Rican soldiers in Korea who "together with other free nations are combating radicalism, communism, anarchism" while fighting "for the cause of liberty." This posturing rearticulated the pro-Independence Party and the Commonwealth's support of the war while also offering moral reassurance to the soldiers and their families.[99]

Although it is extremely difficult to summarize all the themes that were part of *El tremendo hotel*, primarily because of the historical and cultural specificity of the texts, the narratives directly and indirectly articulated the political, economic, cultural, and social negotiations that characterized Puerto Rico from the late 1940s to the mid-1950s.[100] At the margins of these transformations was the fictional character Calderón. While both the Puerto Rican and U.S. governments were disseminating the message of the social and economic success of the U.S. development plan for Third World nations, Calderón and the other characters of *El tremendo hotel* represented ideological reminders of the groups who remained at the bottom of the economic and social ladders.

As Abelardo Díaz-Alfaro notes regarding Rivero's creation, "it was the wretched man's revenge," a man who was "underestimated because of his plebeian background."[101] Calderón was a trickster, a picaresque character who transgressed the law, the official norms of conduct, and challenged the habitus of the Puerto Rican modernized middle upper class. In addition, he ridiculed (albeit in contradictory ways) Puerto Rico's dominant ideologies of Spaniards' cultural superiority (aristocracy and language) and defied American economic and cultural imperialistic practices on the island. Conversely, in the process of assessing Puerto Rico's social, economic, political, and colonial conditions along with the subjugation of the working class, Rivero produced an essentialist view and stereotypical representation of CubaRican black subjects.

I contend that Calderón and all of Rivero's blackface and black voice characterizations were CubaRican, not only because of the influence of the

Cuban actor Leopoldo Fernández and Cuba's Bufo comedy but also because, at least in radio, Rivero appropriated a Cuban accent. In other words, Rivero's "black" voice was equivalent to a *habanero* (accent from Havana) cadence. This categorization of CubaRican does not erase the local elements of Rivero's personifications. After all, and as I previously mentioned, Calderón identified himself as being born and raised in Puerto Rico and constantly addressed the island's political, social, and economic issues. Significantly, the audience read him as Puerto Rican. Furthermore, while Rivero signed all of his radio, theater, and television scripts as the writer, director, and producer (including the radio show *El tremendo hotel*, the television shows *La taberna India* and *La farándula Corona*, and the theater scripts of *Hay que defenderse* and *El tremendo hotel*), Diplomacia (Rivero's characterization of the poor black man from Old San Juan) was announced as the performer of the black voices and described as the actor who impersonated the black characters in theatrical texts and television shows. Accordingly, Rivero's black voice and blackface performances operated through various masking processes that produced layers of dissociations between himself and his representations of blackness. These levels of masking were articulated through (1) blackface, (2) the character Diplomacia, and (3) the appropriation of a Cuban accent.

The first level of masking was the use of blackface. With the theater piece *El chico mambí* and the use of burnt cork, Rivero physically obscured his whiteness and constructed a generic CubaRican black subject. This generic representation was informed by Cuba's and Puerto Rico's hegemonic racial ideologies and the location of black citizens at the bottom of the CubaRican sociocultural space. However, Rivero's generally CubaRican blackface masking was transformed into a uniquely black Puerto Rican cultural artifact via Diplomacia.

Rivero's Diplomacia created a second level of masking that differentiated his blackface performances from the Bufo tradition. Diplomacia, Rivero's colonized gaze and construction of a singularized yet unknown (and thus imaginary for the audience) poor black male, became the stage, voice, and televisual body for performing Other black subjects. As the character's name suggests, Diplomacia (Diplomacy-Diplo) created a safer body and a space of negotiation for Rivero's political and social criticism. In the case of *El tremendo hotel*, Diplomacia, a politically informed black man, performed Calderón, a morally dubious, yet highly intelligent character. Thus, figuratively, the political satire was not performed by Rivero, but rather by Diploma-

Ramón Rivero donning blackface. Courtesy of Fundación Ramón Rivero.

cia/Diplo. Furthermore, to develop another level of distance, Diplo's Calderón did not have a Puerto Rican accent; he had a Cuban accent. Consequently, the third level of masking functioned through voice.

By performing with a Cuban accent, Rivero returned his blackface and black voice characters to the CubaRican space. Calderón operated within ongoing ethnic ambiguity: he sounded Cuban, but he talked about Puerto Rico. He had a habanero accent, but the audiences read him as Puerto Rican. And I would state the obvious here: the audience translated Diplomacia and Calderón as Puerto Rican, not only because of the topics addressed in *El tremendo hotel* but also because Rivero was Puerto Rican. Given these multiple significations the repercussions of Rivero's levels of masking warrant consideration.

On the one hand (and as I indicated in the beginning of this chapter), the audiences merged Rivero and Diplomacia into one signifier: Diplo. On the other hand, even though Rivero (through Diplo) created various black characters and despite the fact that Calderón was the first black character who appeared on Puerto Rican television (in *La taberna India*), all of his creations were united in the figure of Diplo (Diplomacia). These negritos were similar stereotypes and they were read as the same: they were all the clever and poor negrito Diplo.[102]

Symbolically, a black man became a theatrical, radio, and televisual vehicle for criticizing Puerto Rico's colonialism and the oppressive conditions of the working class. In one respect, the negritos became the jíbaro nemesis. The negritos functioned in opposition to the conceptualization of the white jíbaro as the symbol of Puerto Ricanness. Although the fictional negritos were CubaRican and black, the jíbaro was the autochthonous representation of the Puerto Rican mestiza (nonetheless white and Spanish) identity. Whereas the hybrid negritos were urban and clever yet also self-centered and lazy, the jíbaro was a skillful and hard-working bucolic man. While the negritos could be read as pro-independence advocates, the jíbaro became the iconic figure of pro-Commonwealth status.[103] Most significantly, the negritos were engaged in an ongoing dialogue with their audiences about various problems in Puerto Rican society. On the other hand, the jíbaro was an abstract cultural symbol appearing in literature, in the flag of the pro-Commonwealth Party, and in the local government's reconstruction of the island's national culture and identity.[104]

Nonetheless, in Rivero's efforts to distance himself from his black voice and blackface characters, la negritud became part of the trans-Caribbean and

CubaRican modernity as ambivalent subject and subjected gendered symbols. Rivero's (and others') black voice and blackface characters fixed the social location of blackness in Puerto Rico's mediascape. The masking of blackness reassured the colonized Others of the distance between themselves (a racially and culturally mestiza nation, yet discursively white and Spaniard) and the presence of the black antimodern element that was part of the culture and society. One needs to keep in mind that through newspaper photos and movie newsreels, the audience was aware that Rivero (and also Mona Marti, the actress who performed the black voice female characters in radionovelas and mamá Yoyo in *El tremendo hotel*) were white actors performing blackness.

Unquestionably, the political criticism and the pro working-class elements that were part of Rivero's negrito personas need to be considered. Then again, while the negritos were fictional citizens who transgressed the rules and questioned the social, political, and economic systems, their actions were framed through a rhetoric of individualism. Even as Rivero tried to evoke a class-based collective political empowerment, the negritos were narrated, remembered, reproduced, and caricatured as noble and sentimental, yet also as lazy and individualistic.

For example, in several descriptions of Rivero's creations (all of them referred to as Diplo), the negrito was narrated as "a portion of the tropics' humanity, a man who philosophizes, who thinks and acts between the waves of greatness and meanness," "a character extracted from our people's roots. He is el negrito who played to be shocking, yet harmless," and a "sentimental negrito who possessed the 'Cuban wit' and used his ingenuity for personal gain."[105] The tropics, Puerto Rico, and Cuba became an imaginary borderless Caribbean space that was merged by a masqueraded blackness. As a result, black men were part of both the Puerto Rican nation and the CubaRican symbolic space, portrayed as infantilized youthful figures who never assumed the responsibilities of adulthood. More importantly, the negritos were structured through the discourse of whiteness. They were not Puerto Rican or CubaRican black subjects; rather, they were hegemonic representations of a trans-Caribbean embodied blackness.

It is unclear why Rivero imposed this distance between himself and his embodiment of blackness. Nor is it comprehensible why he adopted a Cuban accent, besides the fact that he was influenced by the Cuban actor Leopoldo Fernández and Bufo theater. However, this posturing raises several questions.

Did Rivero want to protect himself from the repressive political environment of the 1940s and 1950s by assigning his political and social criticism to fictional and hybrid CubaRican characters? Did he think that Diplomacia's impersonation of Other black characters incarnated the voice of the oppressed black Puerto Rican subject? Did he believe that the main problems in Puerto Rico (and the Spanish Caribbean) were colonialism (and neocolonialism) and class stratification? Did he thus perform the voice of the working class despite his own social status? Or was he appropriating the hegemonic discourse of la gran familia puertorriqueña while concomitantly presenting a paternalistic, racist, and reductionist view of blackness? All of these issues might have informed Rivero's constructions of blackface and black voice. Regardless of the reasons, his representations of blackness, his political and social satire, and his popularity with audiences recreated the complexities and contradictions of race in Puerto Rico and the ideological negotiations within the colonized sociocultural space during the late 1930s, 1940s, and 1950s.

Be that as it may, the audience adored Rivero and his negrito personifications. I argue that in addition to identifying with the ambivalent (and masqueraded) negritos who defied the system and always triumphed, along with admiring the actor's talent, audiences venerated Rivero's public persona. In other words, the audience might have perceived Rivero's social and political activism and his negritos as a unified emblem of the working class. This love for Rivero was demonstrated at his burial where "50,000 people attended Diplo's funeral" and the casket was carried by "the port workers who practically snatched it from the funeral procession."[106] This devotion can also be seen in photographs of poor people crying in front of the casket. After Rivero's death, despite ongoing televisual representations of blackface negritos during the late 1950s and 1960s, none of these characters became popular figures. The political and social commentaries that were entrenched in Rivero's (Diplo) creations disappeared. The negritos became playful, childish, uncultured, and laughable elements in Puerto Rico's 1950s and 1960s mediascape.

Screening Blackness: Normalizing Puerto Rican and Cuban Whiteness

The immediate successor to Rivero's Diplomacia and Calderón blackface negritos was Reguerete, a character who became the central figure in Telemundo's *La taberna India*. In Puerto Rico's vernacular language *reguerete* signifies "a mess." As the word suggests, and based on descriptions of the character, Reguerete was the source of ongoing misunderstandings in *La taberna India*. According to Paquito Cordero, the actor who created this character, Reguerete was "a playful and innocent *negrito caribeño* who was always involved in trouble."[107] Cordero's primary influence in creating Reguerete was his admiration for the blackface characters of both Rivero and the Cuban actor Leopoldo Fernández (the actor from whom Rivero borrowed blackface).[108] Because there is only one clip available from *La taberna India* and Reguerete and no available scripts, it is extremely difficult to conduct an analysis of this racialized character. However, based on the existing clip, I position Reguerete as another version of the CubaRican negrito. Still, in contrast to Calderón, Reguerete was constructed as a confused individual who lacked intelligence.

Unlike Diplomacia and Calderón, Reguerete did not become an iconic figure in Puerto Rico. Reguerete's lack of popularity with audiences might relate to two factors. First, in contrast to Rivero's blackface characters, Cordero's Reguerete apparently did not address Puerto Rico's political, economic, and social issues and was generally portrayed as an idiotic black male figure. Second, perhaps audiences did not identify with Paquito Cordero's public persona or did not deem him as talented as Rivero. Regardless of these possibilities, blackface negritos were already established as a televisual tradition in Puerto Rico. While Reguerete disappeared in 1965 (largely because of Cordero's interest in television production), the character was replaced with the negrito Doroteo.[109] Performed by the Cuban actor Tino Acosta, the negrito Doroteo signaled an important sociocultural transformation in Puerto Rico during the early 1960s: the Cuban migration.

The first Cuban migration to Puerto Rico after the 1959 Cuban Revolution occurred during 1960–1961 when Governor Luis Muñoz Marín invited professionals to the island.[110] According to José A. Cobas and Jorge Duany, successive Cuban migratory influxes were influenced by language, the similarities of cultures and climates, the economic growth that Puerto Rico experienced during the 1960s, and the political, social, and economic ties between Puerto Rico and the United States.[111] Of significance to this migration is the fact that most of the individuals were part of the migratory group classified as the "Golden Exiles," a categorization that referred to their upper socioeconomic status in Cuba. Before migrating to Puerto Rico, most of these exiles' occupations were related to business, manage-

The negrito Doroteo. Courtesy of *Teve Guía* Archives.

ment, or other professional enterprises.[112] Furthermore, racially speaking, most of them were white.

Initially, Puerto Ricans received the group with enthusiasm, but the positive environment eroded when some members of the Puerto Rican middle class perceived that many of the immigrants were being hired over Puerto Ricans. Thus, the prejudice against Cuban immigrants in Puerto Rico was primarily rooted in the migrants' rapid economic success and the fact that they were viewed as people who took jobs away from Puerto Ricans. Cubans in Puerto Rico were pejoratively constructed as the "Jews of the Caribbean" and as "opportunistic and ungrateful parasites."[113] As well, in Puerto Rico's vernacular culture in general and certain sectors of the population in particular, Cubans were depicted as *gusanos* (worms), a derogatory term for Cubans who abandoned and opposed the Cuban Revolution.

With the post-1959 Cuban migration, Cuban actors (for example, Leopoldo Fernández and Tino Acosta) performed the negritos, adding another dimension to the embodiment of blackness. Considering the social, racial, and previous economic positions of the Cuban immigrants who came to Puerto Rico and the fact that the actors who donned blackface were white middle-class Cubans, these negritos can be viewed as impersonations of the black underclass who stayed in Cuba after the revolution. In other words, through the Cuban actors' blackface performances and through the disruption of the anastomosis flows between Cuba and Puerto Rico due to the 1959 Cuban Revolution, blacks would now (supposedly) remain in socialist Cuba. With these racial, political, and social discursive constructions, negritos can be read as a class and racial self-reaffirmation of the Cuban migrant community's whiteness.

In addition to the CubaRican negritos, a new stereotype of blackness appeared on Puerto Rico's commercial television in 1955 in the character of Lirio Blanco. Performed by the black actress Carmen Belén Richardson, Lirio Blanco was part of Tommy Muñiz's (producer and writer) and Telemundo's highly successful comedy *El colegio de la alegría*.[114] This show presented the daily routine in a Puerto Rican elementary school where all the child characters were performed by adults. I position Lirio Blanco as a translation of the U.S. pickaninny stereotype. Similar to the pickaninny depicted in Hollywood movies and U.S. television, Lirio Blanco was a harmless, pleasant, and eyepopping character.[115] Lirio Blanco's comedic persona relied on the hyperbolic use of her wide open eyes to show elements of surprise.

Lirio Blanco from *El colegio de la alegría*. Courtesy of *Teve Guía* Archives.

Another element of Lirio Blanco's racialized characterization was her name (lily white), which was an ironic reaffirmation of what the character's black body could not possibly be: white. Although Lirio Blanco was represented as just another Puerto Rican child in a typical school environment, the character also posited recurring racial differentiation between herself as a black girl and the other children, since none of the other characters were identified by their race (white). It should be clear that Lirio Blanco did not reproduce the black CubaRican accent of the blackface negritos; neither did she have the Puerto Rican black accent that was later acquired by 1970s blackface negras. Furthermore, she was not constructed as a self-centered and individualistic child, nor was she less intelligent than the other children. Still, her name and physical reactions created a racial distinction between the way white children and black children supposedly behaved.[116] Although the CubaRican negritos and Lirio Blanco were different stereotypes and even though Lirio Blanco was performed by a black actress (something extremely important since black actors and actresses were almost nonexistent in Puerto Rico's commercial television during the 1950s and 1960s), these characters legitimized whiteness by positioning negritud as an Other amusing element in Puerto Rico's televisual space.

It should be noted that during the 1950s when *La taberna India* and *El colegio de la alegría* were being broadcast, black musical performers (such as Rafael Cortijo y su Combo) and Afro Puerto Rican musical elements were also part of Puerto Rico's televisual space.[117] As Frances Aparicio asserts, "Rafael Cortijo's historical significance lies in the *visual* presence of blacks on television (in his show *La taberna India*) and in their musical prominence in radio; in other words, they 'occupied' the social space of media and entertainment that threatened and contested the 'whiteness' [*blanquitismo*] of social clubs and dance halls."[118] Also, prominent Puerto Rican black figures such as Juan Boria (a black Puerto Rican poetry reader) recited *poesía negroide* (black poetry) in *La taberna India* and in the 1950s variety program *Show de shows*.[119] Nonetheless, what Aparicio does not discuss is the fact that while black and mulatto performers were indeed part of local television during the 1950s and 1960s, these musicians were introduced on multiple occasions by a blackface Master of Ceremony Caribbean or CubaRican negrito.

For example, the only clip available from *La taberna India* presents the blackface character Reguerete introducing Rafael Cortijo and his band. In a similar fashion, a photo provided by Rivero's family depicts Juan Boria next to Rivero in blackface. Finally, neither Rafael Cortijo nor any other black performer was a television producer in Puerto Rico during the 1950s. In the beginning of Puerto Rican commercial television, local production was in the hands of several actors-producers who took advantage of the new medium's financial opportunities. Racially speaking, these actors-producers were white.[120]

Needless to say, black and mulatto audiences might have been able to create counterhegemonic readings of the negrito performances. Or, using José Esteban Muñoz's concept, black and mulatto television viewers may have engaged in an ongoing process of "disidentification." In other words, they likely "recycled and rethought the encoded messages" embedded in *La taberna India* (and also in *El colegio de la alegría*) and focused on the cleverness of Calderón, on Lirio Blanco as a black child performed by a black actress, or on the key participation of black musicians in the beginning of Puerto Rico's commercial television.[121] Still, Puerto Rico's commercial television entertainment programming was dominated by white actors and actresses. Hence, televisual constructions of blackness were framed through whiteness.

Consequently, Rivero's characters, subsequent blackface Caribbean negritos and negras, and Lirio Blanco normalized the whiteness of the Puerto Rican nation and the Cuban immigrant community while concomitantly reaffirming the marginal location of blacks in Puerto Rico and the CubaRican borderless cultural space. This interconnection of blackface and the stereotypical construction of a black child as a reaffirmation of whiteness should not be understood as an emblematic desire to whiten the Puerto Rican nation and facilitate assimilation into the U.S. white melting pot. On the contrary, I argue that black voice, blackface, and black televisual representations in Puerto Rico functioned through the Eurocentrism engrained in la gran familia puertorriqueña discourse and also in the CubaRican hegemonic mestizaje ideology.

I emphasize this local and CubaRican discourse of whiteness partly to distance this analysis from the multiple studies on how Irish and Jewish immigrants in the United States "became white" by—in addition to other processes—performing in blackface. Furthermore, I am also responding to Gladys Jiménez-Muñoz's theorizing and questioning of Rivero's televisual blackface as possible ideological and racial negotiations of Puerto Rican whiteness in relation to U.S. whiteness. Although I agree with Jiménez-Muñoz's positioning of Rivero's blackface as a class and racial objectification of the black Other, I also believe Rivero's "racial transvestism" (as Jiménez-Muñoz categorizes it) needs to be contextualized through his performances before the arrival of television and his public and private political personae.[122]

Rivero became an iconic cultural figure in Puerto Rico by way of his theater and radio shows and through his social and political activism before 1954. Rivero, a self-proclaimed nationalist, created a show (*El tremendo hotel*) that directly and indirectly criticized the U.S. presence in Puerto Rico. Thus, why would he be concerned with U.S. whiteness when his political public persona rejected U.S. imperialism? Additionally, the analysis of Rivero's blackface negritos must be examined through the influence of Cuban Bufo theater and the political and anticolonial connotations associated with this theatrical genre and more specifically with the negrito catedrático type.

That said, I would like to suggest that since its beginnings, Puerto Rico's commercial television depictions of blackness were contained within three specific televisual locations: variety shows, comedies, and telenovelas. First, the variety shows (one of the most popular television genres in Puerto Rico since 1954) integrated Afro Puerto Rican cultural traditions and bands composed of black and mulatto musicians but also—during the 1950s and 1960s—included blackface characters. Second, the locally produced comedies presented a few black actors and actresses alongside white actors in blackface. Third, the telenovelas were dominated by white actors and actresses, some of whom (specifically actresses) performed in blackface. As I discuss in chapter 2, these televisual spaces and the ongoing use of blackface drastically limited the opportunities for black actors and actresses in Puerto Rico's commercial television.

Finally, the Cuban Revolution and the United States' intricate relations with the island destabilized the anastomosis flows between Puerto Rico and Cuba. Indeed, cultural relations between these two islands have persisted since Cuban singers, theater groups, and scholars continue to visit Puerto Rico and vice versa. Furthermore, as Cesar Salgado observes, pockets of the CubaRican cultural space still exist. These spaces are evident in the vernacular cultures (for example, salsa music), in theater (for instance, the Spanish-language and Latino theater scene in New York City), and in literature (the work of Magali García Ramis, Sonia Rivera-Valdés, and Mayra Montero). Nonetheless, as I previously indicated, the results of the post-1959 Cuban migration spawned a strong resentment toward this migratory group in Puerto Rico.

As I discuss in the following chapter, the love-hate sentiment that emerged after the Cuban migration transformed the CubaRican negrito into a Puerto Rican blackface jíbara version during the 1970s. However, the civil rights and black power movements; the reemergence of the Puerto Rican Left and its ideological connection with both the Cuban Revolution and the black power struggles; and the influence of U.S. (and global) alternative political, social, sexual, and cultural practices in Puerto Rico partially altered televisual representations of blackface blackness during the 1970s. More significantly, during the 1970s black actors and actresses mobilized to protest stereotypical images in local productions, thus challenging the white ideological normativity that characterized the industry, its representation of the Puerto Rican people, and Puerto Rican society in general.

Bringing the Soul Afros, Black Empowerment, and the Resurgent Popularity of Blackface

I hope that the make-up they [white performers] use on their faces
cannot be taken off and that it transforms itself into tar!
    Raquel Rey, *Teve Guia*, May 13, 1973, quoting Sylvia del Villard

On January 26, 1967, Stokely Carmichael, head of the Student Nonviolent Coordinating Committee (SNCC), flew to San Juan, Puerto Rico, to sign a "protocol of cooperation" with Juan Mari Brás, the leader of the Movement for Puerto Rican Independence (MPI).[1] In a joint statement Carmichael and Mari Brás indicated that both organizations were "in the vanguard of a common struggle against U.S. imperialism." According to Carmichael, Puerto Rico's main site of oppression was the island's colonial status. He observed that "just as 'Black Power' signifies a struggle for liberation and control of Afro-American communities by black people, the independence struggle in Puerto Rico is for control by Puerto Ricans of their own lives and the wealth of the country. Black people constitute a colony within the U.S. Puerto Rico is a colony outside the U.S."[2] For these two leaders, Puerto Rico's political sovereignty was the primary goal in the fight against imperial domination.

This brief news story, entitled "Stokely's Castroite Links" and published in the right-wing newspaper *Human Events* as an example of the alleged communist influence in the black power movement, hints at the intersections of 1960's local and transnational anticolonial fronts.[3] In addition, the Mari Brás-Carmichael meeting alludes to the sometimes intertwined and sometimes disjointed political, racial, and cultural mobilizations that took place in Puerto Rico during the late 1960s and early 1970s. Although seemingly disconnected, it is precisely within this Puerto Rican–African American and, even though not included in the conversation, U.S.-based Puerto Rican radical left context that one should consider the highly critical statement of the Puerto Rican black and diasporic (Puerto Rico–New York City) performer Sylvia del Villard: "I hope that the make-up they [white performers] use on

their faces cannot be taken off and that it transforms itself into tar!" The re-
birth of the Puerto Rican Left in both Puerto Rico and the United States and
the U.S.-based Puerto Rican–African American political coalitions serve as
a background for understanding the racialized contestations that took place
in the island's commercial television during the 1970s.

Although the political repression of the 1940s and 1950s drastically reduced anticolonial political movements in Puerto Rico, the triumph of the
Cuban Revolution in 1959 precipitated a reemergence of the pro-independence ideology.[4] The island's struggle for independence and working-class
politics defined the Puerto Rican Left during the 1960s. Groups such as MPI,
the Federation of University Students Pro Independence (FUPI), and the Federation of High School Students Pro Independence (FEPI) organized demonstrations and strikes against military service, created coalitions to fight the
exploitation of the working class, and wrote petitions to the United Nations
in favor of Puerto Rico's political freedom and the liberation of political pris-
oners.[5] Notwithstanding the anticolonialist political rhetoric of the Puerto
Rican–based Left, the inequalities experienced by Afro Puerto Ricans on the
island were rarely the concern of pro-independence groups.

Alternatively, on the mainland, Puerto Ricans (and specifically Afro
Puerto Ricans) were actively involved in African American political, social,
and cultural organizations from the early 1960s to the black power movement of the mid-1960s.[6] Certainly these associations should not come as a
surprise because Puerto Ricans residing in the United States had been relegated to racial and class locations that were similar to those of African Americans.[7] More important, in the United States many Afro Puerto Ricans were
indeed read as African Americans. As Pablo "Yoruba" Guzmán (one of the
leaders of the 1970s Young Lords Party) recalled, "before people called me a
spic, they called me a nigger."[8] Guzmán hints at the intertwined processes of
racialization that Afro Puerto Ricans experienced (and probably still experience) in the states. Through the U.S. mainstream's black and white binary
racial discourse, the racialization of Puerto Ricans in general, and the rejection of blackness that has characterized Puerto Rico's culture, Afro Puerto
Ricans were subjected to multiple levels of oppression. This spectrum of
racial and racist practices informed the 1960s and 1970s African American–
Puerto Rican–Afro Puerto Rican coalitions and the political platform of the
Young Lords.[9]

In both Chicago and New York, the Young Lords Party (a group that was part of the Black Panthers' Rainbow Coalition alliance) mobilized to re-gain community control and established political ties with other minority groups to challenge the racial and class subjugation of Puerto Rican and Latino communities in the United States.[10] In addition, the Young Lords in-cluded women's rights as part of its platform and criticized the machismo and homophobia ingrained in Puerto Rican and Latino cultures.[11] Similar to the island's leftist movements, the Young Lords focused on Puerto Rico's in-dependence. But, as Roberto Rodríguez-Morazzani argues, "for Puerto Rican radicals in New York, the legacy of Black Nationalist Malcom X was to occupy a place equal in importance to that of Don Pedro Albizu Campos [leader of the Nationalist Party of Puerto Rico]."[12] Therefore, for the U.S.-based radical left anticolonialism signified political freedom as well as racial conscious-ness. From the appropriation of names associated with Africa (for example, Yoruba), to the use of au naturel hair styles, to the ongoing dialogues with African Americans, race and blackness occupied important positions within the Young Lords' political and cultural platforms.

The political awareness and action of Puerto Ricans on the mainland were palpable not only in terms of grassroots community-based mobilizations but also in their use of media outlets to represent their struggles. For example, in separate studies Chon Noriega and Lillian Jiménez have demonstrated that Boricua (Puerto Rican) and Chicano activists have fought for media access, protested mainstream media stereotypes of Latinos, and co-produced tele-vision programs on PBS addressing the Latino cultural heritage and issues pertinent to these communities since the late 1960s and especially during the early 1970s.[13] Furthermore, similar to Asian American, Native American, and African American filmmakers, Puerto Ricans and Chicanos used documen-tary filmmaking to represent their identities and civil rights struggles.[14]

Although the problem of racism in Puerto Rico was apparently not in-cluded in these media artifacts, all the aforementioned political, cultural, racial, mediatic, and diasporic intersections had both a direct and an indirect impact on the island. The writers from *La generación de los 70* (the 1970s generation), researchers, and theater groups examined race, class, and gen-der within the context of colonialism and incorporated Afro Puerto Rican and Caribbean themes in their cultural and intellectual productions.[15] More-over, several key individuals developed sociopolitical discourses that cen-tered on blackness, racism, and the exaltation of Afro Puerto Rican cultural elements.[16]

In addition to these intellectual, literary, and theatrical cultural fronts, black identity politics were also performed in another, more visible location: Puerto Rico's commercial television. Through the appropriation of cultural elements associated with the U.S. black power movement, black performers' protests against racist casting practices and the production of shows that focused on blackness, as well as television in general (the industry, media professionals, and audiences), newspapers, and TV magazines, fostered a dialogic space that challenged the whiteness that characterized the industry.

The 1970s televisual (and media cultures) transformations emanated from three divergent levels of political, cultural, and commercial signification: (1) the black performers' activism against racism, (2) the appropriation and adaptation of U.S. television programs and concepts that addressed the topic of blackness, and (3) the U.S. and European fashion industry's commodification of blackness. In other words, Puerto Rico's commercial television and media were influenced by multiple local and global political mobilizations of the 1960s and early 1970s and by the processes of desegregation that took place in U.S. media cultures.

Indeed, as numerous scholars have argued, the incorporation of blackness in the U.S. media in general and commercial television in particular functioned through the ideologies of middle-class whiteness and the de-politicization of racial struggles.[17] However, what I foreground here are the ways in which various radical vernacular movements and commercial changes had a partial, but nonetheless crucial, impact on Puerto Rico's commercial television industry. In sum, the 1970's televisual debates directly challenged the ideology of racial equality at the heart of la gran familia puertorriqueña discourse.

The limited representation of black bodies and the ongoing use of blackface in entertainment television programming occupied the center of the 1970s racialized struggles. Although, as I discussed in the introduction, racial categorization in Puerto Rico does not translate to racial consciousness, it should be clear that the few black performers who were working in the industry were pivotal in televisual contestations in the 1970s. Although some artists combined their pro-independence ideology with their racial, gender, and sexual politics, blackness and racism nonetheless served as the catalysts for their mobilization.

The 1970s televisual symbolic and actual transformations operated both individually and collectively, with some being politically motivated and others commercially driven. Nevertheless, even as these performers and media producers articulated distinct political and racial agendas, they were all fighting against the same oppressive condition: antiblack racism. By the 1970s, the antiblack racism in Puerto Rico's commercial television operated within three venues: blackface, cosmetic whitening, and discriminatory casting practices.

As I discussed in chapter 1, televisual blackface began with the arrival of commercial television in 1954. For the most part, and as in radio, the negrito continued to be a stock buffoon-like representation in comedies and the comedy sketches included in variety shows, while the negra characters were depicted as submissive maids in telenovelas. In addition to the ongoing use of blackface to masquerade whiteness, a process that I refer to as cosmetic whitening was pervasive. I identify cosmetic whitening as the practice through which features associated with a black phenotype (such as hair or darker skin) are purposely concealed to re-construct a mulatto body into a more white body. In other words, cosmetic whitening functioned as a camouflage that refined or disguised the flaws of racial mestizaje. Cosmetic whitening included tactics such as using a wig to hide the black hair or applying a light makeup foundation to whiten the trigueña/o face. Obviously, mulatto bodies were primarily involved in the process of cosmetic whitening. Still, in contrast to blackface, which can be categorized as a theatrical or televisual performance, cosmetic whitening required perpetual masquerading because the televisual mulatto performer needed to maintain the illusion of whiteness not only in front of the camera but also in public spaces.

Although both the practice of blackface and the process of cosmetic whitening drastically reduced the opportunities for black actors and actresses in Puerto Rico's commercial television, discriminatory casting practices further limited their access. As I discuss later in this chapter, the logic used by television producers and directors (particularly in telenovelas) was simple: there were no good black actors; thus, they had to use white performers in blackface to perform the maid characters. These media professionals never questioned their own racist equation ("blacks" were synonymous with maids in the fictional telenovela world) or the racial constraints that informed the island's television. Consequently, in Puerto Rico's commercial television entertainment programming, blacks occupied a particular space, one that was already fixed for them and not by them.[18] Although through various genres television constructed the nation as mestiza (composed of blacks, whites, and mulattos), racial masking and processes positioned whiteness as the most desirable racial element within the televisual space, and thus, the nation.

In the following pages I focus on particular events, artists, characters, and shows that shaped debates or that symbolized a transformation in terms of racial representations. I begin with the 1970 appropriation of the Afro hairstyle by Luz Esther Benítez (Lucecita), a renowned singer in Puerto Rico and Latin America. I then examine shows that directly and indirectly dealt with race and blackness and the resurgent popularity of blackface. Finally, I discuss the selection of a mulata to represent Puerto Rico in a world beauty pageant, paying special attention to the ways in which the media constructed her racialized body.

In this chapter I argue that although whiteness was still the norm in local television entertainment programming, and while, similar to Rivero's (Diplo) construction of blackness, a new blackface character became a vehicle for political and social satire, the 1970s was a critical stage in the history of Puerto Rico's commercial television and media discussions of racism. The performers' militancy created an imaginary circuitry that connected Puerto Rico's black populations to marginalized communities in the United States and to the struggles against racial oppression that informed other parts of the world.

The Racial, Gender, Sexual, and Political Ramifications of a Televisual Afro

During April 1970 Luz Esther Benítez (Lucecita), a renowned performer who was (and still is) considered one of the most talented singers in Puerto Rico and Latin America, inadvertently shocked local television audiences.[19] After years of straightening her hair and wearing wigs, Lucecita (who since the mid-1960s had been marketed as a whitened *nueva ola* [rock and roll] ballad singer) appeared with an Afro in her *El show de las 12* segment.[20] The so-called "African look" stunned the press and fans, creating a controversy that not only reaffirmed the racism that is part of Puerto Rico's culture but that also re-articulated the multi-axial system of oppression related to race, gender, and sexuality. Within a period of three years Lucecita became a televisual and popular culture figure who defied Eurocentric, patriarchal, heterosexual, and right-wing political ideological discourses.

It should be clear that the African look debate that emerged in 1970 was

not the first incident of racism against Lucecita. According to Javier Santiago, toward the end of the 1960s some television fans sent letters to TV
magazines questioning Lucecita's whiteness (i.e., her continual use of wigs
to allegedly hide her black hair).[21] In addition, fans established an indirect
racialized comparison between Lucecita and Lissette (a white Cuban immigrant who also became a youth icon in Puerto Rico during the mid-1960s).
Regarding the fans' contestations, Lucecita later recalled, "There was racism.
And when Lissette dyed her hair blond, the debates acquired another ingre-
dient — the blond with the American 'look' versus the Puerto Rican trigueña.
People said that she [Lissette] was white and that I was supposedly black.
People screamed at me all the outrageous things characteristic of an audience inflamed with a very evident racist problem."[22] While the fans' racist
debates affected Lucecita's public persona at the end of the 1960s, ideologies
of cultural nationalism and the emerging prejudice against the Cuban immigrant community in Puerto Rico re-inscribed Lucecita as a mestiza, and
more important, a Puerto Rican body.

As I indicated in chapter 1, after the 1959 Cuban migration, Cubans were
socially constructed as people who took jobs away from Puerto Ricans. This
anti-Cuban sentiment also permeated the television industry because many
Cuban media professionals (actors, actresses, directors, scriptwriters, and
producers) had begun to work in Puerto Rico's commercial television, with
some occupying important positions. Thus, even though Lucecita's blackness
and Lissette's whiteness precipitated discussions among their respective fans,
Lucecita's Puerto Ricanness juxtaposed to Lissette's immigrant and progressively unwelcome Cubanness temporarily disrupted some of the fans' racist
contestations.

Furthermore, in 1969 Lucecita's symbolic Puerto Ricanness reached a new
level of signification when she won first prize as the most talented singer at
El Primer Festival de la Canción Latina del Mundo (The First Festival of Latin
World Music) in Mexico City. Lucecita's international success and her still
televisually constructed whitened body (her use of wigs), intertwined with
Puerto Rico's cultural nationalism, delayed the racist public outburst that
emerged in 1970. The Afro, however, completely destabilized her — until this
point — racially, socially, culturally, and somewhat acceptable whitened tri-
gueña/mestiza televisual body. By wearing an Afro, Lucecita disrupted the
televisual containment and locations of blackness, thus instigating a televisual racial crisis.

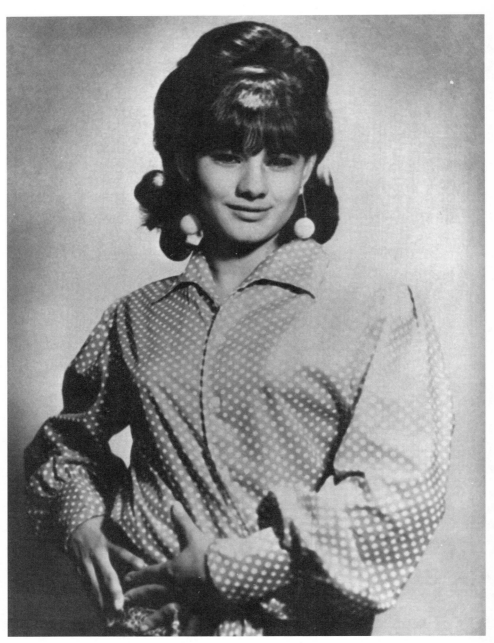

Lucecita as a nueva ola singer wearing a wig, circa mid-1960s.
Courtesy of La Fundación Nacional para la Cultura Popular.

Television magazines played a key role in framing the debates. The media always narrated Lucecita's hairstyle as an "African look" instead of an Afro. Although the phrase (used in English) suggested a direct association with the United States, none of the magazines considered the racial, political, cultural, and social signification of the Afro within African American communities. Instead, the unexplored term *African look* seemed to associate Lucecita's hair with Africa. Still, the phrase might have contained other meanings, particularly within the context of Puerto Rico's cultural and racial ideologies and Lucecita's public persona. By appropriating this phrase the media were foregrounding and, as I will further explain, rejecting the supposed Africanness of Lucecita's body and thereby indirectly re-articulating official and vernacular discourses that situated Africa (and blackness) as a present yet negligible and unwelcome element within the national body.

Initially, the media, not Lucecita, generated the public's racialized discussion. Lucecita had not intended to use her hairstyle as a symbolic reaffirmation of her blackness. Her decision to grow an Afro was a response to an allergic reaction caused by her ongoing use of wigs.[23] Still, regardless of Lucecita's medical condition and actual intentions, audiences and TV magazines initiated an informal campaign to censor her hairstyle and conceal her blackness.

Following Lucecita's first television appearance with what TV magazines and newspapers categorized as an African look, audience members called the office of Paquito Cordero (the producer of the *El show de las 12*, the creator of the late 1950s blackface character Reguerete, and one of the most powerful media professionals during the 1970s) and voiced their opposition through remarks such as "when Lucecita appeared with that Afro, I just turned off the TV."[24] A group of Lucecita's supporters appeared with signs outside of Telemundo's building that read "with Afro or without it, with Lucecita until the end."[25] Other fans de-politicized the Afro and Lucecita's controversy by writing letters supporting the hairstyle that was, according to them, the new fashion trend in New York City.[26] However, those who were in favor of the African look apparently represented a small minority. *Vea* (a television guide magazine) initiated a survey asking readers whether they were in favor of or opposed to the African look. *Vea*'s survey received 248 votes in support of the Afro and 2,823 against it.[27]

During this unexpected controversy, Lucecita, who had plans to film a movie in Spain and who was required to get rid of her Afro by the film's

Lucecita with a big Afro, circa 1970. Courtesy of *Teve Guía* Archives.

producer, began to show signs of her politically radical transformations. In reference to her fans and the Spanish film producer's censorship of her Afro, Lucecita remarked, "this is nothing, wait until my hair keeps growing and I show up in Spain with this huge and forceful 'African look' . . . I will stop the traffic in Madrid."[28] The Afro kept growing, increasingly challenging her televisual and deliberated whitening.[29] However, alongside this racial re-presentation of her body, Lucecita also transgressed dominant constructions of femininity by wearing "masculine" garments during her shows and public appearances.

While Lucecita began changing her style of dress at the end of the 1960s, after her appropriation of the Afro, newspapers and TV magazines began to target not only her race but also to question her femininity. For example, with her 1970 acclaimed success at the Caribe Hilton hotel's prestigious Club Caribe, one reviewer stated that "coiffed with an Afro out to here, and dressed in a rakish grey suit with tails (she is famous for not wearing skirts or dresses) Lucecita empties a cauldron of emotion onto the Caribe stage."[30] Although her talent was never doubted, her personality had now become the focus of public debate.

Lucecita, who during the beginning of her career was narrated as a shy, quiet, and humble woman, grew progressively more outspoken. Gradually, she became famous for constantly transgressing proper norms of feminine conduct by using bad words. Subsequently, she began to be categorized as difficult. Disc jockeys stopped playing her music on Puerto Rico's commercial radio stations. Finally, in March 1972, due to ongoing pressures from the television industry, publicists, and Rambler Toyota (the sponsor of *El Show Rambler Toyota* in which Lucecita was going to participate), Lucecita straightened her hair.[31] Soon after changing her hairstyle, Lucecita decided to stop working in television and indeed, she let her Afro grow again.

The final dramatic changes in Lucecita's public persona occurred during 1973, when she released the album *Raza Pura* (Pure Race) with *nueva canción* (new song) left-oriented political songs. The album openly affirmed her pro-independence political stance, symbolically represented her ideological position as a sympathizer of the Cuban Revolution, and reiterated Lucecita's pride in her blackness. These racial and political affirmations were articulated not only in the song *Soy de una raza pura* (I am from a pure race) but also on the album cover.

The song *Soy de una raza pura*, written by two men who identified with

Lucecita wearing a "masculine" outfit, circa mid-1970s.
Courtesy of *Teve Guía* Archives.

Puerto Rico's political left movement (Tony Croatto and David Ortíz), rejects Eurocentrisim, the oppressive condition of slavery, racism, and whiteness. The lyrics detail the subjugation of black people and the rebellious and combative "essence" of this marginalized population. *Soy de una raza pura* also positions blackness as an integral part of the Puerto Rican nation while concomitantly ignoring the Spanish cultural and racial influences. This ideological position is clearly revealed in the stanzas, "I am borincano [from the island's Taíno name], black, and gypsy" and "I am Taíno, I am tears, and I am also pain."[32] Although the song in itself is an embracement of non-European cultural and racial elements, the fact that it was performed by Lucecita brought a second level of political and racial signification to its lyrics.

The album cover, designed by Antonio Martorell, a renowned Puerto Rican graphic artist and pro-independence activist, is dominated by a drawing of Lucecita. Her face and torso are painted in red and her hair is depicted as an Afro. The background for Lucecita's red figure is blue, making a connection between her blackness and Puerto Rico's flag. Therefore, as with the song *Soy de una raza pura*, the album cover positions blackness as a central element in Puerto Rico's culture, identity, and society.

With this album, Lucecita became one of the popular cultural symbols of the Puerto Rican Left and alternatively a pariah among Puerto Rico's politically conservative groups. Obviously, she became the devil incarnate for some sectors of the powerful media and right-wing anti-Castro Cuban immigrant community in both Puerto Rico and Miami. In the eyes of the Cuban immigrant community Lucecita became a cultural attaché for Fidel Castro and the Cuban Revolution; therefore, she had to be expunged from the popular culture landscape. As was expected, Lucecita was blacklisted.

Furthermore, her transgressions of femininity went beyond "male" outfits and inappropriate language. Lucecita began to use masculine adjectives when singing some of her songs and on some occasions when describing herself. Contrary to many singers who usually changed the gender-specific adjectives in song lyrics to accommodate their gender, the lyrics of *Soy de una raza pura* kept the masculine construction in phrases such as "*soy borincano, negro, y gitano* (I am Puerto Rican, black, and gypsy)." Moreover, when a journalist asked Lucecita about fashion and her "masculine" outfits, she, in some parts of the interview, characterized herself as a man. As Lucecita remarked, "I am a simple and humble negro [black male] who does not know about luxurious dresses and fine jewelry. I dress as I am, as Luz Esther Benítez is. I have my own criteria as an individual, and that 'I' does not stick to fashion nor to anybody. I believe that all of us have the right to be as one feels one is, not what society imposes."[33] Later during the same interview, she re-appropriated her female gender, declaring, "I am a negra [black woman] who has struggled a lot in life." Judith Butler argues that, "performing one's gender wrong initiates a set of punishments both obvious and indirect, and performing it well provides the reassurance that there is an essentialism of gender identity after all."[34] In the case of Lucecita, because of her self description as a male together with what was considered her nonfeminine appearance and the fact that publicly she was not romantically involved with any man, rumors began to spread about her possible lesbianism.

Besides playing — in the performative and socially contravening sense — with gender, Lucecita intertwined her racial, gendered, and left-wing public performances with direct criticisms of the Catholic Church, women's oppression, and homophobia. For example, while touring in the Dominican Republic in 1973, she declared, "I am not a virgin. That is an obsolete myth . . . the Catholic Church is wrong and outdated . . . we have to accept homosexuality as an expression of love."[35] Although Lucecita never came out as a lesbian, one might say that these statements in the context of Puerto Rican, and more generally, the Spanish Caribbean's conservative and homophobic culture fueled doubts about her sexual orientation. Lucecita became a black, pro-independence, pseudo-communist, pseudo-lesbian, butch, a direct menace to the patriarchal, white, mestizo, pro-commonwealth, pro-statehood racial, political, cultural, and gendered social order. Mainstream TV magazines and newspapers made Lucecita a media spectacle and by 1973 she had become an outcast.

During an interview published in a left-wing magazine in 1973, Lucecita finally discussed the racism that she had experienced and the process that she endured to mask her blackness while working in Puerto Rico's commercial television:

> I am not a puppet, I never wanted to be that but they [the television industry] wanted to erase the blackness that is part of me. They forgot that my father was black. They wanted to refine my nose. They demanded a white Lucecita, who would fill up their requirements. I felt bad but accepted. They told me that it was going to be better for me and I believed

them. But the day that they took away my Afro, I cried and cried . . . I still remember and it hurts.[36]

Lucecita, the black, pro-independence woman, who sometimes constructed herself as male and at other times as female, and who retained her African look, was marginalized from Puerto Rico's commercial television and mainstream culture until 1980. Within a short period of three years (1970–1973) Lucecita had moved from being portrayed as the beloved humble, working-class, trigueña woman who sang love songs to one who was described as a communist and Castroite *camionera* (a word used to describe a woman as vulgar, nonfeminine, and a lesbian) and as a foul-mouthed, difficult woman. Certainly, Lucecita was an active agent in her ideological and bodily transformations. Yet, equally important in these narrations was the fact that Lucecita's African look and her subsequent revolutionary performances revealed the mainstream media's and some audiences' aversion to practices and discourses that challenged Puerto Rico's (and I should also say, the Spanish Caribbean's) dominant culture.

I position Lucecita as the televisual signifier of the alternative racial, political, feminist, and sexual discursive transformations that were part of some sectors of Puerto Rico's society.[37] Lucecita's African-look incident was the beginning of the portentous changes in her career, and it also signaled shifts in the activism of black actors in Puerto Rico's commercial television. Indeed, no other televisual performer directly transgressed Puerto Rico's dominant multi-axial ideological discourses in the ways that Lucecita did. Moreover, her aggressive and politically up-front performances cost her many employment opportunities. Nonetheless, Lucecita's Afro was emblematic of the racial and cultural challenges that erupted in Puerto Rico's commercial television during the early 1970s.

I would like to suggest that in Puerto Rico the Afro functioned as a discursive iconography of multiple and sometimes intertwined, sometimes autonomous counterhegemonic movements. It should be noted that, as I will further explain, just a few years after the uproar over Lucecita's hair, the Afro and soul music — by way of the locally produced and hybrid version of *Soul Train* — became imported and commodified cultural artifacts.[38] Granted, many audiences may have been unaware of the hairstyle's political implications. Robin D. G. Kelley argues that in the United States the Afro became an essentialist and manufactured representation of the black power movement, black com-

Lucecita, circa mid-1970s. Courtesy of Gabriel Suau.

munity struggles, and soul music.³⁹ In Puerto Rico, some rebellious teenagers may have appropriated the Afro void of any political connotations. After all, in the island's vernacular culture, the Afro was characterized by some as *un criadero de piojos* (a breeding place for lice). It follows that some young people might have used the Afro to rebel against their parents. In contrast, others might have simply appropriated the hairstyle to be defiantly fashionable. Nonetheless, I contend that the Afro acquired other meanings.

First, the hairstyle served as a reaffirmation of Puerto Rico's African heritage and as a direct affront to the island's racist ideologies and practices. Considering that in Puerto Rico's vernacular culture, phrases such as *mejorar la raza* (improve the race) and *pelo malo* (bad hair, in reference to blacks' curly hair) represent the whitening in sexual mixing and the white constructed normativity of the body (i.e., straightening the hair to hide the bad, black hair), the Afro was an in-your-face resistance to hegemonic racial discourses.⁴⁰ In other words, the Afro signified a transgression of the whitening that informs the mestizaje discourse.

Second, at least in television and in Puerto Rico's media cultures, media professionals (actors, actresses, singers, composers, etc.) who identified with Puerto Rico's independence movement appropriated the Afro. Thus, for members of this racialized, gendered, and heterogeneous group, the Afro may have been a symbol of black empowerment, of racial struggles (in Puerto Rico, in the United States, and in other parts of the world), and of freedom from colonialism. Consequently, this racial symbol galvanized a number of political movements, some racial and some that extended beyond the boundaries of race.

The multiplicity of meanings associated with the Afro are important given that some U.S. scholars have positioned the commercialization of the au naturel hairstyle as a negation of any political signification without considering the ways in which Other transnational and Afro diasporic communities might have *translated* and re-appropriated the hairstyle. For example, Maxine Leeds Craig identifies 1970 as the year when the Afro was "drained of its meaning."⁴¹ She contends, "the natural, once it had become acceptable, became a mere style. As the social activism out of which the style was born fractured in array and defeat, the style referred to an increasingly distant historic period of activism."⁴² In addition, Robin D. G. Kelley asserts that, "by the early 1970s, on the eve of the Afro's ultimate demise, the whole 'natural' movement took another turn. . . . The Afro began to lose its specific political meaning, or at least the connection to black nationalist politics seemed to fade into the background."[43]

The commercialization of the Afro that took place during the 1970s is undeniable. And indeed, as Kelley argues, the hairstyle's political specificity was transformed. Still, I prefer to treat the Afro as a symbol of African diasporic racial struggles, which instead of being shattered of its political meaning, acquired other radical significations"[44] In the case of Puerto Rico, I would locate the Afro as a cultural artifact that symbolically connected Puerto Ricans on the island with the African American–Puerto Rican–Afro Puerto Rican radical mobilizations that had taken place in the United States since the early 1960s. In other words, the Afro can be seen as a performative bodily practice that integrated the black power "black is beautiful" discourse, the Young Lords, and pro-independence activism. Additionally, in the case of Puerto Rico's commercial television in general and Lucecita in particular, the Afro directly defied the practice of cosmetic whitening because, as I have previously discussed, Lucecita went through various masquerading processes to disguise her blackness.

However, through Lucecita's televisual persona, the Afro became more than a sign of black or anticolonial empowerment. According to a member of Lucecita's fan club during the African look controversy, the imminent menace attached to Lucecita and her Afro was its racial connotation.[45] Yet, was it only her blackness that the mainstream culture rejected? My answer is no. Although Lucecita's Afro linked Puerto Rican blackness to the U.S. black power movement and the anti-U.S. imperialism rhetoric that characterized alternative political discourses in Puerto Rico, Latin America, the United States, and other parts of the world, her Afro also became an emblem of gender, feminine, and even sexual transgressions. Lucecita needed to be eliminated from the island's media cultures because her Afro signified multiple and intertwined ideological contraventions. I would also argue that this is precisely why, when Lucecita staged her television comeback in 1980, she stopped performing most of her political left-wing-oriented songs, no longer constructed herself as a male, and removed all traces of an Afro or an African look. Lucecita, while still identified with the Puerto Rican Left movement, became (for the most part) a bolero singer.

Nonetheless, Lucecita's official Web page states that, "the fight for her ideals is not over, her commitment is apparent, and her voice, along with a talent to make poetry and music meld into a whole that touches our soul with a laser that cuts deep within our feelings. Lucecita is more than a light that leads the path, she beams a course with her talent and commitment to higher ideals."[46] The African look controversy is not documented on her Web page. She is now described as "the national voice of Puerto Rico." First and foremost Lucecita has embraced Puerto Rico's cultural and political nationalism as her main artistic and political battle. Yet, if one examines, for example, her 2000 Carnegie Hall CD, one sees that the first song is *Soy de una raza pura*. And, if one listens to the obviously heart wrenching bolero *Que tal te va sin mí* (How are you doing without me), she clearly sings "Me alegro de encontrarte nuevamente [I am happy to see you again]. Te juro que te vez maravillosa [I swear that you (a female) look wonderful]."[47] The racial, political, gendered, and sexual ramifications of the 1970s televisual Afro still permeate Lucecita's public persona. The difference is that today, and contrary to the 1970–1973 African look controversy, one has to pay closer attention to the subtexts of Lucecita's corporeal and verbal representations.

However, besides Lucecita's 1970–73 debate, the ideologies of race and blackness in Puerto Rico's commercial television acquired a variety of complicated meanings during the early 1970s. Black actors and actresses protested the use of blackface in local television, soul music became popular and—at the same time—a blackface female character became an iconic cultural figure in Puerto Rico.

Resistance and Fragmentary Accommodations: *Soul Train* and Other Shows

In 1971, while Lucecita was in the midst of her African look battle, Sylvia del Villard (a black Puerto Rican theater and nightclub performer and president of *La Asociación Panamericana*, an organization targeting Afro Puerto Rican culture), sent press releases to television magazines and local newspapers to criticize racist casting practices in television, the limited opportunities for black actors and actresses, and the ongoing use of blackface. In response to del Villard's accusations, commercial television station managers indicated in a newspaper article that racism was nonexistent in Puerto Rico's television industry and that the allegations were absurd.[48] As one of the interviewees responded, "if there are limited black artists [in television], it is simply because they have not been interested in that career."[49] In addition, Carmen Belén Richardson (the actress who performed Lirio Blanco in the comedy *El colegio de la alegría*) also accused the industry of racial discrimination.[50] Even though CubaRican blackface negritos were still part of local shows, and despite the fact that Lucecita was being pressured to re-whiten herself, industry officials, audiences, and the government apparently did not see any form of racial discrimination.[51]

During the early 1970s, as in previous decades, television "blackness" was accepted as long as these representations operated within the parameters of what the mainstream considered black or mulatto Puerto Rican popular culture (for example, Afro Puerto Rican and Afro-Caribbean musical styles); reproduced hegemonic constructions of blackness (i.e., blackface negritos and negras); or functioned as a comedic element. Any performer who directly transgressed these racialized spaces and depictions was labeled as a ridiculous, difficult individual or as someone who had appropriated an imported (U.S.) racial or political ideology (the perception of a U.S. influence was not completely off the mark). Then again, given that after the civil rights movement and the commodification of the black power "black is beautiful" discourse, "blackness" appeared in limited forms in U.S. media cultures, lo negro became *partially* in vogue in Puerto Rico's commercial television.

I want to make it clear that while black musicians continued to be part of local variety shows, during the early 1970s media professionals embraced new types of programs, ideas, and racial depictions. Significantly, these televisual and fragmentary accommodations at least temporarily, and *often inadvertently*, destabilized the normalized televisual "whiteness." In other words, the 1970s shows were either purposely designed to address issues of race and blackness or were conceptualized by adapting U.S. black-oriented programs. Still, contrary to the transformations that occurred on U.S. commercial television during the 1970s, Puerto Rico's televisual and racialized adjustments did not arise from a massive social mobilization to have more roles and more complex representations of blackness in its commercial media in general and television in particular. Instead, the island's fragmentary accommodations responded to the potential for producing and portraying something different, and therefore, profitable. Thus, while Lucecita was dealing with the last stages of her televisual African look debate, a *glocalized* version of *Soul Train* began to air on Puerto Rico's commercial television.[52]

In January 1973, WAPA-TV (channel 4) began to broadcast a slightly different version of the U.S. music show *Soul Train*. Produced by Promotores Asociados and hosted by Carol Myles and Malín Falú each Saturday from

12:30 P.M. to 1:30 P.M., the pair interviewed soul music artists who were per-forming their acts at *El Flamboyán* (a local hotel located in Condado, Puerto Rico).[53] For the most part, the show included segments from the U.S. *Soul Train* and served as a televisual promotion for the soul music artists visiting the island. In addition, the local *Soul Train* was an artistic venue for singer Carol Myles, who was described as "the white soul singer of Puerto Rico."[54] The only indigenous elements in the Promotores Asociados' *Soul Train* were the hosts and a train track painted on a flat in the back of the studio where each track was named for an island's town (for example, Moca, Bayamón, Ciales, Utuado, etc.).

Despite the sparse local elements, *Soul Train* and soul music were being *translated* to Puerto Rico's culture. The simple verbal translation from En-glish to Spanish of what James Brown or members of the O'Jays trio were saying and the selection of the local hosts and their participation on the show were part of the process of accommodating to Puerto Rico's culture and racial ideologies. Accordingly, the front cover of the July 8, 1973, issue of *Vea* de-picted the white Anglo-looking, green-eyed, and blond-haired Carol Myles at the center of the photo (and therefore, of *Soul Train*) while the black Malín Falú was relegated to the background (thus, a secondary, yet somewhat re-quired, racial element for the show). The train track was the ultimate trans-lation. The train with soul music and performers was going to pass by all the towns in Puerto Rico . . . even the smallest and most remote ones (in relation to San Juan).

Targeting local audiences, newspapers and television magazines explained the Spanish meaning of the word *soul* (*alma*), the origins of soul music, and the racial struggles in the United States. The periodicals also promoted *Soul Train* and singers such as James Brown, Aretha Franklin, The O' Jays, and Roberta Flack who were performing on the island.[55] Soul music and its con-tagious, already commodified and fashionable, yet distant and mediatized blackness became hip within Puerto Rico's popular culture. These depictions of blackness apparently did not represent a racial threat to Puerto Rico's tele-visual culture and audiences. They may have functioned as symbolic remind-ers of the differences between Puerto Rican and U.S. racial discourses, thus reaffirming Puerto Rico's racial ideologies as the superior antithesis to Jim Crow segregation and racism in the United States. Conversely, Malín Falú (*Soul Train*'s black host) wore an Afro on the show and was never criticized by the press or audiences because of her hairstyle.[56] Just three years after the pandemonium caused by Lucecita's Afro, the hairstyle became (to some extent) a trendy style on Puerto Rican television.

After *Soul Train* began to air, there was a proliferation of short-lived local shows focusing on blackness and racism in Puerto Rico.[57] In March 1973, channel 7 began a segment during its noon program called *El cafetín oveja negra* that included a contest that specifically targeted young and amateur black singers.[58] In addition, *El cafetín oveja negra* contained comedy sketches that centered on a black couple who had a white son. Through inverting the ideology of antiblack racism, the comedy sketches depicted the black parents' racial prejudice toward their white son. According to a television magazine description, the comedy segments "tried to present a problem that exists in Puerto Rico" (i.e., racism).[59] It should be noted that two of the three black characters were performed by white actors in blackface.[60] At any rate, the segment's success prompted the production of a situation comedy called *Black Power*.

In its review of *Black Power*, a *Vea* article explained that "racial discrimination in Puerto Rican society is something of the past, although sometimes there are vestiges with no major importance. It is precisely those vestiges that 'Black Power' ridicules."[61] With no actual connection between the show and the U.S. black power movement, the sitcom focused on a white aristocratic, yet poor Puerto Rican family who had a trigueña daughter and a rich black family who had a white son.[62] Apparently, the humor resided in both sets of parents' racial and class prejudices. In addition, it seems that the narrative positioned class, not race, as the defining element for social mobility in Puerto Rico. Based on the show's descriptions, the white parents did not object to their trigueña daughter dating the white man (with black parents) after they discovered that the black family was financially solvent. In other words, class could erase someone's blackness.

Furthermore, according to *Black Power*, nobody in Puerto Rico could claim the purity of the white race because even those who looked and asserted their whiteness were racially mixed. Although the show's title and narrative represented a de-contextualization of the U.S. black power movement's political and social struggles, it redefined and rearticulated the hegemonic obliteration of blackness that informs Puerto Rico's society. In addition, an English title might have been used as a catchy phrase to attract audiences who were already fascinated with *Soul Train*, while concomitantly creating a symbolic detachment from the situation comedy theme. In other words, using the Spanish title (*Poder negro*) would have been a direct confrontation and fragmentation of the hegemonic national culture and Puerto Rico's mestiza identity. Even if these were the creator's intentions, the visual depiction of the family contradicted the show's thematic premise since *Black Power*, like the *El cafetín oveja negra* noon segment, used performers in blackface. What is more, the premise of both shows implied that racism in Puerto Rico was a product of interpersonal relationships, not a systemic social problem. Therefore, the shows did not question the ideology of racial democracy but instead they reaffirmed it.

Soul Train, *El cafetín oveja negra*, and *Black Power*'s televisual accommodations functioned through commercialized, yet distinct racial, political, cultural, and social discursive significations. First, one should consider the glocal version of *Soul Train* in relation to the U.S. *Soul Train*. According to Mark Anthony Neal, the U.S. *Soul Train* was a "visual affirmation of the black communal ethics" and "black expressive culture."[63] Although the show was a manufactured cultural product, it represented an important avenue for what Neal categorizes as the local cultural elements of the African American diaspora in the post–civil rights era. On the other hand, Promotores Asociados' *Soul Train* was a de-politicized translation of soul music and its community-centered, African American discursive significations.

Indeed, multiple local newspaper and magazine stories explained the cultural and political meanings of soul music to audiences in Puerto Rico. Furthermore, some audience members might have created connections between African Americans' oppressive racial conditions and diverse cultural expressions and Puerto Rico's marginalization of black and mulatto populations and vernacular cultural artifacts that had emerged from these communities. Still, the Puerto Rican version of *Soul Train* never mapped the routes and African diasporic relations between the U.S. racialized African American communities and music and Puerto Rican (on the island and in the United States) cultural expressions.

Additionally, in Puerto Rico's mediascape, *Soul Train* may have been considered a possible threat to local musicians because television programs had been key spaces for singers and bands since 1954. The Puerto Rican version of *Soul Train* never created a space for local singers (with the exception of Carol Myles singing soul) or even local audiences dancing to soul music. Thus, this incomplete glocalization and the fact that Promotores Asociados' *Soul Train* was basically a re-broadcast of the U.S. program may have been a key factor in the show's cancellation in 1974.[64] What did emerge in the early 1970s were the highly successful salsa music shows. The salsa shows can be viewed as an indirect cultural answer to the U.S. *Soul Train*, but more importantly, as a commercial opportunity to attract salsa fans.[65]

According to an *El Mundo* newspaper article, the first salsa show in Puerto Rico's commercial television was *Factoría de la salsa*, which began broadcasting in October 1973 on channel 7. Produced by a Puerto Rican salsa musician (generally known as Pijuán), *Factoría de la salsa* was described as "an innovative show" where "all salsa groups would have an opportunity to perform."[66] During the 1970s and the 1980s, salsa programs, which presented local, translocal, and transnational Puerto Rican, Caribbean, and Latin American salsa performers, became popular cultural artifacts in Puerto Rico's commercial television. Although these programs functioned through the contained locations of blackness that had characterized the medium since 1954, they were primarily designed as a venue for salsa performers, music, and dance. Thus, salsa shows created a televisual (and even exclusive) place for the representation of a musical genre that articulates working-class and racial struggles in Puerto Rican, U.S.–Puerto Rican, Spanish Caribbean, and various Afro Latin American communities.[67]

Conversely, I position *El cafetín oveja negra* and *Black Power* as responses to the importation of a foreign product (*Soul Train*) and as commercial opportunities to create potentially profitable programs in Puerto Rico's television market. Although the situation comedy genre had been part of Puerto Rico's local television since 1954, the issues of race, racism, and mestizaje were never its main thematic concept.[68] Therefore, *El cafetín oveja negra* and *Black Power* were commercially attractive products that also served as partial (yet ambivalent) answers to the lack of opportunities for black performers (*El cafetín*) and the problematization of Puerto Rico's racial ideologies (*Black Power*).

Still, both cultural artifacts were off the air by the mid-1970s. Perhaps their themes were among the factors that prompted the cancellation of *El cafetín oveja negra* and *Black Power*. With their demise the possibility of providing more opportunities for amateur black performers or for examining Puerto Rico's racial discourses was eliminated. What remained part of Puerto Rico's commercial television for years to come, and which also emerged in 1973, was Chianita, a blackface female character.

Chianita: The Puerto Rican Black *Jíbarita*

In February 1973, Telemundo began to air the telenovela *El hijo de Angela María*. With a cast of the best actors and actresses in Puerto Rico, *El hijo de Angela María* represented a major investment for Telemundo.[69] This was the first locally produced telenovela to go to a one-hour narrative instead of the traditional thirty-minute format. In addition, *El hijo de Angela María* incorporated previously filmed scenes and Telemundo had big commercial plans to export the telenovela to Latin America.[70] Considering the novelty of this cultural product, television magazines and newspapers devoted a good deal of attention to *El hijo de Angela María*. And, as had been expected, the telenovela became an immediate success.

El hijo de Angela María included two secondary black maid characters (Panchita and Chianita), both performed by white actresses in blackface (Mona Marti and Angela Meyer).[71] Panchita was the main servant at Angela María's home (the rich owner), while Chianita was Panchita's granddaughter. Panchita was the old negra-type character who had been part of locally produced radionovelas and telenovelas since the 1940s and 1950s. In addition, Panchita was performed by an actress (Mona Marti) who had previously played Caribbean negras. However, none of the reviews about *El hijo de Angela María* described Panchita as a *negra caribeña* (Caribbean black woman). Although there were comparisons between Panchita, mamá Dolores (the principal character in the Cuban radionovela and telenovela, *El derecho de nacer*), and other negras performed by Mona Marti, Panchita was apparently Puerto Rican.[72] This constructed black Puerto Ricanness could be assumed by the reviewers' omissions regarding the character's ethnicity and, more importantly, by the ways in which the actress performed Panchita. Panchita's black Puerto Rican ethnicity was revealed in her accent and speech pattern. Her words were divided into syllables and the "s" was omitted at the end of the words (*tu no me quie-re* [s] *má* [s]).

Whereas early radio and television programs positioned blackface blackness in a geographically ambiguous location (the Caribbean), Panchita was located in a marginal Puerto Rican space. This marginality was articulated not only through the character's class and lack of education but also in the distinctions that Panchita created between the ways in which black and white Puerto Ricans supposedly talked. Based on *El hijo de Angela María*'s narrative, blacks were part of the nation, but something intrinsically and racially distinct separated them from the hegemonic white majority. Con-

Panchita in *El hijo de Angela María*, 1973. Courtesy of *Teve Guía* Archives.

versely, Chianita was a newly formed, yet hybrid televisual stereotype. In *El hijo de Angela María*'s texts, Chianita combined the buffoon elements of the CubaRican negrito with the submissive traits characteristic of the negra maid stereotypes. Nonetheless, in contrast to the earlier blackface negritos, her gender, ethnicity, and voice constructed her as a black and humble jíbara (Puerto Rican peasant). What defined and differentiated Chianita from previous blackface negritos was her hyperbolic (and thus stereotypical) jíbaro self.

Chianita's constructed jíbara persona was informed by her manner of dress, her jíbara speech patterns, and her personality. First, she was depicted as an uncultured and uneducated poor, black, and young woman from the countryside who was unaware of fashion trends and wore bold jewelry and brilliantly colored nonmatching outfits. Even though Chianita thought she was being fashionable, in reality she looked ridiculous. Second, Chianita's magnified accent, frequent loudness, and constant mispronunciation of words suggested her lack of formal education and her jíbara identity. Based on Puerto Rican stereotypes of *jíbaro/as* (similar to the U.S. hillbilly stereotypes and their televisual representations), they sometimes scream because when working in the fields they have to communicate with people who are far away. Simply put, jíbaros/as yell even though they are talking to someone who is next to them. Besides having these traits, Chianita's vocal intonation exemplified the island's vernacular Spanish, which is also associated with jíbaro/a speech patterns (i.e., she substituted the "r" for "l" and omitted the "s" at the end of words). Third, Chianita's exaggerated reactions to various situations defined her personality. Taken together, these elements reaffirmed her jíbara persona.

Although Chianita, like Rivero's CubaRican negritos, was a picaresque character, she was constructed as innocent, cheerful, hard-working, and content with her socioeconomic position. If Chianita transgressed her servant status it was not because she wanted to defy the system (as did Calderón in the radio comedy *El tremendo hotel*); rather, she was unaware of middle-upper-class cultural-social rules and proper norms of conduct. Finally, contrary to other somewhat asexual blackface characters (for example Calderón and mamá Dolores), Chianita was interested in romance and thus, she was a sexual being. In *El hijo de Angela María*'s narrative she was romantically involved and actually married (at the end of the telenovela) an aspiring white working-class singer.[73] Thus, the class-based racial mixing that informs

Chianita, the maid, circa 1973. Courtesy of *Teve Guía* Archives.

the mestizaje ideology in Puerto Rico and other Latin American nations was re-articulated in the telenovela texts.[74] All of the aforementioned elements, together with the actress's talent, positioned Chianita as a clownish figure and as one of the most popular characters in *El hijo de Angela María*.[75]

When Panchita and Chianita appeared in the telenovela, Sylvia del Villard (who in 1971 had protested the industry's racist practices) condemned Chianita, Angela Meyer (the actress who created Chianita), Telemundo, and the use of blackface. Del Villard used the United States as a parameter for comparison and indirectly referenced the mobilization of African Americans to eliminate blackface in U.S. entertainment industries. As she remarked, "in the United States no white person can paint his/her face to play a black character. There are organizations such as Equity, AGMA, and AGVA who send representatives to plays. If they discover that someone is in blackface, both the actor and the producer are in a lot of trouble."[76] In addition, Carmen Belén Richardson (who in 1971 also complained about racial discrimination) criticized the industry and Puerto Rican society, noting that in Puerto Rico "racial prejudice transcends the television industry."[77] Similar to their 1971 protests, these two black performers became the voice of the marginalized black actors and actresses in Puerto Rico.[78]

In response to these criticisms, Angela Meyer (the actress who created Chianita) stated in an interview that, contrary to the United States, in Puerto Rico "there are not many black actors to play the parts" and that Puerto Rico "is a country that has distinguished itself for its lack of racism."[79] During that same interview, the journalist included comments by a renowned black *Bomba* and *Plena* (names for musical styles) performer from Loiza (a coastal town with a large Afro Puerto Rican population) to demonstrate the Puerto Rican black population's support for Chianita's character. In reference to a recent Chianita visit to Loiza, the interviewee stated that "Angela and her Chianita character provoked traffic congestion. People were on top of her kissing and hugging her."[80]

This magazine story suggested that if Puerto Rico's black population supported Chianita, then del Villard's and Richardson's accusations were the product of isolated, invalid, and U.S. assimilated voices. In other words, by using a nationalistic rhetoric to marginalize the black actresses' comments (the opinion of a *Bomba* and *Plena* performer), the discussions activated the distinct histories of these two nations' race relations while concomitantly articulating Puerto Rico's hegemonic constructions of a racially democratic society. Furthermore, regarding the scarcity of black actors observed by Meyer, nobody questioned the whiteness that had informed local television since 1954. Thus, the beloved Chianita continued to perform in *El hijo de Angela María* until the end of the telenovela and then appeared in some of Paquito Cordero's comedy productions on Telemundo during 1973 and 1974. Even though the immensely popular Chianita was appearing in multiple television shows and numerous town festivals, Sylvia del Villard continued her protest against Meyer's donning of blackface.

A second major controversy between del Villard and Meyer occurred in August 1974 at Telemundo's *Telecine de la tarde*, an afternoon show targeted to housewives where, in addition to screening Mexican, Spaniard, and Argentinean movies, the host incorporated interviews and entertainment-related news segments. Sylvia del Villard, who had been invited to talk about one of her club shows, used her live televisual appearance (to the surprise of the suddenly speechless host) to once again condemn racial discrimination, the use of blackface, and Chianita. Del Villard indicated that watching white actors in blackface was "repulsive" and that "blacks in Puerto Rico were tired of this situation."[81] Approximately a week later, Angela Meyer also had the opportunity to express her opinions on *Telecine de la tarde*. This time she stated that *la gente de color* (the colored people) in Loiza loved Chianita, that the "great Diplo" (Ramón Rivero) performed in blackface, and that in the United States Al Jolson also played a black character donned in blackface.[82]

Alongside Meyer's foregrounding of black Puerto Rican support for Chianita and the iconic figure of Ramón Rivero, the interesting aspect of the 1973–1974 del Villard and Meyer debates is the way in which the United States was used as a key point for comparison and validation of both positions. On the one hand, the mobilization of African Americans symbolized racial liberation and the potential for transforming the oppressive conditions of Afro Puerto Ricans. On the other hand, blackface was constructed as a performative and legitimate tradition, not only in Puerto Rico, but more importantly, in the United States. The historical specificities of African Americans' political mobilizations pre- and post–civil rights movement and the U.S. early cinema black and blackface film representations merged, creating a chronological disorder that was never clarified in the magazine stories. By translating selective historical moments, political activism, and the media's racial depictions into a nonspecific time frame, both actresses' opinions were narrated as historically accurate positions.

Sylvia del Villard performing African dances. Courtesy of *Teve Guía* Archives.

Sylvia del Villard. Courtesy of *Teve Guía* Archives.

The 1974 del Villard and Meyer *Telecine de la tarde* debate became a short-lived but nonetheless important media event. Audiences wrote letters supporting and opposing del Villard's accusations. For example, one female viewer indicated that even though she was *de color* (colored), del Villard offended "*la gente de nuestra raza*" (the people of our race), while another individual referred to del Villard as "una racista" (a racist). On the other hand, one woman indicated that she agreed with del Villard, noting that she had wanted to "be an artist," but white people objected to that idea because she was black. Finally, although several audience members agreed with del Villard's arguments, they criticized the way she expressed herself, specifically her use of the word *asco* (repulsion) when referring to Angela Meyer's donning of blackface.[83] Still, this controversy soon became old news. While del Villard continued to protest the use of blackface throughout her entire career, the industry and the majority of the audience ignored her up-front confrontations.[84] What did become a new contestation in 1974 was Angela Meyer's, and consequently Chianita's, possible Cuban ethnicity. The characterization of Meyer and Chianita as Cuban was connected to the reinforcement of the anti-Cuban discourse as a result of Puerto Rico's critical economic condition.

During the early 1970s, and as a product of the U.S. recession and Puerto Rico's dependent economy, the island suffered an economic crisis. Whereas the unstable economy was detrimental to certain sectors of Puerto Rico's society, the changes had little impact on the educated and financially affluent Cuban immigrant community in Puerto Rico.[85] Throughout this period, Puerto Rican prejudices against Cubans intensified because members of this ethnic group were viewed as getting the limited jobs that would have belonged to Puerto Ricans. This financial and ethnic crisis also affected Puerto Rico's commercial television.

While situation comedies, noon shows, and variety shows continued to be produced, local stations stopped the production of local telenovelas, leaving many media professionals without jobs. Because many Cuban immigrants worked as performers, producers, scriptwriters, and directors (among other media-related positions) in Puerto Rico's commercial television, much of the public believed that Cuban actors and actresses (the most visible entities in television production) were taking jobs away from Puerto Rican artists. Thus, an actress such as Angela Meyer, who was born into a family of circus performers and who thus spent most of her childhood traveling throughout Latin America, was included in the "foreign"-Cuban group despite her

Puerto Rican birth. Along with Meyer's upbringing outside Puerto Rico, there was also the association of blackface with Cuban culture.

As I discussed in chapter 1, after the 1959 Cuban migration to Puerto Rico, Cuban actors began to perform the negrito characters in locally produced comedies. Although Ramón Rivero's negritos Calderón and Diplomacia and Paquito Cordero's negrito Reguerete might have been remembered by some of the television audience, in the early 1970s the negritos were mostly performed by Cuban actors (Tino Acosta and Leopoldo Fernández). Consequently, for Puerto Rican audiences, this televisual and racialized representation was mostly associated with Cuba's vernacular culture and Cuba's Bufo theatrical tradition. All of the aforementioned economic, social, and cultural factors might have influenced the 1974 public outburst against the supposedly Cuban Meyer and Chianita.

In a November 1974 newspaper article entitled *Es más boricua que el maví*, Meyer responded to audiences' "multiple calls" to Paquito Cordero's office denouncing the hiring of a "foreigner" (i.e., Cuban).[86] Although Meyer was appalled by the prejudice against non-Puerto Ricans, the main purpose of the article was to authenticate Meyer's Puerto Ricanness. Both the title and the article used the island's Taíno name (*Borinquen*), categorized Meyer as *boricua*, and made direct reference to an autochthonous beverage (*maví*), indicating that Meyer was so Puerto Rican that she transcended the maví.

In the article Meyer mentioned that audiences might have thought that she and Chianita had descended from Cuba's vernacular theater (i.e., Bufo theater). However, she made it clear that Chianita was not "la clásica mulatica" (the classic mulata, in reference to one of the stock characters in Bufo theater). Obviously, Chianita was not the sexualized mulata; she was a version of the negrito. However, neither Meyer nor the journalist made connections between Chianita and the Cuban Bufo negritos or between her character and Rivero's (or others') CubaRican negritos. In the article, Chianita was constructed as an original, made-in-Puerto Rico cultural artifact. The last element to demonstrate Meyer's (and Chianita's) Puerto Ricanness (which at the same time illustrated the prejudice against Cubans during the 1970s) was the journalist's reaffirmation of her nationality: He informed readers that he had seen Meyer's birth certificate.

In sum, to occupy a space in Puerto Rico's television and to be accepted by Puerto Rican audiences, both Angela Meyer and Chianita needed to distance themselves from any traces of Cubanness. And they publicly did that with the 1974 newspaper (quasi-advertisement) article on their Puerto Ricanness. Additionally, Chianita's constructed Puerto Rican jíbara identity acquired a new level of signification by the end of 1974.

In 1974 Angela Meyer (as Chianita) released a Christmas album that became a mega hit in Puerto Rico. Using jíbaro music rhythms, the songs incorporated themes related to Puerto Rico's high cost of living, Christmas traditions, and the possibility of having Chianita as the island's governor. This last tune (*Chianita gobernadora*) became a huge success in Puerto Rico. Presenting a feminist position, the song used comedy to criticize the subjugation of women in the island's *machista* culture. According to the lyrics, if Chianita were elected governor, women would have more power in Puerto Rico's society. With this album, Chianita was transformed into an iconic figure in Puerto Rico. After Meyer and Chianita certified their Puerto Rican ethnicity, Chianita continued to perform on Puerto Rico's commercial television, with segments on Telemundo's and WAPA-TV's noon shows. However, as a result of Meyer's allergic reaction to the makeup, Chianita disappeared in 1985. Thus, whereas Lucecita's body rejected the whitening process through the use of wigs, Angela Meyer's body rejected the chemical process that darkened her skin. For each, the body undermined racist cultural practices.

One important aspect regarding Chianita's popularity with audiences after the telenovela *El hijo de Angela María* was Meyer's alteration of the previously socially content Chianita through her re-definition of the character as a televisual vehicle for political and social commentary and satire. Chianita was re-constructed as an intelligent, well-informed, clever, and humble jíbara who kept in touch with local and global political, economic, and cultural issues. Using local newspapers or the most recent news as a point of departure, Chianita discussed the events and transformations in the Puerto Rican (and on occasion, the U.S. and global) political arena. More importantly, Meyer (as Chianita) used her television segments and character as an agent for helping people in need. For example, if a poor family needed money for an operation, a dialysis machine, or a wheelchair, they called Chianita. If a neighborhood did not have electricity for months, and the government did not respond to the citizens' complaints, they went to Chianita's television segment and both the character and the individuals demanded action.

Chianita became a continuation and validation of Ramón Rivero's complex and contradictory racial constructions. Although neither Meyer nor Chianita identified with Puerto Rico's nationalistic or pro-independence

movements (as Rivero and his characters directly and indirectly did), Chianita represented the economically and socially oppressed sectors of the population. Once again, blackface became a safe and ambivalent masquerade for
social and political commentary and was constructed as the voice of the
working class. What is more, by becoming a jíbara, Chianita transformed
the gender-specific (male) symbolic cultural figure and narrated herself as
an assertive, liberated, and feminist woman. A (blackface) jíbara discussed
politics, criticized the system, and provided political-social commentaries to
audiences.

Through Chianita's character, televisual blackface was nationalized. Key
to the process of national authentication was the construction of a blackface
jíbara identity. Simply put, to televisually represent the oppressed sectors of
the population and, more significantly, to criticize Puerto Rico's political,
economic, and cultural conditions, the character needed to be constructed
and read as unquestionably Puerto Rican. As I have previously discussed, in
Puerto Rico's cultural imaginary the jíbaro is the primary emblem of Puerto
Ricanness.

I locate this nationalization of blackface as a televisual discursive response
to the prejudice against Cubans that informed Puerto Rico's society during the late 1960s and early 1970s. The ethnic and geographical (Caribbean,
CubaRican) ambiguity that characterized previous negritos was eliminated.
Chianita's character represented the final translation from CubaRican blackface negritos into a stereotypical Puerto Rican blackface. However, as Sylvia
del Villard claimed until her death in 1990, Chianita and blackface in general
were a mockery of lo negro.

It should be clear that some of del Villard's public assertions presented a
de-contextualization and even denial of U.S. racist practices and the oppression of African Americans and other racialized groups. For example, once she
expressed that "the vision that the United States people have toward blacks is
different from the one that Puerto Ricans have. The North American sees me
as I am, as a black woman. There, I do not have any problems with racism.
Here, I have problems because there is another vision of a black person.
My appearance and behavior do not correspond with the vision that people
here have of blackness."[87] Based on this statement and other interviews, for
del Villard, the most important aspect of her identity was her race, and she
understood that her black reaffirmation and questioning of racist practices
challenged Puerto Rico's mestizaje and racial democracy discourses. Perhaps

Sylvia del Villard. Courtesy of *Teve Guía* Archives.

her identity formation was a result of spending years in New York City during the 1960s, where indeed, she was probably perceived as African American. Thus, when del Villard said that in the United States people saw her as black and that Puerto Ricans had another vision, she was indirectly referring to la gran familia puertorriqueña discourse and the construction of ethnicity as the main symbol of unity within the nation.

Even though some of del Villard's statements (like the one previously mentioned) were contradictory interpretations of U.S. racial ideologies and practices, her multiple and constant protests against racism and blackface on Puerto Rico's commercial television represented important confrontations that questioned the ideological and visually real whiteness that characterized the industry. On the other hand, it seems that for the majority of audiences during the early 1970s, the Puerto Ricanness of a blackface character was more relevant than problematizing the national culture, the mestiza identity, and Puerto Rico's colonial and racial discourses and racist practices.

Still, thanks to the black performers' ongoing protests regarding the limited opportunities for black actors and actresses in telenovelas, there were some changes in Puerto Rico's commercial television blackface representations. Although the comedic Puerto Rican blackface negrito/a type remained part of local television, the use of white actresses to perform the blackface negra maid characters gradually disappeared during the 1980s. The stereotypical representation of negras as servants remained essentially the same. The main difference was that black actresses began to perform these characters. Furthermore, a few black actors were able to enter the telenovela genre even though they were usually confined to minor roles.[88] Whereas the locally produced telenovelas provided some (still problematic) spaces for black performers, these cultural artifacts began to disappear in the late 1980s due to the local cost of production. Comedies became the principal working vehicle for local performers. Thus, while a few black actors and actresses had some job opportunities in locally produced variety shows and comedies, it was not until the 1990s that, as I discuss in chapter 4, a situation comedy focused on a black Puerto Rican family.

In addition to the controversies surrounding the Afro of Lucecita, blackface, and racist casting practices during the early 1970s, there were other changes in the island's mediascape. Even though there was never a public or government acknowledgment that racist practices permeated Puerto Rico's society in general and commercial television in particular, during the mid-

1970s one media event partially transformed the whiteness that characterized Puerto Rico's world of beauty. At the same time, similar to other televisual debates during this period, the selection of a nonwhite Puerto Rican woman as a symbol of national beauty and the dialogues that emerged after her triumph at the Miss World pageant reiterated the conflictive terrain of gendered blackness in the national imaginary.

"A Mulata Was Selected to Compete in England"

The year 1975 marked the first time in the history of Puerto Rico's beauty pageants that a mulata was chosen to represent the island in an international beauty contest.[89] Wilnelia Merced, a young working-class woman who was beginning her career as a fashion model, was handpicked by the Fontecha Modeling School, the locally owned organization that had the rights to the pageant in Puerto Rico, as the island's representative at the Miss World contest in England. To the surprise of the majority of the people on the island — who did not know that Puerto Rico was even participating — Wilnelia Merced became Miss World 1975.

Although the selection of Wilnelia marked an ideological distance from Eurocentric ideals of female beauty, Wilnelia's body became a complex site where her *mulataje* or blackness was constantly scrutinized, and therefore, her nontraditional (i.e., nonwhite) beauty was questioned. As I discussed in the introduction, in Puerto Rico (as in Cuba, Brazil, and Colombia) black and mulata women have been socially constructed as hypersexual and sensual bodies.[90] Thus, when a Puerto Rican mulata was chosen as Miss World, the racialized lines that demarcate sex from beauty (defined as female whiteness and purity) were blurred, leading to some confusion among locals. Simply put, based on some descriptions of Wilnelia Merced in local media outlets, it was one thing to have sex with a mulata and quite another to have a mulata as a national symbol of beauty in the global arena. In a moment when national pride and dominant ideologies of beauty and sex collided, local journalists became the intermediaries who, through their descriptions of Wilnelia, elucidated why she should be considered and accepted as a Puerto Rican beauty queen.

Similar to the fragmentary accommodations that occurred on Puerto Rico's television during the early 1970s, the local selection of Wilnelia Merced needs to be considered through the lens of the U.S. civil rights movement, the black power movement and its "black is beautiful" discourse, and the

Wilnelia Merced, Miss World 1975.
Courtesy of *Teve Guía* Archives.

Wilnelia Merced, Miss World 1975.
Courtesy of *Teve Guía* Archives.

subsequent Western (European and U.S.) fashion industry construction and commodification of female blackness as exotic chic. In the United States, one of the outcomes of integration efforts in the late 1950s and 1960s was the inclusion of blacks within the mainstream and clearly Eurocentric fashion environment. By the mid-1960s, a few black models were appearing on the pages of magazines such as *Harper's Bazaar, Life,* and *Ladies Home Journal.*[91] In terms of beauty contests, in September 1968, the NAACP organized the first Miss Black America pageant as a protest against the segregation of black women in the Miss America pageant. Following the politics of integration, in 1970, Miss Iowa became the first black woman to participate in the Miss America contest. As Maxime Leeds Craig argues, besides nationally demonstrating and celebrating the beauty of black females, the NAACP, community activists, and young African American women were trying to desegregate the mainstream world of beauty.[92]

On the other hand, by the mid-1960s advocates of black power were rejecting this ideology of integration. Denouncing assimilation into a white-dominated society, black power proponents emphasized the need for economic and political control centered around black communities and business. In addition, merging politics and culture, the black power's "black is beautiful" ideology created what Robin D. G. Kelley categorizes as "the politics of style."[93] The "natural look" (i.e., Afros), African garments, and the celebration of blackness became sites of militancy and resistance. Yet, as I previously mentioned, by the 1970s, the "black is beautiful" discourse, Afros, and soul music had become commodified cultural artifacts.[94] That said, the integrationist approach of the civil rights movement together with the European fashion industry's construction of black women as desirable bodies nonetheless opened spaces for black Puerto Rican female models.

Beginning in the late 1960s in the United States, some mainstream modeling agencies such as Wilhelmina, Elite, and Ford began to include black women as talent.[95] As was expected, modeling agencies in Puerto Rico (for example, Fontecha and D'Rose) who wanted to tap into the U.S. and European market followed this commercial trend. In addition, in 1972 Malín Falú (*Soul Train*'s 1973 host) and Siba Routté established Azabache, the first and only agency for black models in Puerto Rico.[96] During the early 1970s, the fashion sections of newspaper and television magazines in Puerto Rico (for example, *El Nuevo Día, El Mundo, Vea,* and *Angela Luisa*) began to include a few black and trigueña females as models. For the most part, black and mulatto models were confined to participating in local fashion shows and photo shoots, not television commercials.[97] Yet, keeping these transformations in mind and given that by the mid-1970s gendered blackness was already constructed as fashionable in the lucrative U.S. and Western fashion market, it should not come as a surprise that a nonwhite Puerto Rican female was selected by a modeling agent to participate in the Miss World pageant.

Wilnelia Merced as a Miss World contestant was practically ignored by the local press. It was not until Wilnelia won the pageant that newspapers and TV magazines devoted some attention to her. As one journalist noted, "for Puerto Rico the triumph of Wilnelia was a surprise since few people knew that a Puerto Rican was participating in the pageant."[98] However, in several newspaper and magazine stories, Wilnelia was not described as a beautiful woman per se.[99] Instead, she was depicted as having a "special beauty" or as being "exotic." Regarding gendered beauty in Puerto Rico, graphic artist and political activist Antonio Martorell observes that "women with black eyes and hair and darker skin are described in Puerto Rico as exotic. Nonetheless, this physical type constitutes the majority of women in Puerto Rico. Thus, for Puerto Ricans, the logical thinking would be to consider a blond or a red haired woman as exotic. But no, our aesthetic models continue to be Eurocentric therefore, we are exotic to ourselves."[100] Framed by the Eurocentrism that informs Puerto Rico's beauty culture, Wilnelia Merced was narrated as an exotic Puerto Rican gendered Other.

For example, an *El Mundo* journalist wrote, "Wilnelia is captivating. Her beauty is special. Her epidermis, a little toasted by the crushing Caribbean sun, produces sights of admiration from men and forces women to say that she is a *morena* [a racial categorization sometimes used for blacks and mulattos] that has appeal. Miss World possesses a sensual and fleshy mouth."[101] In this article, it seems that the journalist was trying to explain Wilnelia's victory by disconnecting her beauty from her mulataje but then also implying that her sexualized-mulato body had played an important role in her selection. Three main elements are pivotal in this description: first, the Caribbean sun that makes people look black; second, the imaginary and apparently white gendered audience; and third, Wilnelia's socially constructed and sexualized black body parts.

According to this interpretation of Wilnelia's race, her dark skin was not related to racial mixing or black ancestry. The Caribbean sun was so powerful that it was capable of completely transforming the supposedly white skin of Wilnelia into a *café con leche* (coffee with milk) skin. Therefore, due to external and geographical influences, Wilnelia had become a morena. Actually, because of the sun Wilnelia was performing in blackface and black body given that, according to this narration, she was really white. And because Wilnelia was white, there was no need to include references to the African elements that are part of Puerto Rico's culture and society.

At the same time, her morena skin apparently elicited different reactions from men and women. All men, regardless of race were taken by Wilnelia's "special beauty." After all, black and mulata females have been historically constructed as primitive sexual objects. Consequently, the main dilemma was convincing women—especially white women—of Wilnelia's attractiveness. The blatantly racist sentence, "Wilnelia forces women to say that she is a morena that has appeal," directly addressed this issue while concomitantly rearticulating dominant constructions of beauty as synonymous with whiteness. Actually, according to this journalist, it is rare to find an attractive morena (and thus black woman). However, to demonstrate Wilnelia's magnetism, the journalist appropriated some of the sexualized and desirable body parts of black and mulata female bodies: Wilnelia had a "sensual and fleshy mouth." In focusing on her lips and mouth, the journalist dissected Wilnelia's body and reconstructed it as the body of a sensual mulata that was a little dark but not as dark as a black female because in reality she was white.

Another article directly addressed Wilnelia's blackness. Instead of focusing on her physical attractiveness, the journalist philosophized about the spiritual and metaphysical beauty inherently present in black people. He noted, "Puerto Rico knows better than anyone that Wilnelia can be called Miss World because within herself palpitates and vibrates a beauty more deep and significant than any other: the beauty of a moreno spirit."[102] Certainly, the rhetoric used by this journalist did not make any sense. After all, can anyone explain the essentialist and confusing phrase, "the beauty of a moreno spirit"? Furthermore, the fact that he focused on her spirit instead of her body raises this question: Why did he not talk about Wilnelia's physical beauty? Still, this description positioned Wilnelia's blackness as a crucial element within herself and definitively within the nation. More important, for this journalist, Puerto Rico, as a mulata society, should accept Wilnelia.

Finally, an *El Nuevo Día* article entitled *De su pueblo con amor* (From Her People with Love) paid special attention to the comments expressed by people who were present at Wilnelia Merced's welcoming party in Old San

Juan. By purposely including some of the public voices, this story hinted at both the bewilderment caused by Wilnelia's race and also the apparent happiness expressed by trigueño/a individuals. According to the journalist, "a young woman opened her arms and with astonishment exclaimed 'ay, she is trigueña.' . . . An old trigueña woman waved various flags, symbols of Wilnelia's triumph and screamed 'hurrah for our queen. She is the one!' "[103] It is unclear whether some of the public members were black because this racial categorization was never mentioned in the article. Yet, this was the only story that focused on the allegedly mulatto and probably black segment of the population who might have been delighted to see a Puerto Rican trigueña recognized as a national and world beauty.

During an interview with a black Puerto Rican male who worked in Puerto Rico's modeling industry during the late 1970s and early 1980s, the interviewee assured me that Wilnelia's crowning was very important for aspiring mulatto and black models. According to this model, Wilnelia brought hopes to many nonwhite individuals who thought, "if Wilnelia did it, I can do it too." Although since the early 1970s mulatas and black women have participated in local beauty contests and a few have been selected as finalists, Puerto Ricans had to wait twenty-eight years to witness another nonwhite Puerto Rican woman representing the island at an international beauty pageant. As I discuss in chapter 5, in 2003 for the first time in the history of Miss Universe–Puerto Rico, a young woman racially described as morena was selected as Puerto Rico's representative at the Miss Universe 2004.[104] Still, even though gendered blackness was not considered beautiful enough to wear the crown of Miss Universe–Puerto Rico for nearly three decades, after Wilnelia Merced became a world queen some changes were made in the local beauty pageant and fashion industry.

By way of international modeling contests in New York City, U.S. modeling agencies such as Wilhelmina and Elite, and the U.S. Ebony Fashion Fair, some black Puerto Rican models were able to enter the U.S. and global haute couture industry during the mid-1970s.[105] On the other hand, since 1976 Puerto Rico has held Miss *Piel Canela* (Cinnamon Skin), a beauty pageant for black and mulata women. According to another interviewee involved in Puerto Rico's modeling industry, the original intention behind the Miss Piel Canela pageant was to send the Puerto Rican participants to compete at the Miss Black America contest.[106] However, this U.S.–Puerto Rican Afro-diasporic gendered and commodified beauty connection never occurred.

Even though it is not clear why Puerto Rico has never participated in the Miss Black America pageant, the possibilities of this black beauty intersection would have certainly challenged hegemonic constructions of Puerto Rican-ness. Miss Black America–Puerto Rico would have represented a direct fragmentation of the discourses of ethnic and national homogeneity while concomitantly (and televisually) re-articulating the marginalization of blackness in Puerto Rico's cultural imaginary. Maybe this is why Miss Piel Canela has remained local.

Although Miss Piel Canela has provided a space for nonwhite women and has given some participants (the lighter skin mulatas) the opportunity to enter the television and fashion industries, this pageant is mostly ignored by the media. As Colleen Ballerino Cohen, Richard Wilk, and Beverly Stoeltje contend regarding beauty pageants, "by choosing an individual whose deportment, appearance, and style embodies the values and goals of a nation, locality, or group, beauty contests expose the same values to interpretation and challenge."[107] In Puerto Rico, the media outlets' and audiences' obsession regarding beauty pageants have focused on Miss Universe, a pageant for which until 2003 whiteness had been the hegemonic norm for beauty.

As with television, blackness in the local fashion industry during the 1970s was a new, marketable, and therefore profitable commodity. Even though lo negro in Puerto Rico's fashion and beauty pageants functioned as a translation of the U.S. and global objectification of racialized Otherness, at least these partial transformations provided negotiable spaces for black and mulatto individuals in some of Puerto Rico's commercial media outlets. Nonetheless, for the racialized Others who wanted to be actors and actresses and who were not as beautiful as models or who did not have the talent to be salsa performers, ballad singers, or musicians, *it was almost impossible to enter the local television industry.*

Filtering Televisual Blackness

The racialized debates and constructions of blackness in 1970s commercial television were informed by the ideological intersection of nationalism, whiteness, the racial stereotypes of earlier radio and television eras, and the translations of local and transnational cultural and political movements. Televisual blackness was accepted as long as its depictions functioned within the parameters of the mestizaje ideology and reaffirmed a Puerto Rican constructed raceless society. Even though whiteness was still the norm throughout the 1970s, the performers' activism emerged as an open and public statement whose roots were in what James C. Scott defines as *hidden transcripts*, the "offstage speeches, gestures, and practices that confirm, contradict, or inflect what appears in the public transcript."[108] In other words, the black performers' challenges to antiblack racism in Puerto Rico's commercial television publicly intertwined the oppressive condition of black citizens in Puerto Rico's society and in la gran familia puertorriqueña hegemonic discourses with the marginalization of blackness that has informed the industry since 1954. To use Scott's astute analysis of public articulation of the hidden transcripts, the 1970s televisual racialized debates were a time when "truth [was] finally spoken."[109]

I position the civil rights and black power movements together with the changes that occurred in U.S. society and mainstream television during the late 1960s and 1970s as key influences on Puerto Rican television's and more generally the media's partial negotiations during the 1970s. I am not suggesting that prior to the 1960s and 1970s racial consciousness was nonexistent in Puerto Rico. Instead, what I contend is that throughout the 1970s multiple voices and some televisual representations directly and indirectly challenged the racism that characterized the industry and Puerto Rican society. These contestations where in some ways connected to the racial struggles that had taken place in the United States during the 1960s.

Certainly, Puerto Rico's pro-independence movement, the Cuban Revolution, and global anticolonial struggles influenced some performers who, besides situating their blackness as a central component of their identity, also identified with political positions against U.S. imperialism. Lucecita's radical performances and artistic transformation during the early 1970s exemplified the ideological intersections that interconnected alternative ideological discourses in the United States, Cuba, and Puerto Rico (as well as other nations). Then again, in terms of Puerto Rican television's partial negotiations, the few shows that dealt with blackness or problematized race can be seen as cultural products influenced by U.S. mainstream television.

Another element to consider regarding the black performers' mobilization is the racialization of Puerto Ricans in the United States and the circular pattern that characterizes Puerto Rican migration to the mainland. As Arlene Torres suggests, some black and mulatto Puerto Ricans who have lived on the mainland and who have been categorized as minorities return to the island and appropriate alternative political ideologies that challenge the hegemonic construction of la gran familia puertorriqueña.[110] In Puerto Rico's media cultures, Sylvia del Villard represented a vivid example of this circular migration pattern and the translation of the U.S. African American, Puerto Rican, and Latino minority politics. Furthermore, while scholars have not fully explored the U.S. Afro Puerto Rican and Puerto Rican–African American potential influence in Afro Puerto Rican communities on the island, the examples provided in the previous pages attest to these intersections.

As I mentioned in the beginning of this chapter, Stokely Carmichael and leaders of Puerto Rico's pro-independence movements created coalitions during the late 1960s. In addition, the Puerto Rican Left supported Fidel Castro's Revolution, and the Young Lords were influenced by Puerto Rico's nationalist movement, the black power movement, and the Cuban Revolution. But beyond those connections, Afro Puerto Rican communities were also likely influenced by an ideologically diverse array of voices such as Martin Luther King Jr., Frantz Fanon, Malcom X, Robert F. Williams, and Angela Davis (among many others).[111] One can even argue that Afro diasporic influences could have come from other movements in Latin America such as the Afro Brazilian mobilizations for racial equality.[112] It is precisely within this context of Afro diasporic and transnational protest movements that one should position the political activism of Puerto Rican black performers during the 1970s. Still, these intersections become extremely complicated, particularly when one considers Puerto Rico's television translations of blackness during the 1970s.

U.S. commercial television and African American popular culture influences on Puerto Rico's television functioned through an ongoing process of cultural translation, sometimes creating an ideological racial filtering. This ideological filtering of blackness can be seen not only in the examples discussed throughout this chapter, but also in the creation of a local Angela Davis. In 1975, while Angela Davis was involved with grassroots political activism in the United States, a translated Angela Davis (with the same name but with a Spanish pronunciation), who spoke perfect Spanish and wore a huge Afro, dark glasses, and hippie outfits, began to appear in the comedy show *Esto no tiene nombre*, an indigenous and adapted version of *Rowan & Martin's Laugh-In*.[113]

According to Carmen Belén Richardson, who created and performed the local Angela Davis, the character was a mixture of "feminist liberation and racial protest" and was used as a vehicle to criticize "the deficiencies of governmental institutions."[114] Even though these were the intentions of the actress, the character progressively became a parody of political activism. Angela Davis defiantly complained about everything and eventually became a lonely, loud, and comedic voice in the *Esto no tiene nombre* sketches. While the translated Angela Davis was protesting anything possible to the point of mocking political dissent, Chianita, the blackface jíbara, was analyzing and criticizing various political and social issues that were prevalent in Puerto Rico's society and in particular communities. In contrast, the political activism of the real Angela Davis was filtered. In the eyes of industry officials and a majority of the audiences, racism was a U.S. problem; thus, it was not necessary to address racial discrimination in Puerto Rico. However, the displacement of racial prejudice outside the national space became more complex during the late 1970s and throughout the 1980s when a new antimodern, undesirable, and foreign group appeared in Puerto Rico: the Dominicans.

In some ways one could argue that, in the national imaginary, blackness was still situated in the Caribbean. Yet, in contrast to previous decades, this Caribbean and stereotypical blackness was not geographically or ethnically ambiguous. In Puerto Rico, the socially constructed and unwanted blackness began to be associated with the Dominican Republic and its citizens, especially those who migrated illegally to Puerto Rico.[115] Although the 1980s television depiction of Dominicans did not contain the negative stereotypes that, according to Jorge Duany, permeate contemporary jokes about this ethnic group in Puerto Rico's media, by the mid-1980s and particularly throughout the 1990s, Dominicans became the "illiterate, poor, with limited intellectual capability, and dirty," criminal, and illegal Other in Puerto Rico.[116] Given that the new foreign Others were Dominicans, that the Cuban immigrant community was already established in Puerto Rico's society as an upwardly mobile and white group, and that, as I explain in the next chapter, Cubans were in charge of writing most locally produced comedies and situation comedies, it should not come as a surprise that in the early 1980s Cubans became part of a blood-related Puerto Rican and fictional televisual family.[117]

The CubaRican Space Revisited

Don Angel [Telemundo's founder] was first in love with the Americans and later he fell in love with the Cubans. That is why today they (Cubans) rule the roost.
  Interview with Telemundo technical staff, July 1997

Beginning in the mid-1970s and continuing through the 1980s, Puerto Rico's commercial television experienced two important business and cultural transformations. First, as I mentioned in the introduction, all commercial stations were gradually sold to U.S. media corporations.[1] Although television stations remained autonomous in terms of programming, audience viewing measurements, and business arrangements with independent producers, the production of local programming declined. Locally produced telenovelas, which had previously represented a major source of work, disappeared by the late 1980s. As a Telemundo media professional observed, "producing locally is expensive. You spend around twenty to twenty-five thousand dollars per telenovela episode [to produce it], but if you buy it, it costs you between three to four thousand dollars."[2] Consequently, it became more profitable for the local commercial stations to buy Mexican, Venezuelan, Brazilian, and Colombian telenovelas. Because the FCC regulated (and continues to regulate) all media industries on the island, and because the Commonwealth's government had no legal rights over its communication systems, local officials had no authority to establish quotas for the importation of television shows or, subsequently, to protect the jobs of media professionals in Puerto Rico.

At about the same time that local stations were being sold, another transformation was underway. Cuban immigrants were beginning to dominate various areas of television production, particularly the writing of most locally produced comedies and situation comedies. As I discussed in chapter 1, during the early years of commercial radio and television in Puerto Rico, most radionovelas, telenovelas, and some comedy scripts were purchased from Cuba. Because U.S. advertising agencies turned Cuba into the capital of mass-produced radionovela and telenovela scriptwriting for the Latin

American region, there was no space—at least during the 1940s and 1950s—for Puerto Ricans to develop their scriptwriting skills. In terms of comedy shows, although a new cadre of Puerto Rican comedy scriptwriters worked in television beginning in 1954, some writers rejected the low salaries paid by local actors-producers and advertising agencies.[3] Others, from an artistic standpoint, rejected the fast pace of commercial television production.[4] For all these reasons, many Puerto Rican television actors-producers continued with the tradition of buying inexpensive and commercially successful Cuban scripts.

In the first few years following the Cuban Revolution, Puerto Rican producers and television station managers (similar to Latin American station owners and producers) purchased some telenovela and comedy scripts that were originally written for Cuban television.[5] In addition, as occurred in Mexico, Brazil, and Venezuela, a few local producers commissioned scripts from Cuban exiles who were living in other parts of Latin America. For example, while still residing in Venezuela, Cuban scriptwriter Felipe San Pedro wrote some of the scripts for the late 1960s locally produced situation comedy *La criada mal criada* and was commissioned by Puerto Rican producers to write the 1970s situation comedies *Soltero y sin compromiso* and *Tres muchachas de hoy*.[6] This practice of buying Cuban scripts and hiring Cuban scriptwriters solidified a Cuban hegemony, for which Puerto Rican producers were largely responsible. Thus, by the 1980s, the majority of locally produced comedies, situation comedies, and comedy sketches in variety shows were being written by two Cuban immigrants who had been living in Puerto Rico since the mid-1970s: Felipe San Pedro and Manuel Montero "Membrillo."[7]

What follows is an analysis of the construction of Cubans both behind the television scenes and in locally produced programs. In this chapter I argue that while the love-hate relationship that permeated social and cultural discourses of the post-1959 Cuban migrant community continued in Puerto Rico, by the early 1980s Cubans were being televisually depicted as foreign, yet somewhat welcome members of the televisual fictional family. The inclusion of Cubans in the Puerto Rican family not only reasserted the whiteness of both ethnic groups, but this racial representation also operated discursively in relation to a new racialized Other in Puerto Rico—Dominicans, a group that had been situated outside the imaginary borders of the Puerto Rican and CubaRican sociocultural spaces.

To understand how Cubans were gradually incorporated within the Puerto

Rican televisual family, I first address some media professionals' perceptions of the origins of the Cuban scriptwriters' predominance in Puerto Rico's commercial television. I then examine the portrayal of Cubans in local programs, paying special attention to the highly successful 1980s situation comedy *Los suegros* (The In-Laws). Through an exploration of the relationship between Puerto Ricans and Cubans within *Los suegros*, I argue that this situation comedy created a new fictional televisual family. Via marriages and the second generation of Cubans born and raised in Puerto Rico, the post-1959 migratory group was merging into one blood-related group: CubaRican. This televisual representation re-connected Puerto Ricans and Cubans while incorporating the external colonial and neocolonial element that had permeated the CubaRican space since 1898: the United States. Although they were constructed outside the CubaRican family, it was clear that—at least in the *Los suegros* fictional world—Americans were an undeniable cultural, political, and economic presence in Puerto Rico.

Cubans behind the Television Scene

A pervasive theme in my conversations with Puerto Rican media professionals was their admiration for pre-1959 Cuban television, particularly the shows produced by the Cuban commercial television station CMQ. As I mentioned in chapter 1, from the beginning of commercial media in Puerto Rico there was a desire to emulate the quality of both Cuban radio and television programming. Actually, some Puerto Rican media professionals attributed "the golden age" (the 1960s) of both television and advertising in Puerto Rico to the Cuban influence. The categorization of 1960s television as the golden age related not only to production values but, equally important, to the exportation of Puerto Rican shows to Latin America and the internationalization of Puerto Rican actors, actresses, and performers across the region. As one interviewee remarked, "they [Cubans] revolutionized the [Puerto Rican] industry. It was an injection of energy, talent, and business ambitions."[8]

A key figure in Puerto Rico's television internalization during the late 1960s and 1970s was Cuban producer Gaspar Pumarejo. Founder of Cuba's first commercial television station (Union Radio TV, channel 4, October 1950) and also a pioneer in the establishment of color television in Cuba (1957),[9] Pumarejo migrated to Puerto Rico in 1960. Soon after his arrival, Pumarejo started the television production company Antillana de Televisión, wherein he, for the most part, produced variety and game shows. However, through his previous connections with some Latin American television owners and producers, Pumarejo created a space for local performers in a trans–Latin American television production market still in its infancy.

For instance, in the late 1960s Pumarejo, a close friend and business partner of the Delgado-Parker brothers (owners of the Peruvian television station Panamericana), sent several Puerto Rican performers to participate in Panamericana's productions. By way of this association, Puerto Rican actor Braulio Castillo became the male protagonist of *Simplemente María* (1969–1970), the first Latin American telenovela with a trans–Latin American cast and the first megahit in the region.[10] To be sure, in the late 1960s Telemundo, which had incorporated videotape (1966), color television (1968), and satellite broadcasting (1968),[11] began to sell its locally produced telenovelas in Latin America. In fact, the first local exportation was the 1968 *La mujer de aquella noche*, which also featured Braulio Castillo in the leading role. Nevertheless, contrary to Puerto Rican producers, Gaspar Pumarejo had long-established relations with powerful television owners in the region and equally important, vast experience in exporting cultural artifacts.

Although many of the interviewees acknowledged the talent of the Cuban media professionals such as Pumarejo, and the value of their cultural products, some interviewees expressed resentment toward Cubans. This resentment presumably related to the Cuban community's power in Puerto Rico's commercial television and their predominance in the area of scriptwriting during the late 1970s and the 1980s. As I discussed in chapter 2, this bitterness should be contextualized within the parameters of the social, political, and economic transformations and prejudices that emerged after the 1959 Cuban migration. Whereas media professionals held diverse opinions regarding the origins of the Cuban scriptwriters' hegemony, those opinions tended to revolve around four interrelated factors: the Cuban community's prestige, the low cost of its cultural products before 1959, the alleged dearth of Puerto Rican scriptwriters, and the commercial success of shows written by Cubans.

According to a media professional who began working in Puerto Rico's commercial television during the mid-1980s, the Cuban dominance was associated with the fact that most television producers in Puerto Rico had been working in the industry for many years and were familiar with the "old modes of production."[12] In other words, given that during the radio era and the beginning of television, some Puerto Rican actors-producers had purchased inexpensive and what were generally described as "excellent" programs in

Cuba, and because these actors-producers who began working in 1954 increasingly controlled television production in Puerto Rico, they continued to hire Cuban scriptwriters.[13] However, producer Paquito Cordero offered a different explanation regarding the prevalence of Cuban scriptwriters in local commercial television. Although Cordero praised the work of various creative people from Puerto Rico, he believed that there was a lack of Puerto Rican writers. As he observed:

> In Puerto Rico we have a problem. In Puerto Rico we did not cultivate scriptwriters. The main reason was that at the beginning, the scripts came from Cuba. We were able to find telenovela and sitcom scripts very cheaply. One can count excellent [Puerto Rican] scriptwriters on one hand. When I began my company, I had to hire Cuban writers who came from Cuba. Recently, we have hired new scriptwriters. On many occasions, we tried to incorporate our scriptwriters [from Puerto Rico] . . . but if you ask me now about Puerto Rican scriptwriters, I have a short list.[14]

The realities of this transcultural influence became evident when specific examples were discussed. When asking some television professionals about successful sitcoms, three titles consistently came to mind, *Los García* (The García's), *Los suegros* (The In-Laws), and *En casa de Juanma y Wiwi* (In Juanma and Wiwi's House). Only *Los García* was written by a Puerto Rican (Tommy Muñiz) while the other two, like most of the sitcoms produced locally, were written by Cubans (Manuel Montero "Membrillo" and Felipe San Pedro, respectively). Although one should not assume that these programs were successful simply because they were written by Cubans, one should realize that local producers tended to hire people who had mastered comedy writing techniques or who had experience in television production. Thus, it seems that for many years, an ongoing pattern of hiring already commercially successful (Cuban) writers was common.

Nevertheless, some media professionals diverged from Cordero's opinion regarding the lack of Puerto Rican scriptwriters. Pablo Cabrera, a highly respected Puerto Rican theater and television director, praised the talent of many Cuban scriptwriters.[15] Still, Cabrera argued that the problem was not the lack of talented Puerto Rican writers. As he noted, "I do not think there was such a scarcity. To put it simply, they were not given the opportunity that should have been given to them. They were not offered a fertile ground for their development. During the 1960s, at WIPR [the Commonwealth radio and television stations] we had excellent Puerto Rican writers in radio and in television. Commercial television did not want to spend the money to pay the local talent."[16]

In considering these two diverse postures, one should reflect on the power hierarchies and struggles within the field of cultural production and the fact that commercial television is a business enterprise.[17] As Cordero recognized, Cuban scripts were inexpensive; therefore, it was more profitable for local producers to buy these already made and low-cost products that had originally been made for Cuban television. Additionally, although no one ever disclosed the scriptwriters' salaries, it is likely that in the beginning, Cuban scriptwriters—new immigrants trying to establish themselves in Puerto Rico—worked for less money than Puerto Ricans. Therefore, even though Puerto Rican society in general harbored a strong resentment toward the Cuban immigrant community, top-level television officials professed great admiration for the Cuban media professionals' expertise even as they felt aversion regarding Cubans' power in the medium. This love-hate relationship was part of both the behind-the-scenes television production environment and the construction of Cuban characters in locally produced comedies and situation comedies.

From the late 1960s through the 1980s, televisual Cubans were portrayed as white, upper-middle-class, and right-wing conservatives who supported Puerto Rico's annexation to the United States. In addition, through their habanero accent and Cuban vernacular language, Cuban characters usually made references to the sugarcane industries they owned in Cuba and their hope that someday, when Fidel Castro died, they would return to the island and reclaim their property. In these constructions, Cuban men were depicted as greedy and pushy business owners who dressed in *guayaberas* (semiformal shirts), smoked cigars, and wore multiple gold chains. Cuban women were commonly represented as sensual and attractive ladies who dressed in bright colors, wore gaudy jewelry, and constantly made reference to the prestigious club Casa Cuba and its parties.[18]

Puerto Rican and Cuban actors, actresses, and scriptwriters constructed these representations for Puerto Rico's commercial television.[19] The performers' and scriptwriters' depictions of Cubans were a recurring comedic element in locally produced programs. Although television's stereotypical representations of Cubans narrated them as culturally and politically different, they were nonetheless portrayed as active participants in Puerto Rico's

Puerto Rican actress Awilda Carbia performing the Cuban character
Dulce María, circa early 1980s. Courtesy of *Teve Guía* Archives.

"imagined community."[20] The placement of Cubans into the island's social, cultural, and economic environments and the conflictive relations between Puerto Ricans and Cubans can be clearly seen in the highly successful 1980s prime-time situation comedy *Los suegros* (The In-Laws).[21]

Los suegros: The New CubaRican Family

Conceptualized and written by Cuban scriptwriter Manuel Montero "Membrillo" and produced by Puerto Rican actor-producer Elín Ortíz (Producciones Ayax) for WAPA-TV (channel 4), *Los suegros* (1981–1991) centered on a Puerto Rican couple (Tito and María Rivera) and a Cuban couple (Ñico and Caridad Fernández) who became family members when their respective daughter and son (Jackie and Cuco) married. Paralleling what David Marc defines as the four stages of the U.S. situation comedy formula (familiar status quo, ritual error made, ritual lesson learned, and familiar status quo), the *Los suegros* narrative revolved around the ongoing tension among the older generation of Cubans and Puerto Ricans.[22] Nevertheless, the familiar order was never fully restored in the *Los suegros* episodes because the domestic family lifestyle operated through the incessant and unresolved contingencies between Puerto Ricans and Cubans in general and Tito and Ñico in particular. These ethnic-cultural nationalistic clashes were so ridiculous and exaggerated that the Puerto Rican and Cuban interactions represented the principal comedic element in *Los suegros*.

Although the Riveras were disappointed over the fact that their daughter Jackie had married a "hard-working and good man, but still a loud Cuban," and the Fernándezes could not understand why Cuco had fallen in love with a "nice young Puerto Rican woman, but not as nice as *las muchachitas cubanas*" (young Cuban women), the Riveras also had another source of dissatisfaction. Junior, Tito and María's highly sentimental mama's-boy son (he cried at the least provocation), married Katy, an American woman from Kentucky. For the Riveras (especially Tito), it was difficult to comprehend why their son and daughter had not married Puerto Ricans. As Tito remarked to Jackie and Junior at their double wedding ceremony, "You are in love with a Cuban and the other idiot is in love with an American woman. None of you consumed what the country produces!"

The various migrations and political, economic, and cultural intersections in Puerto Rico's society were transforming the ethnic family. Even as the discourse of la gran familia puertorriqueña and Puerto Rico's cultural nationalism continued to be solid ideological forces, it was clear that by the 1980s multiple influences and levels were permeating the nation. While Cuban immigrants were still viewed as outsiders in the island's cultural imaginary, after twenty years of the first (post-1959) massive migration to Puerto Rico, their presence could not be ignored. On the other hand, although the United States was still politically characterized by the Puerto Rican Left as the colonial, imperialistic, and oppressive external force, as the foreign yet necessary constituent for the economic survival of the nation by pro-commonwealth supporters, and as the future country by the pro-statehood followers, Americanness was an indisputable influence in Puerto Rico. Therefore, the *Los suegros* episodes served as televisual locations that re-appropriated, re-packaged, and re-presented what had been socially constructed as the cultural and ideological differences among these groups in Puerto Rico.

Los suegros's narrative portrayed the ways in which each character and ethnic group perceived itself and the Others. For the most part, being the Other in *Los suegros* was contextualized within notions of Puerto Rican and Cuban cultural nationalism (i.e., positing one of these two nation's island, population, and customs as better than the other) and Puerto Rican and Cuban stereotypes of Americans. Although the Fernández couple reproduced hegemonic discourses regarding Cubans in Puerto Rico (overconfident individuals who identify politically with the ultra right), the narrative, through secondary characters and general references, also represented some of the internal political conflicts and class divisions that inform the Cuban diaspora. In contrast, Puerto Ricans were depicted as xenophobic, especially toward the Cuban immigrants. However, even though the Puerto Rican characters (particularly Tito) were fixated on the anti-Cuban sentiment, the situation comedy, as I will further discuss, problematized the power differences among Puerto Rico's immigrant groups.

The third ethnic group (the Americans) was the epitome of cultural Otherness. The Puerto Rican and Cuban characters (especially the older generation) did not have anything in common with the SSL (Spanish as a second language), liberal, and annoyingly perky Americans. Nonetheless, even though Americanness was an important element at the beginning of *Los suegros*, its central theme focused on the ethnic contestations among the Puerto Rican and Cuban characters, and above all, between Tito and Ñico.

In addition to ethnic Otherness, *Los suegros* articulated Otherness within the fictional Puerto Rican and Cuban clans. For the most part, this internal Otherness revolved around political dissent within the Cuban family and the socially and culturally constructed machista ideology prevalent in Puerto Rico and Cuba. In other words, the characters who disagreed with the anti–Fidel Castro political rhetoric and the individuals who transgressed the gendered places in both the private and public spheres were still situated as family members, yet were *different* from the dominant majority. Whereas *Los suegros* did not address the issue of racial Otherness in Puerto Rico, the narrative generated several discursive spaces for the articulation of racial and class differences within the Cuban diaspora.

Los suegros had two secondary American characters: Katy and Mr. Morrison, Katy's widowed father. The Americans were depicted at the opposite end of the cultural spectrum from Puerto Ricans and Cubans and their behavior challenged what Tito, María, Ñico, and Caridad (and sometimes Cuco and Jackie) perceived as normal, polite, and correct. For example, Tito detested what he considered Katy's bossy personality. This domineering trait was expressed primarily as Katy's transgressing the gendered role of a submissive, sacrificing, and dedicated Puerto Rican and Cuban woman and housewife. Perhaps more important, her rejection of the traditional gender role emasculated Junior, who carried out all the housewifely tasks at home. Katy challenged Puerto Rico's (as well as Cuba's and Latin America's) machista culture by juxtaposing the socially and culturally constructed positions of men and women in the private sphere.

According to *Los suegros*'s narrative, the worst transcultural matching occurred in the pairing of a Puerto Rican man and an American woman because the American's (imported) feminist behavior had the potential to destroy the patriarchal system within the family. Katy's dominant, and therefore, "masculine" personality amplified Junior's passive and "feminine" persona and ultimately transcended the realm of the private sphere. Junior was proud of being the housewife and he happily told stories to the extended family members regarding how nicely he cleaned the house or how happy he was with the new iron that Katy had bought for him. Junior assimilated some of the socially constructed negative elements associated with the U.S. culture in Puerto Rico and thus did not behave as a Puerto Rican macho. As was expected, Ñico and Cuco made jokes at the expense of Junior, while Tito felt ashamed of his "weak" son.

In addition to being an unfit and "manipulative" wife, Katy was described as *"fea"* (ugly). Both the Rivera and the Fernández couples were perplexed over the fact that Junior had married *"una mujer tan fea, flaca, y jincha"* (a woman so ugly, bony, and sickly pale). As I discussed in the previous chapter, the Eurocentric ideals of beauty inform the construction of a beautiful female body in Puerto Rico. However, as I also explained, the mulata is positioned as a sexual and sensual body. Although discourses of beauty are intertwined with whiteness, in general, Anglo-Saxon, Germanic, Nordic whiteness (culturally codified as excessive and as a symptom of an unhealthy body) is deemed as nonattractive and nonsexual in Puerto Rico. For example, in Puerto Rico (and probably in the Spanish Caribbean in general), Halle Berry (who would be read as a mulata, not as a black woman), Penélope Cruz, and Sofia Loren might be considered more beautiful and sensual than Jennifer Anniston, Calista Flockhart, and Candace Bergen. Actually, Flockhart would be described as very fea because, as Frances Aparicio observes, "for the Latin gaze, both male and female, . . . wider hips and fuller bodies have been generally established as ideal aesthetic standards for women. The thin and tall bodies signal deficiency, not beauty."[23] Within this gendered and cultural ideal of beauty, Katy was perceived as sexually unappealing by both Cuban and Puerto Rican characters. Even Junior thought that Katy was ugly but as he always responded to his family, "I know that Katy is ugly, skinny, and *jincha* [sickly pale]. That she looks like a broom stick and that she is whiter than a glass of milk. But you know what? I love her."

Beyond being fea, Katy did not know "how to dress," thus Tito, María, Ñico, and Caridad constantly criticized her "inappropriate" clothing. Regardless of the occasion or place, Katy usually dressed in very short pants and tiny or revealing blouses. Considering Puerto Rico's tropical climate, Katy's dress code was practical. Still, for the more conservative-traditional sectors of the population (which in *Los suegros* were represented by the older generation of Puerto Ricans and Cubans), this type of clothing is used for the beach not, for example, as appropriate attire for a nice restaurant or a family reunion. Therefore, for the Rivera and the Fernández families, Katy had no taste for clothing nor did she have a sense of decorum regarding dress codes.

Both Junior and Katy were seen as cultural Others by their extended families. Junior, negatively influenced by his American wife, publicly abandoned some of the traditional elements of the Puerto Rican and Cuban cultures by becoming a pathetic, dominated man. Alternatively, Katy never accommodated her behavior to the socially constructed gendered place in the private or public spheres. While Tito criticized Katy behind her back ("that woman controls my son!" and "look how she dresses!") and sometimes confronted her directly ("your last name is not Morrison, it is Rivera. Riveraaaa! In Puerto Rico, married women adopt the husbands' last names!"), he was generally polite to Katy. The main reason behind Tito's behavior was the economic power of Katy's father, Mr. Morrison.

Together with Tito, Mr. Morrison co-owned a *tembleque* (dessert) factory. While all the families were represented as upwardly mobile, Mr. Morrison owned 51 percent of the factory shares, which positioned him and Katy as the most financially solvent individuals in this extended family. Additionally, Mr. Morrison, who owned several successful businesses in the United States, did not have to work for a living. Ñico Fernández was also very courteous to Mr. Morrison partly because of his financial status but primarily because he was the manager of the factory. At least at the beginning of this sitcom, both Puerto Ricans and Cubans were financially dependent on Mr. Morrison's investments.

Whereas *Los suegros* presented a class-ethnic-based hierarchical economic structure (Americans at the top, Puerto Ricans in the middle, and Cubans on the bottom), none of these families or characters ever made references to being financially constrained. They were *modernized* Americans, Puerto Ricans, and Cubans who had secure jobs even though Puerto Rico was undergoing a difficult economic period. During the 1980s, many U.S. and global corporations moved their plants from Puerto Rico to other Third World countries in search of a cheap labor force.[24] Hence, contrary to the economic realities of 1980s Puerto Rico, Tito and Ñico had the financial support of Mr. Morrison (and thus, the United States).

Mr. Morrison's and Katy's characters symbolized the U.S. political and cultural presence on the island and, evidently, Puerto Rico's economic dependency. Although Tito lost his temper on several occasions and told Mr. Morrison that, "like always, you Americans are involved in our internal problems!," Ñico always reminded Tito that he had to control himself. "Tito you should keep in mind that Mr. Morrison owns 51 percent of the shares," Ñico usually responded, forcing Tito to contain his stereotypical explosive reactions. Whereas some of Tito's and Ñico's comments situated Mr. Morrison as an emblem of the U.S. colonial authority in Puerto Rico, Americanness in *Los suegros* was first of all synonymous with economic power. However, contrary to the late 1940s to mid-1950s radio show *El tremendo hotel* and the characters Ruth, la americana, and Mr. Sandwich, the portrayals of Katy and Mr. Morrison did not emerge from an imperialistic racial and cultural ideological discourse that characterized the locals (Puerto Ricans and Cubans) as the colonized and intellectually inferior primitive Others. Both Katy and Mr. Morrison appreciated Puerto Rican and Cuban cultures, participated in the local festivities, and highly respected the members of their extended family. In addition, Mr. Morrison never complained that his only (and precious) daughter had married a Puerto Rican man.

That said, Mr. Morrison displayed some of the stereotypes that are associated with the U.S. dominant culture. For example, regardless of his family connections with Tito and Ñico, for Mr. Morrison business and profits were the most important things in life. Thus, when Mr. Morrison returned to Puerto Rico after residing in the United States for a year, he expected Tito to re-sell him the 51 percent of the tembleque factory shares, which he had sold when he migrated to the states. After Tito refused to sell, Mr. Morrison countered, "If you do not want me to do business with you, I will then have to open another tembleque factory." Tito, María, Ñico, and Caridad were befuddled by Mr. Morrison's plans, primarily because for them, the possibility of competing with family members was not seen as morally correct or ethical. On the other hand, for Mr. Morrison opening another business was the normal action to take, and he simply replied, "Well, that is the American way. Business is business."

Mr. Morrison did not want to destroy the local family, community, or nation as Ruth, la americana, intended with Doña Polita's hotel in the *El tremendo hotel* narrative. He was constructed as an American man who functioned through the ideology of individualism that is associated with the U.S. capitalistic culture. For Mr. Morrison there was a clear distinction between the public (business) and private (home-family) spheres, and he did not consider that opening another tembleque factory would affect the family. Nevertheless, for the Puerto Rican and Cuban characters, the family was the most important entity in their lives. Therefore, Mr. Morrison's American slogan and ideological discourse, "business is business," was interpreted as a conflict that could potentially disturb the family unit. While Mr. Morrison's plans caused confusion and dissatisfaction within the extended family, he put aside his capitalistic goals and accepted a job at Tito's factory. Tito did not re-sell the shares and Mr. Morrison accommodated himself to the new economic and family reality.

Los suegros, in some ways similar to *El tremendo hotel*, placed local businesses and, indirectly, the control of the nation, in the hands of Puerto Ricans. However, from the perspective presented by *Los suegros*, the intricate U.S.–P.R. relations needed to operate through ongoing re-negotiations. Regardless of economic benefits, Puerto Ricans were required to be attentive to the shifts of power since these transformations could affect the family. On the other hand, the show suggested that Americans (and thus, the United States), rather than imposing their imperial-economic force, should be conscientious of the ways in which their power affected local structures. In *Los suegros*'s fictional and utopian space, the debates between Americans and Puerto Ricans were easily resolved. After all, in this imaginary televisual world, the Riveras and the Morrisons were members of the same family. Regardless of the history of colonial exploitation, the union between these two groups was already established. The key was to work through the ideological, cultural, economic, and political discrepancies.

In comparing *Los suegros* and *El tremendo hotel*, one needs to keep in mind the two comedies' ideological objectives, temporal contexts, and the perspectives of their scriptwriters. As I discussed in chapter 1, *El tremendo hotel*'s narrative centered on class divisions in the late 1940s and early 1950s Puerto Rico and the nation's economic and social modernization processes. Ramón Rivero used his radio comedy as a vehicle to directly and indirectly question Puerto Rico's new political environment (the island's Commonwealth status) and its economic transformations (industrialization). In contrast, *Los suegros* focused on cultural differences and ethnic conflicts within the nation during the 1980s. Manuel Montero "Membrillo" (the *Los suegros*'s scriptwriter) utilized the show to examine the ways in which the U.S. presence and the Cuban diaspora constituted distinct sociocultural influences in Puerto Rican society. More to the point, and as I will further discuss, Montero used the narrative to criticize certain sectors of the Cuban community in Puerto Rico and Puerto Rico's xenophobic culture. Consequently, even though both authors were critical of the U.S. presence in Puerto Rico, the differences in time, location, and authorship permeated the constructions of Americanness in the two comedies.

Still, mirroring *El tremendo hotel*, the American characters in *Los suegros* served as the target of jokes solidifying a common ground between the Cuban and Puerto Rican characters. During these comedic moments, the Puerto Ricans and Cubans performed some of the cultural elements of the CubaRi-

can space and the familial interactions that informed these two groups before the 1960s Cuban migration to Puerto Rico. From ridiculing the dressing styles of Katy and Mr. Morrison ("they have no taste!"), to joking about
the way they danced salsa ("they look like they are killing cockroaches"),
to being amazed that Katy and Mr. Morrison dared to do things that they
did not know how to do (for example, they went to Casa Cuba and presented themselves as, respectively, a Cuban *rumbera* [rumba dancer] and a
Cuban drummer), Puerto Ricans and Cubans teased the constructed, clue-
less Americans. Nonetheless, in addition to being the objects of mockery,
Katy and Mr. Morrison (together with María, Caridad, Junior, Jackie, and
Cuco) served as mediators in the nonsensical disagreements between the
anti-Cuban and extremely xenophobic Tito and the pretentious and ultra
right-wing conservative Ñico.

Clearly, not all the Cuban characters or Cuban themes in *Los suegros* reproduced the stereotypes associated with this community in Puerto Rico.
Quite the contrary. The *Los suegros* narrative opened a multiplicity of spaces
for various interpretations of Cubans. Even though the early 1960s Cuban migration to Puerto Rico comprised white, upper-class, and educated individuals who generally identified with the Right (especially regarding U.S.–Cuba
relations), *Los suegros* transgressed this socially constructed generalization.
Actually, *Los suegros* not only questioned hegemonic class and political ideologies regarding Cubans in Puerto Rico but the show also brought to light
the familial and ethnic complexities that are part of this diverse and transnational group.

For instance, contrary to the antirevolutionary politics of Ñico and Caridad, Cuco Fernández was portrayed as a young man who identified with the
Left. Although politics was not the center of the *Los suegros* narrative, some of
Cuco's comments and several of Ñico's remarks regarding his son positioned
Cuco as a sympathizer of Puerto Rico's pro-independence movement and as a
man who was critical of the United States. For example, Cuco referred to Katy
as the "imperialistic Yankee," who, like her country, "dominated the weak"
(i.e., Junior). Whereas this comedic line articulated Puerto Rico and Cuba's
machista ideology, the comment also had a subtextual meaning regarding
U.S. international and local politics. In another episode that dealt with the
possibility of Mr. Morrison and one of the factory's secretaries having a child
outside of marriage, Cuco indicated that Mr. Morrison's behavior was not
uncommon given that "the Yankees are always invading the territories that

are not officially theirs." Furthermore, according to Ñico, Cuco was becoming a "communist in exile" because he was an avid reader of the far-left Puerto Rican newspaper *Claridad*.

In the world of *Los suegros*, there was an existing Cuban diasporic group that did not identify with the dominant far right, even as political dissent was (and still is) usually silenced by the most powerful sectors within the Cuban community in Puerto Rico (and in Miami). Cuco, whose Cuban ethnicity was a fundamental element of his identity (he always identified himself as Cuban even though he was raised in Puerto Rico), was able to distance himself politically from his parents, and thus, from the Cuban majority. According to *Los suegros*, exilic Cubanness represented much more than anti-Castro politics or an uncritical position toward the United States. Cuco's character defied the monolithic ideological construction of the Cuban community in Puerto Rican society and in previous locally produced comedy shows.

As *Los suegros* addressed ideological differences within the Cuban diaspora, the show also interrogated the socially constructed and standardized affluence of Cubans in Puerto Rico. The Fernández family migrated to Puerto Rico in 1960, which allegorically placed them as part of the golden migration. However, this fictional Cuban family did not do as well financially as their compatriots in Puerto Rico. While the early 1960s Cuban migrants became (for the most part) successful business entrepreneurs, Ñico Fernández worked for Tito and Mr. Morrison. Additionally, after Tito closed the tembleque factory to open a jeans' sweatshop, Ñico survived financially by working several part-time jobs (for example, selling encyclopedias). Even though Ñico and Caridad portrayed themselves as part of the pre-1959 Cuban community of prosperity, it was clear that the Fernández family did not come from old money. Also, contrary to the golden migration group, neither Ñico nor Caridad had a college degree or professional training.[25]

Ñico and Caridad Fernández established their own business during the mid-1980s. Yet, it had taken them more than twenty years to become financially independent. Furthermore, instead of opening, for example, a furniture store, a restaurant, or an insurance company (like many golden migration Cubans in Puerto Rico), they established a *botánica*, a store where people buy the necessary items to perform a spiritual cleansing of a place or person, candles for various saints, or Santería religious artifacts. And indeed they were successful because, culturally speaking, even as the majority of both Puerto Ricans and Cubans identify as Christians (and in the case of Cubans, also Jewish), the Santería religion (a syncretism of the Yoruba tradition with Catholicism) is an integral part of the Cuban culture and has been a major influence in Puerto Rico.[26] Although the elite Cuban community in Puerto Rico categorizes this religion as "witchcraft and superstition" (which can be read as a Eurocentric, class-based, and racial rejection of Cuba's African influences), the *Los suegros*'s fictional Cuban family members were devout believers in Santería.[27] The Fernández family (a white middle-class couple) embraced the African elements of the culture even as Puerto Rico's Cuban middle-upper classes rejected them.[28]

Last, the fact that a cousin of Caridad Fernández was a *marielita* (a person who migrated through the 1980 Mariel boatlift) indirectly addressed the issue of race and class in this new layer of the Cuban migrant community. The majority of Cubans who migrated through Mariel were working-class, black, and mulatto individuals.[29] Moreover, due to the institutional repression of homosexuals in revolutionary Cuba, many Cuban gays and lesbians also migrated through Mariel.[30] Even though *Los suegros*'s narrative never dealt with the problems of racial prejudice within the Cuban community, in Puerto Rico's society, and in Cuba, or problematized Cuba and Puerto Rico's homophobic cultures, the references to the Mariel migration discursively entwined issues of race, class, and sexual orientation. What is more, whereas Fidel Castro categorized the Mariel exodus as the scum of Cuban society, and although the U.S. media to a large degree reproduced Castro's ideological characterization, in *Los suegros* the Fernández family welcomed the marielitos as what they were: family members.

In sum, *Los suegros* created multiple textual gradations for audiences to broaden their understanding of Cubans and Cuban politics in the diaspora, even though Ñico and Caridad were depicted as mega right-wing conservative and arrogant Cubans. However, whereas the older Cubans (and particularly Ñico) embodied some negative stereotypes associated with Cubans in Puerto Rico, this depiction operated through a parallel universe in relation to negative stereotypes of Puerto Ricans. By televisually portraying a Cubanness and a Puerto Ricanness that exceeded the socially constructed stereotypes of the two ethnic groups, *Los suegros* criticized the far right-wing Cuban community's ideological inflexibility, Puerto Rican prejudices toward Cubans, and Puerto Rico's xenophobic culture.

In every episode, Tito and Ñico fought to demonstrate the superiority of Puerto Rican and Cuban cultures and people. While the narrative did not

Caridad and Ñico. Courtesy of *Teve Guía* Archives.

construct one culture as more advanced (modern) than the other, the older Cuban characters were represented as extremely immodest in comparison to the Puerto Ricans. Their conceited personalities came across in the way they portrayed themselves in front of the other characters and in their firm belief that nothing in Puerto Rico—or in any other part of the world—was as good as it was in Cuba. For instance, Cuba was the most beautiful place in the world, had the most intelligent population ("at three months Cuban children were already in kindergarten!"), and possessed its own and definitively much better Cuban Disney (which indirectly meant that the idea to build the amusement park came from Cuba). In addition, according to Ñico, CMQ's television facilities were so huge and technologically advanced that "one studio held one thousand and four hundred actors" and "each of the one hundred cameras per television show was operated by three camera men."

Besides these general and hyperbolic references to Cuba (which Ñico and Caridad firmly regarded as truthful), they talked extensively about themselves and what they had in their *Cubita bella* (beautiful Cuba). Ñico was born and raised in "beautiful Old Havana," while Caridad was born in Matanzillo, "which is bigger than the entire island of Puerto Rico." Also, when they lived in Cuba, they were part of the crème de la crème. As Ñico proudly declared, "I had properties throughout the island. I had two sugarcane plantations in Camaguey, three apartment complexes in Havana, and I owned a button factory in Bayamo." It was impossible to keep track of all of Ñico's possessions in Cuba because he made references to multiple businesses and properties in most of the episodes. On top of being rich in pre-revolutionary Cuba, Ñico and Caridad were the best in everything imaginable. Caridad was a renowned Cuban rumbera, singer, musician, and artiste, while Ñico was the greatest actor, domino player, accountant, lawyer, drummer, and baseball player (among other vocations and hobbies). In addition, Ñico and Caridad claimed to know everybody in both Cuba and Puerto Rico and with every individual they encountered, each maintained that he or she was his closest friend.

Even as Ñico and Caridad were constructed as extremely arrogant to the point of being farcical and, therefore, funny, they were also represented as cheerful individuals who loved to party and enjoy life. They frequently sang Cuban tunes or danced to a Cuban mambo for no special reason. These moments served to recreate Ñico and Caridad as amicable people and placed them in opposition to Tito, a cantankerous man who was always in a bad mood and constantly complaining about the "foreigners that were taking over Puerto Rico."

It is important to note that Ñico and Caridad's ongoing references to their previous life in Cuba did not function as nostalgic longings for their lost homeland.[31] While Ñico and Caridad constantly talked about "the wonders of Cuba," they did not miss the land and nation per se. What they really yearned for were their material assets in pre-revolutionary Cuba. Thus, who was the one to blame for their vanished (and apparently) upper-class status? Fidel Castro. Ñico and Caridad passionately hated Castro and any direct or indirect mention of the Cuban leader or the revolution made them miserable. From Tito's dressing as Fidel Castro for a costume party (which he obviously did to provoke Ñico) to general symbols, phrases, or words that Ñico and Caridad misinterpreted as referring to the Cuban Revolution (for example, the color red or the use of the word *comrade*), the two exiles were endlessly offended. Furthermore, even though Ñico and Caridad constantly claimed that "they did not hold grudges," they used every available opportunity to talk about the evil Castro who "took everything from us," and to express how they would, with the help of the United States, "destroy Fidel." As a result, while Ñico and Caridad reproduced dominant stereotypes of Cubans in Puerto Rico, these characters also functioned as avenues for ridiculing and ultimately criticizing certain sectors and political positions within the Cuban diaspora. And apparently, the powerful far right-wing segment of the Cuban community in Puerto Rico decoded some of the *Los suegros* encoded messages. As expected, there were literal, symbolic, and ideological noises throughout the (mis)communication processes between the *Los suegros* writer and some of the situation comedy's Cuban audience.

In 1984 *La Crónica*, an ideologically conservative Cuban newspaper in Puerto Rico, began a massive campaign within the Cuban exile community demanding the cancellation of *Los suegros* and *Los suegros y los nietos* (The In-Laws and the Grandchildren, a spin-off of *Los suegros* that began airing in 1983).[32] According to several interviews with Cuban exiles published in *La Crónica*, the Ñico and Caridad characters depicted Cubans as "arrogant and as party people," not as "hard working individuals." Although Caridad's role was played by a Cuban actress, the criticism focused on the character Ñico and Manuel Montero "Membrillo," who performed the part in addition to being the situation comedies' scriptwriter. According to the inter-

(From left to right) Ñico in a Cuban rumbero costume,
Tito dressed as Fidel Castro, and producer Elín Ortíz, at the
taping of *Los suegros*. Courtesy of *Teve Guía* Archives.

viewees and the newspaper editorial, Montero's character reproduced previous stereotypes of Cubans by "dressing in guayabera and wearing multiple
gold medal chains."[33] Even though both characters' dressing styles and certain aspects of their personalities were replicas of previous televisual Cubans
(Caridad, like other fictional *cubanas*, dressed in bright colors and wore exaggerated jewelry), and whereas the situation comedies were produced by
a Puerto Rican media professional, *La Crónica* focused its attack solely on
Manuel Montero "Membrillo." However, the most problematic and profes-
sionally dangerous aspect of the anti-Montero campaign, which could have
affected his career and that definitely threatened the well-being of his family,
related to how he was represented politically within the Cuban exile community. Manuel Montero "Membrillo" was labeled as "a spy of Fidel Castro"
and as a "sympathizer of the Cuban Revolution."[34] As a result, Montero and
his family were blacklisted.

Manuel Montero never identified himself as a pro-independence advocate, nor was he a sympathizer of Fidel Castro. Although Montero kept close
ties with Cuba and frequently traveled to the island, his trips were family
related.[35] In *Los suegros* he was critical of the inflexible political position
of far-right Cuban exiles and some community members' fixation on their
material assets in Cuba. As a result, Montero's multidimensional portrayals
of Cubans, together with his close familial ties to the island, were enough
to make him a traitor in the eyes of some Cuban exiles. Manuel Montero
"Membrillo," a man who had left Cuba in 1973 due to government censorship
of his satirical newspaper columns and radio scripts and who was labeled
"anti-revolutionary," was depicted as an "undercover agent" by the elite exile
Cuban community in Puerto Rico.[36] Through his creative work, in disparate time periods and geo-political scenes, Montero was constructed as both
"anti-revolutionary" and "revolutionary." In retrospect, while in Cuba Montero had directly confronted Fidel Castro by writing a letter criticizing the
government's censorship (Castro responded indirectly by finally allowing the
Montero family to leave the island in 1973); in Puerto Rico, he used television
to craft a creative response to the Cuban far right.

Through Caridad's character, *Los suegros* and *Los suegros y los nietos* addressed the need for many Cuban exiles to visit the island, especially when
a close family member was dying. Caridad received news that her mother,
who had remained in Cuba, was extremely sick. Every day, teary-eyed and
sad, Caridad prayed to *la virgen de la Caridad del Cobre* (the Roman Catho-

lic patron saint of Cuba) for her mother's well being. Caridad implored that if this was her "mother's time to go," at least she wanted to see her mother before she died. Because Caridad and Ñico did not have the money for the trip to their homeland, Caridad played the lottery every week. One week she won $4,000, which was enough money for the airplane ticket as well as for gifts for her family residing in Cuba.

In the episodes that dealt with the possible death of Caridad's mother, the characters discussed why some Cubans decided to remain in Cuba after the revolution ("regardless of the suffering, some people made their lives there and do not want to leave") and the fact that traveling to the island was not equivalent to ideological support for Fidel Castro. As Ñico told Jackie, "I hate Fidel Castro, but my wife's mother is in Cuba and she is dying. What do you expect me to do? I need to support her decision." Cuco totally supported her mother's trip to Cuba because "we have family there, and the family is the most important thing in life." The televisual message was crystal clear. Through *Los suegros*'s fictional Cubans, Montero contended that it was both preposterous to assume that the Cuban exiles who visited Cuba were "communist" or "undercover agents" and also that the Cuban community in Puerto Rico, as part of the same ethnic family, needed to support those trips and provide any available help for the extended family members who had remained in Cuba.

Whereas *La Crónica*'s year-long and intense crusade did not damage the popularity of the shows, it did personally affect Montero and his family. During this unforeseen controversy, the Monteros were ostracized by certain sectors of the Cuban community. In addition, although it is not clear who revealed Montero's home phone number, the family received numerous harassing calls during the anti-Montero campaign. Although years later the conservative sector of the Cuban community welcomed Montero and honored him at Casa Cuba, the mid-1980s represented "a very difficult period" for this migrant Cuban family.[37]

The complex ideological struggles within Puerto Rico's Cuban community are not the topic of this chapter, or for that matter, the theme of this book. Nonetheless, I should clarify a couple of points. As *La Crónica* interviewees indicated, and as I previously discussed, both Ñico and Caridad were indeed represented stereotypically. These fictional Cubans were constructed as extremely arrogant people. Yet, contrary to *La Crónica*'s understanding of *Los suegros*'s Cubans as lazy, Cuco, Caridad, and Ñico were actually de-

picted as very industrious individuals. In other words, the show's characterizations reproduced a socially constructed trait and stereotype associated
with Cubans in Puerto Rico. At the same time, *La Crónica* newspaper was
blind to *Los suegros*'s condemnation of Puerto Ricans' prejudice against foreigners in general and Cubans in particular. In *Los suegros*, Puerto Ricans
(specifically Tito) were constantly espousing extreme anti-Cuban sentiments.
Consequently, by reproducing some of the discourses associated with the
Cuban community in Puerto Rico and by depicting Tito in a state of irrational
paranoia regarding Cuban immigrants, the narrative satirized and thus criticized Puerto Ricans' xenophobia. Even as *Los suegros* offered some rational-
ization for Puerto Ricans' dislike of Cubans, which can be read as problematic
(Cubans' fixation on their previous lavishness and their ongoing comparison
of Cuba and Puerto Rico), Tito's prejudice and distrust of Cubans served as
the catalyst for his conflicts with Ñico.

Given that all the episodes available revolved around Puerto Ricans' and
Cubans' ethnic conflicts, I will provide two examples. The 1981 episode entitled *El concurso* (The Sweepstakes) centered (as the title indicates) on a
sweepstakes created by Tito and Ñico to publicize the tembleque factory. Just
one day after the sweepstakes began, two Cuban women appeared at the factory to obtain their car prizes (there were five winning tickets). When Tito
realized the women were Cubans, he thought that Ñico had intentionally dis-
tributed the winning tickets at Casa Cuba. In the end Tito realized that Ñico
had not cheated to benefit Cubans. Nevertheless, Ñico, fully aware of Tito's
mistrust, decided to confront him.

> Ñico: Listen, when you saw that two Cubans won the prize, did you
> think that I had cheated? Tell me the truth.
> Tito: Yes. I thought that you planned something to obtain the five cars.
> Ñico: I am going to tell you something. Similar to other groups, there
> might be a bad seed within the Cuban community. Nonetheless, in
> general, we are honest and hard working people.
> Tito: (Hugging Ñico) I know Ñico. That is why Puerto Ricans received
> you with open arms . . . like brothers. You are already part of our
> community.
> Ñico: And the Cubans who do not recognize this or who do not like you
> [Puerto Ricans] are extremely ungrateful.
> Tito: You arrived in Puerto Rico years ago. Our children have married

your children. . . . Many Cubans have sons and daughters born in
Puerto Rico. Cubans, Puerto Ricans, Dominicans . . . all the people
who live on this little land have to work together and improve the
island's situation.

Ñico: That is right. . . . Cuba and Puerto Rico are . . .

Tito: The two wings of a single bird.

Ñico: They receive flowers and bullets in the same heart.

Contrary to most of *Los suegros*'s scripts, in this episode Tito openly ad-
mitted his prejudice against Cubans. Furthermore, the text also incorporated a reference to Dominicans, hinting at the anti-Dominican sentiment
that was already emerging in Puerto Rican society during the early 1980s.
However, since the main ethnic struggle during this time period was still
between Puerto Ricans and Cubans, the scriptwriter included stanzas from
Lola Rodríguez de Tío's poem ("Cuba and Puerto Rico are the two wings of
a single bird"), thus emphasizing Cuba's and Puerto Rico's shared historical,
political, and cultural ground. Although the episode's ending might be read
as sentimental and nostalgic, the dialogue between Tito and Ñico opened a
space for reasserting the brotherly and familial ties between these two ethnic
groups. Cubans and Puerto Ricans were not only connected through their
shared colonial pasts and struggles but because both groups resided on the
same island, they were also adding another dimension to their familial relations. According to *Los suegros*, it was almost impossible to disregard or
eliminate the Cuban influences in Puerto Rican society and culture or the
Puerto Rican elements in both Cuba and the post-1959 Cuban exile communities. Even though this atypical conflict-resolution episode constructed
Puerto Ricans as being open to their Cuban brothers (and sisters) in general,
Tito (and hence, the Puerto Rican middle and upper classes) did not easily
embrace the historical or familial connections with Cubans.

The 1982 episode entitled *La isla de la fantasía* (Fantasy Island) took place
on an island which, as in the U.S. show, both couples (Tito/María and Ñico/
Caridad) visited to live out a dream. Tito and María's fantasy was to revive
their honeymoon, while Ñico and Caridad dreamed of seeing Fidel Castro
cutting sugarcane under their direct supervision. Because the two couples
were in a fantastic place, they did not know each other. Nevertheless, given
that María was extremely curious about the couple who had flown on the
airplane with them (this nosy behavior was a stereotypical Puerto Rican per-

sonality trait), she and Tito approached Caridad and Ñico and introduced themselves.

> Tito: Is this the first time you have come to the fantasy island?
>
> Ñico: Yes, but we used to live on a beautiful island which is much more beautiful than this one. . . . Have you ever heard talk about the island of Cuba?
>
> Tito: Of course I have heard of Cuba. Are you Cubans?
>
> Ñico: Yes, Mister. My wife and I were born in *Cubita* the beautiful, although we do not live there anymore.
>
> Tito: And I guess that you are from Havana because all the Cubans that I know are from Havana. It seems that in Cuba nobody lived in the countryside.
>
> Ñico: Well, let me tell you something. I was born in Old Havana, but if I would have been born in the countryside, I would have not felt ashamed of telling you. And where are you from?
>
> María: We are Puerto Ricans.
>
> Caridad: Did you listen to that Ñico? They also come from an island!!!
>
> Ñico: Yes, Caridad, but you cannot compare Puerto Rico with Cuba because Cuba is ten times the size of Puerto Rico.
>
> Tito: If there is so much space, why didn't you stay there?
>
> María: Tito, please, they might have had good reasons.
>
> Caridad: The problem was that in Cuba there was a revolution and we had to get out of there. You cannot imagine all the sugarcane that my Mario [Ñico] cut before leaving Cuba. That is the only thing that he cannot forget.
>
> Tito: Tell me one thing. What is your fantasy?
>
> Ñico: Listen my *socio*, my fantasy is to see Fidel Castro cutting sugarcane under my supervision.
>
> Tito: You want revenge.
>
> Ñico: Yes, that's it.

Even as strangers Tito and Ñico cannot get along. Furthermore, Ñico and Caridad's abhorrence of Fidel Castro was so powerful that instead of reviving their lives in pre-revolutionary Cuba, they wanted to see Castro suffer.

Patoo (a version of *Fantasy Island*'s Tattoo) then asked both couples to follow him to perform their fantasies. Still, before leaving the welcoming reception that characterized the beginning of each *Fantasy Island* episode, Ñico approached Patoo to make a comment about Cuba.

> Ñico: Listen my friend, were you born here on the fantasy island?
> Patoo: Yes, mister.
> Ñico: It is so sad that you were not born in Cuba because in Cuba all
>   dwarfs were this size (gesture of a tall person).

Both couples acted out their fantasies. Tito and María re-lived their honeymoon and had all the inconveniences of their first one. Ñico and Caridad watched Fidel Castro cutting sugarcane for eighteen consecutive hours and Castro, although exhausted, was ready and eager to perform another chore. Then Fidel Castro asked to fulfill his fantasy: the execution of Ñico. When Castro was ready to kill Ñico, the viewers discovered that the entire episode had been Tito's dream. *La isla de la fantasía* episode re-articulated Puerto Rican prejudice against Cuban exiles and indirectly addressed the conflictive political relations between Castro's Cuba and some sectors of the Cuban diaspora. According to this episode, Tito (and supposedly Puerto Ricans in general) longed to see the Cuban golden migration vanish from Puerto Rico, while Fidel Castro wished to eliminate the powerful (right-wing) Cuban exile community.

Whereas *La isla de la fantasía* episode and *Los suegros* narrative generally constructed Puerto Rican and Cuban contestations as products of chauvinistic and nationalistic ideologies, these exchanges were also characterized as a generational problem. In other words, the younger generation (Jackie and Cuco) was depicted as more open to cultural and political differences. Moreover, when Jackie and Cuco gave the Riveras and the Fernándezes three grandchildren, the older generation understood that regardless of their ideological and nationalistic differences, they were all part of the same clan. Whether in Puerto Rico or in Miami (where the Puerto Rican–Cuban couple had moved), Puerto Ricans and Cubans were members of a local and diasporic CubaRican group. This transcultural inclusiveness did not, however, extend to Katy and Junior.

Similar to Jackie and Cuco, Katy and Junior had moved to the United States. Junior, the weak mama's boy, was still regarded as part of the community (he was the pitiful member within the family) and Katy remained outside the CubaRican cultural environment. As I previously explained, Katy's exclusion was primarily the result of her never assimilating into Puerto Rican or Cuban traditional machista culture. However, by the mid-1980s another element differentiated Cuco and Jackie from Junior and Katy: the Puerto Rican–American couple did not have children. The U.S. presence in Puerto Rico was inevitable, yet the future of the Puerto Rican family could not possibly be in the hands of an American woman. Not even the potential of blanqueamiento through the white Anglo-Saxon race could overcome the cultural and national order within the ethnic family. With no children and without Katy and Mr. Morrison (who had passed away), the Americans, while symbolically continuing to permeate the CubaRican space, disappeared from the community.

By the late 1980s, several changes had occurred in the *Los suegros* fictional environment. On the one hand, Tito and Ñico had developed a more amicable relationship. While Tito's resentment toward Ñico continued, and whereas one of Tito's worst nightmares of witnessing Jackie and his grandchildren assimilate into the Cuban-Miami culture had become a reality (according to phone conversations and general references, they appropriated a thick Cuban accent and primarily ate Cuban food), Tito had, to a certain degree, come to terms with his extended family. Tito's complaints about "foreigners" persisted, but he now targeted a new group: Dominicans. In 1988 the Rivera and the Fernández families received a new neighbor named Josefito Pascal, a young Dominican man who was described racially as *mulato*.

The Dominican component in Puerto Rico's society was added to the *Los suegros*'s ethnic community. However, instead of reproducing the negative stereotypes associated with Dominicans in Puerto Rico, which have characterized these immigrants as lazy, criminal, and intellectually inferior, *Los suegros* was used as a televisual vehicle for confronting some of the prejudices against this ethnic group. Even though Tito was not pleased by the "invasion of Dominicans" that was taking place in Puerto Rico, and while Ñico was offended by Josefito's questioning of his and Caridad's legal status and their right to be in Puerto Rico ("A green card? Listen, we are more Puerto Rican than the Puerto Ricans who are twenty-eight years old!"), some of the episodes denounced discriminatory practices toward Dominicans.

According to the narrative, Josefito Pascal had migrated to Puerto Rico with his wife and two of his three *chichis* (the Dominican vernacular word for children) to improve the family's economic situation. Josefito did not have any formal education, and in terms of personality, he was a replica of Ñico

(Tito called him "the Dominican Ñico"). This Dominican man described himself as the best in everything and was allegedly financially solvent in the Dominican Republic. As was expected, neither Ñico nor Tito believed Josefito's stories about his opulence in the Dominican Republic. Nevertheless, Josefito was never rejected by the Rivera or the Fernández families, and Tito did not make negative remarks about his Dominican neighbor. Both families provided sporadic jobs for Josefito, lent him money to travel to the Dominican Republic to visit his extended family and his youngest chichi, and tried to help him as much as possible. Even though Josefito was depicted as somewhat arrogant, he was also represented as an intelligent, hard-working, and trustworthy young man—a direct contrast to the Dominican stereotype in Puerto Rico.

One important issue regarding the inclusion of Dominicans in *Los suegros* relates to the narrative's incorporation of comments about the abuses toward this ethnic group. For example, the 1988 episode entitled *Los indocumentados* (The Undocumented) criticized the profit-driven business of transporting illegal Dominicans to Puerto Rico.

> Tito: Maria, did you read the newspaper article about the undocumented?
> Maria: What, Tito?
> Tito: The story about the undocumented Dominicans caught by the authorities.
> Maria: Yes, Tito, it is extremely sad. Those poor souls risk their lives trying to find a better living. Then they get here, the police apprehend them, and send them back to the Dominican Republic.
> Tito: Those things make me really sad. But the real guilty people are the ones who traffic with Dominicans. They do not care about human beings, they only care about money.

By depicting the xenophobic Tito as worried about the ongoing dangers that Dominicans endured (and still endure) to migrate to Puerto Rico, the text tried to appeal to the audience's human and moral side.

In other episodes, Puerto Rican prejudices against Dominicans were addressed by Ñico's and Caridad's characters. For instance, when Tito complained that he was surrounded by foreigners (now exemplified by Dominicans), Caridad replied "Ay Don Tito, you are always talking nonsensical things about foreigners." In another episode Ñico commented to Caridad, "I do not understand why Puerto Ricans dislike Dominicans. It is ridiculous! We are Caribbean brothers. Our cultures are similar. I do not understand." Josefito Pascal was a secondary character in *Los suegros* and based on the scripts available, the character only lasted one year (1988–1989). Nevertheless, the problematization of Puerto Ricans' intolerance of Dominicans was a valuable contribution to the situation comedy's narrative.

Several explanations for this counterhegemonic televisual representation of Dominicans are possible. First, one should consider the creative input and control of producer Elín Ortíz. Ortíz was (and still is) married to a Dominican singer-composer. Given his relationship with a Dominican, he was likely more acutely aware of the prejudice against Dominicans in Puerto Rico. In addition, Ortíz's assistant producer in *Los suegros* (who also played the character Josefito) was Dominican.[38] Consequently, one can presume that these internal Dominican elements might have permeated the character's construction and the ways in which Dominican themes were addressed.

A second factor to bear in mind was the immigrant status of Manuel Montero "Membrillo" and the fact that, contrary to most Cubans in Puerto Rico, he was not part of the golden migration. In other words, Montero did not possess the economic and symbolic power that had characterized the early 1960s Cuban diaspora. More important, during specific periods of time, he was viewed as a political-cultural dissident in certain sectors of the Cuban community in Puerto Rico and in revolutionary Cuba. Therefore, Montero's personal experiences and his social status as the Other likely informed the *Los suegros* denunciation of Dominican prejudice.[39]

Finally, and interrelated to the aforementioned possibilities, was *Los suegros*'s multi-ethnic environment. *Los suegros*'s production comprised Puerto Ricans, Cubans, Dominicans, and even one American (the actress who played Katy). With the exception of Mr. Morrison, each character was played by a member of the ethnic group in question. Thus, one can assume that the participation of people from various ethnic-cultural backgrounds had an impact on the creative processes.

Certainly, the inclusion of an American actress in *Los suegros*'s cast had the potential to present a more holistic depiction of U.S. culture, history, and ethnic diversity. Then again, in the national imaginary, the United States has represented the supreme and external (imperial) power that could destroy the constructed national culture and ethnic unity. Hence, similar to other locally produced comedy shows, *Los suegros* was used as an ideological weapon (through jokes) to symbolically attack the most powerful political and economic entity in Puerto Rico.

Nonetheless, in other ways, *Los suegros* reaffirmed Puerto Rico's dominant racial discourses. In terms of racial ideologies and televisual representations, the description of the Dominican character as mulato re-articulated the location of blackness outside the Puerto Rican nation. In *Los suegros*, neither Puerto Ricans nor Cubans were black or mulatto—Dominicans were black. Actually, according to Josefito Pascal, his youngest and "darkest chichi" remained in the Dominican Republic. Consequently, this televisual depiction reproduced the hegemonic whiteness in Puerto Rican society and in the CubaRican sociocultural space while concomitantly positioning blackness in the Dominican Republic. Similar to previous media constructions, lo negro was symbolically pushed to the margins of the Caribbean, a Caribbean outside Puerto Rico's territorial and cultural spaces.

Even though *Los suegros* did not question the obliteration of blackness that characterizes Puerto Rico's society and culture, this situation comedy was an extremely important venue for a critical exploration of Puerto Rican and Cuban conflicts, and to a lesser extent, Puerto Rican prejudice against Dominicans. Furthermore, *Los suegros* provided multiple representations of Cubans and addressed the complexities that were (and still are) part of the Cuban diaspora in Puerto Rico. In sum, this cleverly written comedy kept audiences engaged for ten years while at the same time directly and indirectly challenging the dominant cultural constructs of ethnic differences, stereotypes, and prejudices.

However, within the larger Puerto Rican context, by the late 1980s and early 1990s, the black and mulatto undesirable and primitive element in Puerto Rico's society was increasingly associated with Dominican immigrants. Derogatory jokes about Dominicans began to dominate the local popular culture arena and the vernacular. While Puerto Rican blacks and mulattos continued to be marginalized, the strongest prejudice was (and continues to be) targeted at Dominicans, a migrant group that, contrary to the Cuban diaspora in Puerto Rico, does not possess economic and symbolic power.[40]

I contend that this social, cultural, and ethnic substitution of Otherness, together with the U.S. and global commercial success of black-oriented situation comedies during the 1980s, created a space for Puerto Rican blacks in the television-situation comedy world. On one level, "blackness" in Puerto

Rico's national imaginary became analogous to Dominicans, thus positioning lo negro, as Jorge Duany argues, as "foreign to the national identity."[41]
On another level, U.S. black situation comedies such as *The Jeffersons* and
The Cosby Show, which articulated U.S. dominant discourses of whiteness,
middle-class status, and social mobility, became highly popular television
shows capturing diverse racial, ethnic, and class segments of U.S. television
audiences. These distinct social, cultural, racial, and media factors—intertwined with the ideology of ethnic unity ingrained in la gran familia puertorriqueña discourse—transformed the local commercial television's racial
depiction of a Puerto Rican (fictional) family.

In 1994, Telemundo (WKAQ-channel 2) began to broadcast *Mi familia*
(My Family), the first situation comedy depicting a black lower-middle-class
Puerto Rican family. Produced by Paquito Cordero and written by Cuban
scriptwriter Felipe San Pedro, *Mi familia* centered on the life of the Meléndez family and their community. Puerto Rican blacks finally "made it" into
the televisual situation comedy families. Nonetheless, as I discuss in the next
chapter, *Mi familia*'s narrative was not about the celebration of Afro Puerto
Rican traditions or the problematization of Puerto Rico's racist culture. Instead, *Mi familia* was about a de-racialized Puerto Rican family "who hap-
pen[ed] to be [look] black."[42]

4

Mi familia
A Black Puerto Rican Televisual Family

We are like monkeys. If the U.S. has a show with black people,
then we have a show with blacks.
  Interview with *Mi familia* production member, July 1997

For nine years (September 1994 to July 2003), Telemundo's network affiliate
in Puerto Rico broadcast the highly successful show *Mi familia*.[1] The idea to
produce a situation comedy featuring a "black" family was largely influenced
by the commercial success of U.S. black-oriented situation comedies such as
The Jeffersons and *The Cosby Show*.[2] However, in the process of translation,
the show's creators transformed the U.S. dominant racial ideologies, middle-
class status, and social mobility represented in the aforementioned U.S. situation comedies. In contrast, *Mi familia* recreated the life of a lower-middle-
class, "colorless," Puerto Rican family (the Meléndez) and its neighbors.

The construction of a "nonracial" Puerto Rican family was the ideological
force behind *Mi familia*'s conceptualization. As one member of *Mi familia*'s
production team indicated, "people sit down to watch *Mi familia* as if it were
a white, yellow or blue [family]. There is no color, there is nothing established. And since we do not touch that subject . . . And it was not that we did
not want to talk about it . . . At the beginning we realized that we did not
have to talk about it. It is a Puerto Rican family, period."[3] This colorless characterization departed from the normalization of "whiteness" that informed
the island's medium since 1954 and the ongoing representation of "white"
televisual families in local situation comedies. Furthermore, the focus on the
Puerto Ricanness of the fictional family hints at the location of "blackness"
outside the national imaginary. What is more, colorless and Puerto Ricanness rearticulate the whiteness that permeates the ideology of mestizaje in la
gran familia puertorriqueña discourse.

Based on *Mi familia*'s nine years on the air, one might be led to believe
that there was an acceptance of blackness in Puerto Rico's commercial television. Obviously, that was not the case. On the one hand, and as I discuss in

Arcadio and Migdalia, the Meléndez couple.
Courtesy of Paquito Cordero Teleproducciones.

Wandita and Willy, the Meléndez children.
Courtesy of Paquito Cordero Teleproducciones.

this chapter, mestizaje and racial equality were at the center of *Mi familia*'s conceptualization and thus created a cultural artifact that normalized Puerto Rico's hegemonic construction of a nonracist society. On the other hand, blackface negrito characters were still part of the local televisual landscape in the 1990s.[4] Although none of these blackface characters became iconic figures (as did Diplo and Chianita), it was clear that in the 1990s, televisual blackface continued to be constructed and consumed as a normalized and de-racialized form of entertainment. The normativity of blackface in Puerto Rico's commercial television was palpable not only in the ongoing comedic performances but also in the 2000 article entitled *¿Y la risa tiene color?* (Does Laughter Have Color?).[5]

¿Y la risa tiene color? focuses on the tradition of blackface in the United States, Cuba, and Puerto Rico, in addition to discussing the popularity of U.S. black comedians. Throughout the piece, the journalist positions blackface as a culturally and racially valid transnational tradition practiced by famous and respected actors such as Al Jolson, Ramón Rivero, and the Cuban comedian Leopoldo Fernández. Similar to the 1973–1974 Meyer and del Villard controversy regarding blackface, this journalist ignores historical context, and her analysis demonstrates a lack of understanding of how blackface "blackness" inscribes racially demeaning messages laden with the historical legacy of racial subjugation. Likewise, the article does not establish any racial, cultural, social, political, or ideological distinction between white actors in blackface and black comedians. Thus, Al Jolson donning blackface and comedians such as Richard Pryor, Eddie Murphy, and Bill Cosby are depicted as equivalent constructions of blackness. In an extremely problematic statement, the piece ends with the phrase, "laughter is therapeutic and colorless."[6] Therefore, according to the article, as long as comedians make people laugh, it does not matter whether the representations objectify certain groups and perpetuate racial hierarchical structures. The contention that "laughter is therapeutic and colorless" circumvents any discussion of race as a social construction in general or more specifically within the sociohistorical context of Puerto Rico.

In 1990s Puerto Rico, racism was still characterized either as a U.S. problem or as an individualized practice.[7] As Kelvin Santiago-Valles argues, the racialization of crime and the historic interconnection of race, poverty, and unemployment that informed Puerto Rico's society during the 1980s and 1990s were not considered endemic symptoms of racial discrimination.[8]

Additionally, as I indicated in chapter 3, the discrimination toward Dominican immigrants and the location of blackness outside the national space were not considered ideological signs of a racist culture. Although publicly and televisually race was either obscured or stereotyped, the island's colonial status occupied the center of public debates. The struggles within local political parties along with the complex relations between the United States and Puerto Rico continued to dominate public discussions during the 1990s.

On December 13, 1998, Puerto Rico held a plebiscite to decide between statehood and independence. The results were 50.2 percent for "none of the above," 46.5 percent for "statehood," and 2.5 percent for "independence."[9] Because "none of the above" was essentially a vote for the Commonwealth status quo, these numbers demonstrated that there was a desire among almost 97 percent of the population to maintain political and economic relations with the United States. Ramón Grosfoguel argues that "they [Puerto Ricans] would rather be exploited with some benefits than be exploited without any benefits (as in the Dominican Republic and Haiti)."[10] Having seen poverty, political instability, and neocolonial status in some Latin American nations, many Puerto Ricans feared that independence could cause the island to suffer the same precarious economic and political conditions as other countries in the region.[11]

Even though the 1998 plebiscite confirmed the desire to maintain relations with the United States, in addition to the fact that the pro-independence political party has never won a governor's election, the U.S.–P.R. cultural contentions in Puerto Rico continued during the 1990s. From the controversies regarding the pop artist Madonna rubbing her private parts with the Puerto Rican flag during a concert on the island, to the English and Spanish official language disputes, to the ongoing protests against U.S. military maneuvers in Vieques, numerous and diverse issues became sites of vocal debates in Puerto Rico's public sphere.[12] Although these debates embodied various levels of political and social significance, many Puerto Ricans took sides on these issues from the perspective that the nation's ethnic, cultural, and political sovereignty was threatened. Therefore, similar to previous historical periods, Puerto Ricans expressed a constant need to reaffirm the island's national culture and identity in relation to the U.S. imported culture.

Considering Puerto Rico's fervent cultural nationalism, it should not come as a surprise that the differences between the United States' and Puerto Rico's way of life directly and indirectly permeated *Mi familia*'s production and textual representations. Similar to the 1970s debates and partial televisual accommodations, *Mi familia* became the location for articulating the distinctions between American and Puerto Rican racial discourses, "blackness," and cultures. However, besides the hegemonic construction of Puerto Rico as a racially equal space, what was particularly prevalent in *Mi familia*'s production was the personal and institutional silencing of the topic of racism on the island. In the context of *Mi familia*'s behind-the-scenes environment, racism in Puerto Rican society was considered either a present but taboo subject or a nonexistent social problem.

In the following pages I discuss *Mi familia*'s encoding processes and perform a textual analysis of the scripts.[13] I first examine *Mi familia* production members' and Telemundo media professionals' conceptualization of the show. To shed light on how the topics of race and racism were purposely silenced in *Mi familia*, I center on the power dynamics among actors, director, writer, and the industry.[14] I then engage in a textual analysis, paying special attention to *Mi familia*'s construction of a lower-middle-class family and community. Because Puerto Rico's cultural nationalism permeated *Mi familia*'s textual representations, I explore the ways in which the narrative defined an "authentic" Puerto Rican. Finally, and interrelated to the theme of Puerto Ricanness, I consider *Mi familia*'s re-appropriations of Puerto Rico's discourses on race and mestizaje.

Mi familia's texts contained multiple problematic representations. Still, I position the show as an important cultural artifact in the history of the island's commercial television. Indeed, similar to the partial accommodations during the 1970s, the main objective behind *Mi familia* was to commodify "blackness" by presenting something "different" within Puerto Rico's commercial television market. Notwithstanding this commercial reality, I contend that the translation of the U.S. black-oriented situation comedy genre represented another transformation of the locations of televisual blackness that had characterized Puerto Rico's commercial television since 1954.

For the first time in Puerto Rico's television history, some of the island's social realities and contemporary issues such as crime, unemployment, and migrations to the United States were encountered and discussed by black and mulatto fictional characters in a situation comedy. The main problem with these discussions was that they did not take into account the racial politics or the power differences and inequalities for black and mulatto characters or citizens within the nation. However, the mere presence of black bodies constructed a new representation of the Puerto Rican family and nation by re-inscribing this marginalized community into televisual, societal, and cultural discourses.

Erasing Blackness, Constructing Puerto Ricanness

In 1994 Telemundo–Puerto Rico found itself in trouble.[15] The station was highly criticized by groups such as Morality in Media and the Catholic Church for what they considered the "vulgarity" of some of its local programming, particularly the variety shows. Even though variety shows were the most profitable local programs in Puerto Rico's television market in 1994, and the public preferred (according to ratings) this format to the family sitcom genre, Telemundo needed a family program that could appease the various protestors. Producer Paquito Cordero took advantage of the station's need to produce a family sitcom and presented his idea for *Mi familia* to Telemundo's programmer. Without even requiring a pilot, the programmer bought the show immediately. Telemundo's response was not surprising given that Cordero had worked exclusively for the station since 1954. More important, throughout his television career, Cordero had produced numerous long-running programs. As he proudly claimed, "none of my programs have been canceled," in reference to the initial thirteen-week contract between Telemundo and independent producers.[16] Simply put, at least until the early 1990s, for Telemundo executives the name "Paquito Cordero" meant profits.

Paquito Cordero, together with scriptwriter Felipe San Pedro, conceptualized *Mi familia*, selected the creative personnel, and sold the entire package to Telemundo. As part of the production arrangement, and similar to other locally produced programs, Telemundo provided the studio facilities, technical personnel, and sets. After shows were taped, Cordero retained ownership. The pre-production of *Mi familia* took approximately four months, and although Cordero did not disclose the compensation he received for *Mi familia*'s episodes, another participant revealed that Telemundo may have paid between five and seven thousand dollars for each program. I was unable to confirm Telemundo's program rates.

Whereas Cordero had obtained a contract for *Mi familia*, he was not the only media professional who wanted to produce a show with black performers. During 1994 three independent producers expressed interest in producing a sitcom with black actors for other local stations. When I asked about this sudden interest, some of *Mi familia*'s media professionals reasoned that because a show with a black cast was something new in Puerto Rico's local television market, it had the potential to become as successful as black-oriented shows in the United States. Nonetheless, despite the possibility that three other shows with a black cast could have been produced, Paquito Cordero was the only producer who achieved his goal. According to some interviewees, the other producers decided to abandon their projects because they were no longer something "unique." Several production members declared that the independent producers had discarded their projects because Cordero had hired the most renowned black comedians on the island, thereby diminishing the likelihood that their programs would succeed because they did not have *ganchos* (actors with market appeal).

Regardless of the perceived interest in shows with a black cast, according to some interviewees, the number of black actors in Puerto Rico was small. One production member stated that *Mi familia*'s main casting problem was finding black actors and actresses. This individual declared that although Cordero had tried to cast as many black performers as possible, he had few from which to select. In this regard, one performer agreed with this justification claiming that "there is a lack of black actors and actresses in Puerto Rico." Although at the beginning some production members tried to bring in black actors, over time the production began to cast white performers to play the secondary roles. This lack of professional black actors and actresses was not coincidental. As I have discussed in the previous chapters, Puerto Rican television has been informed by whiteness, and there has been an ongoing use of white performers in blackface to represent black characters. Yet, despite the small pool of trained black actors, an open casting call advertised in local newspapers would likely have solved the problem. Still, this casting selection issue clearly influenced the situation comedy's racial constructions.

Although *Mi familia*'s principal characters (Arcadio and Migdalia, the Meléndez couple) and their son (Willy) were black, and while their daughter (Wandita) and Migdalia's brother (Cheito) would be considered trigueños (mulattos) according to Puerto Rico's racial categorizations, the rest of the cast members (the neighbors) were white. However, as I will further discuss, one of the main problems regarding *Mi familia*'s racial representations was the program's construction of white women as the objects of desire. Concerning this issue, one of *Mi familia*'s production members acknowledged the construction of "white as beautiful" but mentioned that other people in the production were unaware of this problematic representation. When the scripts described an occasional female character as "sexy and beautiful," the production tended to cast a white woman. Despite the fact that in its first few episodes *Mi familia*'s object of desire was played by a mulata, the character was eventually recast with a white actress. When I asked the participant why the mulata actress was replaced, an explanation could not be provided. The interviewee only said, "*mija, ya tú sabes como es*" (woman, you know how it is), implicating the ongoing racism that characterizes casting practices in Puerto Rico. Consequently, *Mi familia* featured only one black woman: Migdalia, the principal character.

When *Mi familia* began production, one newspaper displayed the headline "Blacks break P.R. television comedy barrier." Another described it as featuring "the first colored family in Puerto Rican television," while an additional article avoided mentioning the family's race by promoting the show as a "new Cordero production."[17] The description of a "colored family" infuriated some production members who argued that the family's race was black and that the term "colored" was racist. As one participant observed, "a colored family? Which color? Yellow, blue, orange?" Nevertheless, not one of my respondents commented on the article that focused on *Mi familia*'s authorship ("a new Cordero production"), thereby avoiding mentioning the family's race.

In addition to the casting problems and the reference to the fictional family as a colored family, some interviewees expressed disappointment over the fact that although *Mi familia* had originally planned to address racism, none of the show's scripts ever dealt with the issue. As one media professional recalled, "when they talked to me about the idea, they told me that this was going to serve as a channel to break with this country's molds, that it was going to be something different, that it was going to deal with themes of racism, social topics such as drugs, everything, everything. Almost nothing has been done." Another participant attributed the absence of racial themes to a combination of factors that included the Catholic Church, politicians, Telemundo, and Puerto Rican society in general. During the interview, this media professional continually used the phrases *la mentalidad isleña* (the island's mentality), "colonialism," and "internal colonialism" to explain the absence of racial themes in *Mi familia* and the racism that prevails in Puerto Rican society in general and local television in particular. As the participant observed, "there is a need to create more work for black people. I have met many talented individuals who are black who do not want to be part of this environment [television] because they think it is for whites. Yes, there is prejudice, but if you have talent, prejudice cannot stop you. It is necessary to untie the internal chains." Although one should not assume that this participant's views are representative of the general population, the remarks depict an illuminating analysis of the various interconnected levels that construct race and racism in Puerto Rico and in other nations with black and Other minority communities.

Despite the fact that some of the production members were displeased with the absence of racial and social themes in *Mi familia*'s narrative, they believed that the show was a "positive space" for the representation of blackness, especially since some white comedians on Puerto Rican television still donned blackface during the 1990s. In several newspaper articles and television magazines, actors identified negritud as a key element in *Mi familia*. Otilio Warrington "Bizcocho," *Mi familia*'s principal actor, noted, "I consider that the show has been successful first, because it satisfies a need, it fills an empty space. Second, because it is the first program with blacks that has been produced in Puerto Rico, something that Paquito Cordero wanted to do for a long time. I think that being the only program in its genre, *Mi familia* causes a sensation and also attracts black people who completely identify with us [*Mi familia*'s black family.]"[18] Furthermore, Judith Pizarro, the show's principal actress, also emphasized the importance of producing a show with black actors. "When Paquito Cordero called me with this in mind, I accepted immediately. In addition, it was the first time that someone created a space for blacks in Puerto Rico [i.e., on television]."[19]

Even though some of the participants recognized the importance of a show featuring a black fictional family, others evaded the topic and instead categorized *Mi familia* as a sitcom with a Puerto Rican family. Most of these participants made references to "colored people," thus avoiding the term *black*. In responding to questions about the process of selecting black actors, some of *Mi familia*'s production personnel and Telemundo's media professionals expressed ideas about race that were completely different from those presented by the interviewees above. One participant observed:

> Here, regardless of the success of *Cosby* and *The Jeffersons* and multiple shows with *colored* families, this topic was never explored. We talked about how we were going to develop the show, what we were going to do. For

me, the interesting thing is that from the beginning we never dealt with that issue [race]. In Puerto Rico, people see them [the black family] as any other family. In the U.S. it is not like that. Those are programs about *colored* people. They have a way of talking, dressing, and we do not have to use that. Here, there is no color [in the program]; it does not frame anything.

It seems that this participant assumed that since the sitcom never addressed racial themes, negritud had been erased from its narratives, leaving audiences to see the Meléndez as "any other family." This reference to "any other family" can be associated both with Puerto Rico's hegemonic whiteness and with previous family sitcoms featuring white performers or families. According to this participant, race was neutralized in *Mi familia* by creating a colorless space whose racial and cultural frame of commonality between audiences and the program was ethnicity. By positioning the narrative as colorless, the participant normalized the mestizaje discourse as the parameter for the family's race.

Furthermore, to sustain the point, the participant highlighted the differences between *Mi familia* and the U.S. black-oriented shows while concomitantly delineating the ways in which racial identities and race operate in Puerto Rico and the United States. According to this media professional, black shows in the United States present cultural elements associated with the African American community ("colored people") that create differences not only in relation to Puerto Rican blacks but also regarding racial, cultural, and ethnic relations in both nations. To be sure, differences between African American and Afro Puerto Rican vernacular cultures and identities exist. However, this participant downplayed cultural aspects that are associated with Puerto Rico's black and mulatto populations and that were evident in some of *Mi familia*'s episodes. In the case of Puerto Rico, the participant understood that there was no need to establish distinct cultural traits since presumably no racial, ethnic, or power differences existed within the island's culture.

A curious aspect of this interviewee's comments relates to the ways in which the interviewee read U.S. black shows such as *The Jeffersons* and *The Cosby Show*. Even though these sitcoms did not explicitly address racial struggles and power inequalities for this participant, the mere presence of black bodies and cultural elements constructed the show as "colored" (black). In other words, this participant might have seen U.S. television's representation of blackness as a unified racial and cultural space. In the case of *Mi familia*, the absence of racial themes positioned the show as colorless despite the fact that the family was black and that, as I further discuss, the show incorporated several cultural elements associated with black and mulatto Puerto Rican communities. Thus, in this participant's view "colored people" and "blackness" were only equivalent to U.S. African American communities, bodies, cultures, and their televisual representations.

Another interviewee noted that "the only difference that exists is that by chance they are negritos, but it could be a white family because racial themes are never addressed, or any type of crime. Actually, you see it [the program] and you would not notice that they are negritos because they are normal." This participant's remarks clearly operated within a racist framework even though the participant might have been unaware of the racism embedded in the comments. As discussed in the introduction, the word *negrito* is sometimes used pejoratively to construct "black" as an inferior category in relation to "white." Furthermore, in Puerto Rico's television culture, negrito was used to describe the CubaRican, and later, Puerto Rican blackface characters. Thus, by using negritos instead of negros and by juxtaposing negritud with "crime" and abnormality, black-bodied citizens became symbols of the Other undesirable sociocultural element in Puerto Rican society. According to this participant, within a dignified representation of a Puerto Rican family in the sitcom's fictional space, negritud had to be neutralized by constructing a "nonracial" and "normal" (white) family. Also, similar to the previous interviewee, the present participant contended that the absence of racial themes erased the family's negritud.

Finally, when addressing the use of black actors and its possible impact on *Mi familia*'s sponsors, one media professional explained that "the fact that the program was about *colored people* [emphasis mine] was never an issue. Besides, you have to understand that Bizcocho [*Mi familia*'s principal actor] is a very commercial actor, the audience likes him. No, the sponsors never had a problem. Besides, here [in Puerto Rico] there are white, black, and trigueño/a people." This media professional presented a commercial position regarding *Mi familia* as a cultural product. According to this professional, the sponsors had no problems with the actors' race, especially since Puerto Rico is a racially mixed society. More important was the fact that the main actor was highly marketable, an aspect that eliminated any possible problems because "Bizcocho" has been a successful and profitable actor for local stations, producers, and for himself.[20] Furthermore, even though "Bizcocho" has openly discussed racial topics, including criticizing the use of blackface in local television in the 1970s, his television characters have never explored these issues. As an actor, Otilio Warrington "Bizcocho" has limited power in television's hierarchical structure, which may account for his characters' silence on these topics.

Nonetheless, as the previous participant mentioned, *Mi familia*'s success and the fact that its audience comprised Puerto Rico's "entire" demographic spectrum resulted in an abundance of advertisers whose products ranged from Pampers diapers to Budweiser beer. In addition to regular advertising time, similar to other locally produced programs airing on Telemundo during the 1990s, *Mi familia* also incorporated product endorsement.[21] Each week the writer included a scene related to a specific product. In these scenes the (black) principal characters expressed the benefits of using Clairol for changing their hair color, of taking Tylenol for the relief of any kind of pain, or of drinking the delicious new juice from Goya. Thus, even though local advertising agencies rarely cast black performers, through its product endorsements, *Mi familia* constructed a (commodified) space where Puerto Rican blacks advertised and consumed products similar to other (white Puerto Rican) fictional characters.[22]

In sum, the sponsors, the station, and some of the *Mi familia* media professionals did not perceive a show with "colored people" as an obstacle; rather, negritud was conveniently marketed. Moreover, even though *Mi familia*'s blackness was allegedly not a problem, institutional, professional, and personal censorships permeated the show's conceptualization, particularly regarding the topic of racism in Puerto Rico.

"What about Doing This?": Working Through Censorship

One of the words heard most often during my visits to Telemundo–Puerto Rico was *censura* (censorship). Every interviewee mentioned censorship as an omnipresent unwritten code that affected Puerto Rican television production in general and *Mi familia* in particular. Each group (Telemundo media professionals and *Mi familia*'s production personnel) blamed the other for the program's censorship. Even the makeup women talked about this, but nobody identified the source of what seemed to be an ongoing anxiety. Thus, I asked each party to provide a concrete example.

According to a Telemundo executive, each program aired on the station was classified according to its content, and all shows were given an advisory categorization for viewers.[23] The participant assured me that the station was on a constant watch to guarantee that its programs were suitable for the target audience. Although race was a very delicate theme and none of Telemundo's media professionals ever mentioned this subject, it was obvious that censorship also permeated this area. For example, various members of *Mi familia*'s production mentioned that the station was "nervous" about broadcasting a program with a black family. This anxiety centered on how to address racism on the island. Thus, after multiple conversations with Telemundo's executives, Cordero decided to avoid references to racism in the program's narratives. Whereas the elimination of the topic of racism was not a direct censorship course employed by Telemundo, *Mi familia*'s production allegedly had to alter the show's original concept (which, according to some of *Mi familia*'s production members, had a sharper political, cultural, and racial edge) to avoid further, contentious debates with station officials. Nonetheless, several Telemundo media professionals contended that the power of censorship and the "conservative" perspective that informed *Mi familia*'s scripts rested not with Cordero or Telemundo but with the writer. As one participant claimed, "the script's censorship comes from the writer [Felipe San Pedro], it does not come from us." To support this point, the individual mentioned Felipe San Pedro's veto power.

Felipe San Pedro's authority to veto narrative ideas was primarily a result of his stature in the industry. As I mentioned in chapter 3, San Pedro (together with Manuel Montero "Membrillo") dominated television scriptwriting in the late 1970s and throughout the 1980s in Puerto Rico's commercial television. Furthermore, the Cordero–San Pedro team produced several commercial successes for Telemundo.[24] Thus, as a result of San Pedro's profitable cultural artifacts, Telemundo and Cordero gave him the authority to veto narrative ideas. For instance, *Fundación SIDA* (AIDS Foundation) offered to sponsor an episode to advertise a new AIDS campaign. After several meetings, Fundación SIDA requested and received complete support from Telemundo's executives and Paquito Cordero. Despite this, San Pedro refused to write an episode about AIDS and the narrative was never developed. Based on this incident, it is plausible that the writer could have also vetoed other episodes, including ones that dealt with racism.

By contrast, some members of *Mi familia*'s production believed the station was responsible for the censorship policy. As one participant remarked, "Look, there are many taboos here. There are themes that you cannot touch, especially if they are realistic." For this participant, realism was associated with sexual themes and jokes that had a sexual twist. Another member of *Mi familia*'s production recalled that the station vetoed an episode because it referred to the movie *Malcolm X*. Apparently, one of Telemundo's media professionals thought *Malcolm X* was a pornographic movie. After various meetings, *Mi familia*'s production team convinced Telemundo that the movie dealt with an important African American leader who had fought against racism and the episode was ultimately broadcast.

The *Malcolm X* debate, while highlighting the ignorance of some of the Telemundo media professionals, also illustrates a central feature regarding the issue of race in the narratives. At first glance, the inclusion of the *Malcolm X* allusion might appear to contradict the assertion that references to racial issues were taboo on *Mi familia*. However, the episode that mentioned *Malcolm X* literally and symbolically transferred antiblack racism to the United States. In other words, as long as the performances and practices of racism reproduced the locally scripted scenario of U.S. segregation, discrimination, and fragmentation, *Mi familia*'s black characters were able to discuss antiblack racism. Thus, the selective censorship regarding the topic of racism in *Mi familia* functioned through the theatricality of nationalism embedded in la gran familia puertorriqueña discourse.

Still, other members of *Mi familia*'s production team attributed censorship to a combination of groups and individuals including Telemundo, the writer, and the advertisers. In addition to recounting the two previous examples (the AIDS Foundation sponsorship and the episode that included a reference to *Malcolm X*), they mentioned Arcadio's (*Mi familia*'s principal character) ambiguous job. At the beginning of the series he was supposed to be the right-hand man for a city mayor, but the station suggested changing this job affiliation to avoid any relationship to a specific political party on the island. Thus, without any reference in the narrative to new employment, Arcadio became the second in command of a private industry. Additionally, the narrative avoided direct references to any particular industry, as some officials believed it could create problems with the show's sponsors.

In light of the interviewees' responses, it is clear that *Mi familia*'s censorship came from three intertwined types of sources: institutional, sociocultural, and personal. Through Telemundo's vigilance, *Mi familia* was constrained to perform within the parameters of Puerto Rico's conservative, ideological discourses. This allowed the show to avoid conflicts with powerful organizations such as the Catholic Church and Morality in Media, advertisers, and specific political parties on the island. Although in my interviews some of *Mi familia*'s production members expressed a desire to address the problem of racism in Puerto Rico, they ultimately remained silent. Within Puerto Rico's commercial television environment, one of the situations the less-powerful individuals (actors in general, but also directors) try to avoid is being characterized as *problemático* (difficult to work with). Local television is a small community, locally produced shows are rare, and creative media professionals know that a mere rumor about being problemático could cost an actor future job opportunities.

During the seven rehearsals and taping sessions where I was a participant observer, some of *Mi familia*'s creative people voiced their opinions.[25] In fact, the actors and the director tried to counteract the writer's occasional "conservative ideological positions" regarding gender relations and the station's censorship regarding the topic of sexuality. The performers negotiated their points of view by establishing a dialogue between themselves and the director. By organizing collective sites, actors and actresses sometimes persuaded the production, via the director, to support their main arguments, change the original script, or provide alternate themes for the show. However, for the most part, the dissent did not target racial issues but instead focused on the machista ideologies entrenched in *Mi familia*'s texts.

For example, in *Mi familia*, Willy (the Meléndez son), was depicted in a perpetual state of sexual heat. He was continually trailing young single female characters and expressing—in all possible ways—his desire to have sex with them. The female actresses who performed these roles were uncomfortable with this characterization and claimed that "many people on the streets" criticized Willy's "heat." The actresses subsequently used every opportunity to denounce this objectification of the female characters.

During one of the July 1997 taping sessions, the actor who played Willy made a sexually suggestive gesture while conversing with a young woman (he slid his hands into his pockets to make it appear as though he had an erection). One of the actresses immediately interrupted the taping, saying that the "gesture was too much," that it was "unnecessary," and that Willy's character "had crossed the line." According to the actress, the character was behaving aggressively toward women, perpetuating the male sexual offensiveness that characterizes Puerto Rico's machista society. At the same time, another actress who was in the scene also complained about the gesture, sparking a gendered argument. Everyone on the set, including the cameramen (all of whom were male), significant others, makeup women, and actors became involved in the dialogue. In general, the men argued that the gesture was not offensive but funny and that it represented a normal male reaction. The women repeatedly said that it was distasteful and that it should not be allowed on the show. After a short discussion, the director eliminated the gesture.

During the taping sessions that I attended, female actresses were constantly on guard for actions and scenes that they considered degrading or otherwise offensive to women. However, this dialogic space for gender issues did not extend to issues of race and racism. Contrary to the ideology of machismo and female oppression, antiblack racism on the island is considered a taboo and an extremely delicate subject. Thus, in the case of *Mi familia*, the lack of general consensus among members of the production team also imposed a level of personal censorship. Alternatively, and based on my conversations with *Mi familia*'s media professionals, none of the production members who possessed more power ever tried to directly counteract the station's directives. As was expected, the intertwined levels of censorship permeated the situation comedy's thematic constructions.

The Framing of a Puerto Rican Lower-Middle-Class Family

During its first five years on the air, *Mi familia*'s opening was changed only once. From 1994 to 1997 the opening showed the family seated in the living room posing for a portrait. In 1997 the opening portrayed the family as local tourists posing for a portrait in a small town plaza. These two openings presented the lifestyle of a Puerto Rican family who, due to financial limitations, spent most of its leisure time either at home or around the island visiting relatives. These images were framed by salsa rhythms that interconnected the family unit to Puerto Rico's cultural, racial, and class spaces.

In addition to the opening, another aspect of *Mi familia*'s packaging was a stamp that read *"Hecho en Puerto Rico para ti"* (Made in Puerto Rico for You). The stamp appeared at the end of each episode and was also included in all of Telemundo's locally produced programs. This nationalistic, strategically placed sign was used to convince the viewers that they were consuming a "Puerto Rican product" even though Telemundo–Puerto Rico was technically part of the U.S. Spanish-language network. Thus, the program's packaging (salsa music and a local plaza), in addition to Telemundo's final seal of approval in the stamp, stood as symbols of Puerto Ricanness.

Mi familia's narratives recreated "a common day in the life of a Puerto Rican family," thus most of the action took place in the Meléndez home.[26] *Mi familia*'s set was divided into four primary spaces: the house's main entrance, the living room, the kitchen and dining room, and the couple's bedroom. A "welcome" sign was perched on the front door, which opened into the living areas. Family photos were placed around the living room. The somewhat standard furniture of a lower-middle-class family decorated the room (a sofa; two recliners in pastel pink, blue, and white; and a coffee table). This furniture perfectly matched the dining room and the kitchen's embellishments. The Meléndez home resembled the domestic architecture presented in 1980s American magazines such as *Better Homes and Gardens*.

Mi familia was a localized version of U.S. domestic situation comedies in which the domestic family lifestyle occupies the center of the narrative. However, this domestic lifestyle rearticulated some elements of Puerto Rico's vernacular culture. In *Mi familia* the home was an open space for extended family members and close friends. The phrases *mi casa es su casa* (my home is your home) and *donde come uno comen dos* (where one eats, two can eat too) were integral to the Meléndez family life. Neighbors visited the Meléndez home without an invitation and brought dishes or food items for no special reason. Visitors such as a policeman and a Roman Catholic priest were frequently part of the Meléndez daily life and that of their neighbors. In addition, these neighbors and friends were the ones who, on numerous occasions, provoked misunderstanding in the Meléndez domestic space. In *Mi familia*'s narrative, the episodic-genre convention of order-confusion-restoration of order related to sexuality, gender relations, or money.

The Meléndez family included Arcadio (the father) and Migdalia (the mother). After more than twenty years of marriage the couple still had a very romantic and passionate relationship. The two other primary characters were their children, Wandita and Willy. The secondary characters appearing in almost every episode (from 1994 to 1999) included Cheito, Karina, Don Pupo, Lola, and Nieves. Cheito, Migdalia's brother, was portrayed as a lazy young man who lived off the Meléndezes' income. Karina, Willy's mulata girlfriend, usually argued with Willy because of his ongoing infidelities. Don Pupo and Lola were the Meléndezes' neighbors. Don Pupo was a white, retired, married man whose primary form of entertainment was gossip. Lola was a young, sexy, single, white dietician who was the object of desire for every male character in the sitcom, including Arcadio. Nieves (which literally means *snow*, a reference to the character's skin color) was Arcadio's secretary. Like Lola, Nieves was a sexy and beautiful woman who constantly flirted with Arcadio. Both Lola and Nieves were constructed as Arcadio's perpetual sexual temptations. Finally, in 1997, *Mi familia* added two secondary characters: Pichón, the neighborhood policeman, a white middle-aged man who loved everything associated with the United States, and Bill, an American exchange high school student.

In the Meléndez family both parents held full-time jobs. Migdalia worked in a beauty parlor as a beautician, while Arcadio was a bookkeeper for a private company. Although it was clear that the financial support of the Meléndez family came from both Arcadio and Migdalia's earnings, the show's narratives presented Arcadio as the breadwinner. Migdalia, as the typical Puerto Rican housewife, was in charge of the family's moral and religious (Catholic) guidance and the restoration of familial order during moments of chaos. Thus, while Migdalia contributed to the family income, her primary duty was in the home.

Nonetheless, the representation of Migdalia's employment outside the domestic sphere reflected the economic pressures that plagued 1990s Puerto Rican families, particularly those in the lower- and lower-middle-class strata. Through references to corporate downsizing and Migdalia's desire to look for a second job, it was clear that the Meléndez family was struggling financially. Arcadio constantly worried about the possibility of losing his job, and to satisfy his employer he frequently worked extra hours without any remuneration. Even though Arcadio worked for the (unknown) company for many years, he knew that the business (and thus Puerto Rico's 1990s economy) was not doing well. As Arcadio often observed, "*la economía está mal*" (the economy is bad). However, no explanations for the island's economic conditions were ever presented. Nor did the narrative explore the difficulties of black Puerto Ricans' real families and communities. Arcadio was depicted as just another Puerto Rican male who made great efforts to sustain his family.

Still, there was a definite class distinction between the 1990s *Mi familia* family and the 1980s *Los suegros* families. Whereas the Meléndezes did not suffer the precarious economic conditions endured by *El tremendo hotel*'s fictional work family of the late 1940s to mid-1950s, Arcadio and Migdalia's financial situation symbolically articulated the residual elements of Puerto Rico's economic development processes (Operation Bootstrap). In the Meléndez community, American investors were nonexistent. It seems that in this fictional space (as in Puerto Rico), many U.S. corporations had already moved to other Third World countries.

The Meléndezes and their neighbors also worried about crime, another element that hinted at the island's economic situation. Yet, when burglaries occurred nobody asked why the neighborhood was enduring these disturbing intrusions. Neither did they establish a correlation between "the bad economy" and the increase in criminal activity. Instead, *Mi familia*'s narratives pursued a "unique" coping strategy. By establishing loving relationships within the family and camaraderie between neighbors, social problems were constructed as something external to the familial living space (home-neighborhood), even though crime sometimes affected their lives. Additionally, similar to many Puerto Ricans, for the characters in *Mi familia*, migrating to the United States became another way of coping with financial instability.

The topic of migration was a recurring theme in *Mi familia*. Throughout various episodes, the narrative directly and indirectly addressed the massive migration during the 1940s and 1950s, Puerto Rican circular migration patterns, and what has been characterized as the "brain drain" migrations of the 1980s and 1990s.[27] One aspect presented in *Mi familia*'s narratives was the close connection between people on the island and their relatives in the United States. The Meléndez family and their neighbors had extended family members in the United States, and they frequently referred to them during informal conversations, phone calls, and visits.[28] By incorporating the familial networks between Puerto Ricans on the mainland and Puerto Ricans on the island, *Mi familia*'s narratives also established the social class spectrum of the fictional community. As discussed in chapter 1, the 1940s and 1950s migration was characterized by people from Puerto Rico's lower-class background. Therefore, because most of the Meléndez community had family members who participated in this migration, one can assume that they were (at some point in their life) members of the lower socioeconomic class.

While *Mi familia* indirectly addressed Puerto Rico's 1990s economic situation, a more prevalent theme in the comedy was the issue of Puerto Rican culture in relation to the U.S. influences. Through sporadic and secondary characters, the narrative rearticulated the socially constructed traits that define a member of the ethnic family. According to the narrative, an authentic Puerto Rican was the individual who was born and raised on the island and who, regardless of political preference, identified him- or herself as Puerto Rican.

Puerto Ricanness vs. Americanization

Mi familia's texts never directly addressed the 1998 plebiscite or the possibilities for the island to become a U.S. state. However, the narratives constantly incorporated Puerto Ricans' experience with what is generally known in the vernacular culture as *el difícil* (the difficult): the English language. Even though *Mi familia*'s characters did not associate themselves directly with a specific political party, the narratives' subtexts attacked the pro-statehood supporters. This anti-statehood criticism was constructed around two themes: cultural assimilation and the reaffirmation of the island's identity through the use of the Spanish language. The theme of Puerto Ricanness versus Americanization can be seen in the depictions of *Nuyoricans*, the born and raised Puerto Ricans who adored anything related to America, and Bill, *el americanito* (the young American).

Nuyoricans is the term generally used in Puerto Rico for Puerto Ricans born and raised in the United States, even though some of these first- and second-generation members were not necessarily born in New York City. The origin of this characterization derived from the large settlement of Puerto Ricans in New York after World War II. Nuyoricans are generally perceived in the island's national imaginary as being Americanized and thus are viewed by some as the Other Puerto Ricans. This Otherness is juxtaposed to Puerto Ricans on the island thereby creating an ongoing discourse regarding issues of cultural authenticity, language, and moral values.[29] Through some of *Mi familia*'s episodes, the narrative reproduced certain island-based stereotypes of Nuyoricans and the socially constructed differences among these members of the same ethnic family.

During 1998 Frida (Fredesbinda), Arcadio's niece and a first-generation Puerto Rican born and raised in Chicago, decided to spend some time with her island relatives. Before Frida arrived, Migdalia began to worry about this family member's visit.

Arcadio: My brother Apolonio called me from Chicago and says that he will send his daughter to spend some vacation time here.

Migdalia: (horrified) Whaaaaaaat? A teenager and from Chicago? God
protect us!

Migdalia's main concern related to her niece's possible sexual behavior and
reflected an understanding in Puerto Rico that U.S. morality is extremely
liberal in terms of sexuality and in relation to Puerto Rico's (Catholic-
repressive) culture. As Migdalia noted in a conversation with Don Pupo (the
neighbor), "well, you know how young people behave in the U.S. nowadays."
Although Don Pupo refuted this stereotypical construction by saying, "like
all places, there are good and bad ones," Frida was the Meléndezes' worst
nightmare. Frida dated many young men, had unauthorized night escapades,
and, "worst of all," spoke Spanglish (a mixture of the Spanish and English
languages). Because of ongoing cultural clashes, Frida shortened her vacation
and departed for Chicago where she felt more at home.

Through Frida's character, *Mi familia*'s narratives reproduced dominant
ideologies in Puerto Rico regarding Puerto Ricans born and raised on the
mainland. As Nancy Morris notes, the rejection of Nuyoricans in Puerto Rico
is based on the perception of cultural differences in general and language
in particular.[30] *Mi familia*'s incorporation of a first-generation U.S. Puerto
Rican established Puerto Rico's translocal community and the ongoing diasporic conditions, but it also rearticulated Puerto Rico's hegemonic identity
discourses.[31] According to the Meléndez family and their neighbors, Frida's
assimilation into the U.S. culture was evidenced by her disrespect for paren-
tal authority (going out without permission), dating many men, and forget-
ting the Spanish language, which has been historically positioned as a pivotal
symbol of Puerto Ricanness. In *Mi familia*, cultural authenticity merged with
the island's territorial space, thereby constructing Puerto Rican communities
on the mainland as distorted spaces of Puerto Ricanness. According to the
Frida episodes, although Puerto Ricans in the United States are part of the
same ethnic family, they nonetheless remain culturally foreign (i.e., American).[32] Through Frida, *Mi familia* portrayed cultural assimilation as unac-
ceptable. Furthermore, even the character who favored statehood rejected
complete assimilation.

In Puerto Rico, regardless of the individual's political preference (pro-
statehood, pro-commonwealth, and pro-independence), there is, as illustrated in the previous chapters, a strong sense of cultural nationalism. Even
people who identify as pro-statehood sympathizers do not consider them-

selves American.[33] This seemingly conflictive dichotomy between politics and culture was presented in *Mi familia* via Pichón, the neighborhood policeman.

Pichón, a recurring character in Puerto Rico's commercial television since 1967 (not coincidentally, the same year the island held its first plebiscite), was born on the island, migrated with his parents to the United States in the 1950s, and returned to Puerto Rico as an adolescent.[34] Pichón was also a U.S. Army veteran and although his first language was Spanish, he preferred to speak English even though he was not fluent. The Meléndez family members and their neighbors knew that Pichón preferred to speak English; thus, they tried to communicate with him by using el difícil (English). However, these attempts at conversing in English succeeded only in fostering misinterpretations since no one understood Pichón and vice versa. These miscommunications were largely a result of the characters' version of English, which was simply to add the suffix "ing" to any Spanish word. For example, *alimentar* became *alimentating* (to feed), *fugarse* became *fugating* (to elope), and so on.

Whereas Pichón's linguistic and (indirectly) political preferences were different from those of the other characters, he was seen as part of the Meléndez communal family. Regardless of his English language preference and his high regard for the United States (according to Pichón, the best things in Puerto Rico's society were obtained thanks to "the great U.S.A."), he saw himself and was seen by the Meléndez family and community as Puerto Rican. Additionally, Pichón's sense of Puerto Ricanness was most strongly reasserted in his interactions with Bill, el americanito.

Bill was a sporadic character who, as I previously mentioned, began to appear in *Mi familia*'s narrative in December 1997. He was a white, blond, tall, and middle-class young man who came to Puerto Rico through a high school exchange program to study Spanish. Bill was always hanging out with Willy, with whom he had established a close friendship. Although Bill did not understand some Puerto Rican traditions (such as eating pork during Christmas or celebrating the Three Kings Day), he was eager to learn everything about the island and its people. Bill, similar to *Los suegros*'s American characters Mr. Morrison and Katy, showed respect for his new cultural experience. The primary difference between *Los suegros*'s American characters and Bill was his wish to be read as Puerto Rican.

Bill's desire to assimilate related exclusively to his lack of appeal to the Puerto Rican girls who considered him "too white" and therefore unattractive. Consequently, similar to other televisual Americans in locally produced programs (particularly sketch comedies and situation comedies), *Mi familia*'s Americanness was synonymous with Anglo-Saxon whiteness, a whiteness that, as I discussed in chapter 3, has been generally depicted as sexually unappealing. Nonetheless, contrary to the character Katy in *Los suegros*, Bill did everything possible to pass as Puerto Rican. For example, he worked very hard to learn Spanish, memorized all the Puerto Rican traditional Christmas songs in order to participate in *trullas* (a Puerto Rican Christmas tradition where people visit and sing to friends during late night or early morning hours without any prior warning), and dressed very properly (slacks and a button-down shirt). Actually, in a moment of desperation, Bill dyed his hair black to "look more Puerto Rican." Regardless of all his efforts, he was always seen by the communal members as Bill, el americanito — a foreigner.

One important aspect of Bill's interactions with the Meléndez family and other community members was that except for Willy, other characters did not even try to talk to him in English. Thus, as with Frida, the narrative constructed U.S.-born individuals and their use of English as cultural invasions. Even the "I-love-the-U.S.A" and allegedly pro-statehood Pichón did not allow Bill to use English during their conversations, as evidenced by a scene from an episode aired in March 1999.

Pichón found Willy and Bill in the neighborhood's park during school hours and immediately confronted them.

> Pichón: Ahh, are you fugating from school? [Are you skipping school?]
> Willy: Officer, officer, we do not criminals. Wasing no no . . . (and continued to mumble incoherent words in English)
> Pichón: Mira, Peter O' Toole, *¿me puedes decir lo que este está tratando de decir?* [Look Peter O'Toole, can you tell me what is he trying to say?]
> Bill: Listen officer, we were just . . .
> Pichón: (disturbed) *¡No me hable en inglés!* [Do not talk to me in English!] That we are in Puerto Rico! (in English)

Based on this scene, and other episodes that included Bill and Pichón, only island-born Puerto Ricans were entitled to use the English language without being considered a threat to the communal cultural order. More than problematizing U.S. colonialism and imperialistic practices on the island, *Mi fa-*

milia's inclusion of Pichón's and Bill's characters served to criticize and mock pro-statehood supporters as well as to re-articulate Puerto Rico's cultural nationalism. Regardless of political or language preferences, Puerto Ricans born and raised on the island were part of the family. Frida and Bill, on the other hand, represented the external U.S. cultural influence and, in the case of Frida, the threat of annihilation of Puerto Rican culture through Americanization. In sum, *Mi familia*'s authentic Puerto Ricanness and family membership were contained exclusively within the island.

The territorially based construction of Puerto Ricanness evidently included black and mulatto individuals. Even though the Meléndez black family lived among whites, the neighbors never used any of the racist phrases that are part of the island's vernacular culture. Indeed, the inclusion of some racist remarks would have provided an opportunity to explore and criticize the island's racial ideologies and racist practices. However, that never occurred. Antiblack racism was not part of this fictional community. Needless to say, the mestizaje of la gran familia puertorriqueña discourse informed not only the daily interactions between the Meléndez family and their neighbors but also the sexual-love relations of Wandita (the Meléndez daughter), Willy, and Cheito (Migdalia's brother).

Racialized Sexuality: Did the Meléndezes Desire Any Body?

Within *Mi familia*'s narrative, Wandita entertained three suitors: Michael, Richi, and Carlos. Racially speaking, Michael was black, Richi trigueño, and Carlos white. Referring to these multiracial suitors, Willy teased his sister, chiding that, "Wandita likes black, white, yellow and American rosy-cheeked men." As with other televisual representations and descriptions of Americans, Willy's construction of Americanness was synonymous with whiteness. Despite the fact that Wandita once had a steady relationship with Michael as well as an opportunity to become romantically involved with Richi, her serious boyfriend and subsequent husband was Carlos, a white man. The racial mixing between Wandita and Carlos in *Mi familia* might be seen as a site where white male desire toward mulata women is socially acceptable because this racial mixing does not promote blackness. Contrarily, their marriage functioned within the mejorar la raza (improve the race) discourse that promotes blanqueamiento (whitening) for black and dark-skinned people.

Yet, even though the liaison functions within the island's mestizaje ideology and Wandita's character might have been constructed as the "sensual mulata," Puerto Rican racialized stereotypes did not directly correspond with Wandita. Instead, Wandita's character was constructed as one of the many pure, virginal young women in the Meléndez community. Therefore, even though her racialized body carried social, cultural, and sexual connotations, in this case, her membership in a morally strict and religious Puerto Rican televisual family neutralized the culturally constructed hypersexuality generally associated with mulatas and black women. In *Mi familia*, female hypersexuality was not particularly related to race; rather, it responded to chauvinistic social discourses that delineate by contrast the characteristics of a respectable, single, Catholic, and family- or domestic-oriented woman. Hypersexuality was presented in Lola's character, the white, single, independent, and "promiscuous" neighbor, while female virginity and purity were embodied in Wandita, Nieves (Arcadio's secretary), and Karina (Willy's girlfriend). On balance, *Mi familia*'s scripts contained some of the racial stereotyping that inform Puerto Rico's society. The following scene illustrates some of the narratives' racist constructions.

Wandita and Carlos, who moved to New York City after marrying (which symbolically positioned them as part of the 1980s and 1990s exodus of professionals to the United States), had decided to spend their Christmas vacation on the island. Migdalia and Arcadio were excited about this visit, especially because they would have an opportunity to spend some time with their newborn grandson.

> Migdalia: Look how beautiful the baby is! And what a cute little pink
>   guy he is.
> Wandita: Mom, do you know how cold it is in New York right now? It is
>   freezing!
> Carlos: Don't you think that he looks like me?
> Arcadio: Let's see. . . . He has his father's eyes, his father's nose, his
>   father's smile (looking down). Yes, but he has something from his
>   grandfather.

Even though the characters did not mention the baby's race, one can deduce that like his father, he was white (pink). However, there was something black about this baby and it was related to his genitalia. In this racial and vulgar stereotyping, Arcadio proudly implied that the baby had inherited his penis, suggesting a distinction between constructions of white and black male sexuality. Black masculinity was thus constructed around black stereotypes of hypersexuality (i.e., a large penis). Although this can be read as another location for machismo and male virility through which "phallocentric" males become more masculine, Arcadio's insistence that sexually speaking, the baby did not resemble Carlos (a white man), produced a distinct reference to black male sexuality.[35] Similarly, the interconnection of blackness and sexuality was also part of Willy's character.

Although Willy flirted with many girls, he maintained a serious relationship with Karina. Willy attributed the girls' fascination with him to his racial body, which symbolized difference and charm. He categorized himself as "a sweet-tasting negrito," as a negrito "with chocolate ears," as a "Leonardo DiCaprio tanned by the sun," or as "a saintly negrito." As the laugh track indicated, these remarks were constructed as humorous in *Mi familia*'s narrative. Although, as previously observed, negrito sometimes carries a derogatory cultural connotation, these references might also be seen as Willy's self-reaffirmation of blackness.

The fact that a young black man was portrayed as attractive and also intelligent (according to the narrative Willy was a very responsible and bright student) was an important representation of gendered blackness in Puerto Rico's commercial television entertainment programming. Given that in Puerto Rico televisual male blackness has been for the most part interconnected to blackface negrito characters, Willy's character functioned as an alternative, and to a certain extent, counterhegemonic depiction, to the idiotic, comical, and uncultured negrito stereotype. Through Willy's character (as well as Arcadio's character) *Mi familia* positioned black males as respectful, smart, and educated members of the Puerto Rican family.

Then again, by expressing his attractiveness and difference in racialized terms, Willy's portrayal of race located his body as a sign-symbol of racial stereotyping. In Puerto Rico (and probably globally) one rarely hears of a white male or female referring to him or herself as "a tasty white" or as "a saintly white." In *Mi familia*, white characters did not have to express anything distinctive about themselves because of their inherent whiteness, their culturally normalized superiority, their power, and their beauty.[36] Although the televisual depiction of this young black man dating several young white and mulata girls re-affirmed racial equality in this fictional community, the character's speech created a second level of meaning associated with both racist discourses and cultural constructions of negritud. Willy attracted young girls not because he was a nice and intelligent young man but because he was a "tasty" and "sweet" negrito. He had a delectable body that all girls yearned to consume. Even though *Mi familia*'s narrative constructed Willy's remarks around machista discourses of male sexual attraction, the racial distinction created a primitive construction of the Other, an Other whom women want to enjoy sexually because of his racialized difference.[37]

The fact that Willy was attracted to white girls but was going steady with a young mulata can also be seen as a sign of his love and desire for negritud. However, this representation could be additionally understood in terms of racialized sexual fantasies. In other words, based on *Mi familia* texts, it was possible for a young black man to play or fantasize across the color lines but not to cross those lines in terms of a serious relationship leading to marriage and family. Because Willy never dated black girls and since constructions of beauty on *Mi familia* were homologous to whiteness, Willy's speeches and behavior functioned within sexualized stereotypes of blackness and whiteness that characterize the mestizaje discourse.

Other examples of racially mixed love affairs were depicted in relationships between Cheito (mulatto) and Brenda (white). During the beginning of the sitcom, Cheito, as a Puerto Rican male stud, flirted with all the single women who visited the Meléndez family or the community. He finally fell in love with and married Brenda, a poor young white woman. As was the case for Wandita and Carlos, *Mi familia*'s narrative did not make direct reference to this racially mixed relationship. Still, Cheito was a light-skinned mulatto while Brenda came from a lower social class. Thus, social class softened racial differentiation by creating a secondary level of permissible racial mixing in this fictional community.[38] Similar to Wandita and Carlos' coupling, the racial mixing occurred between white and mulatto bodies, which posited the mulato/a as a repository of permissible sexual desire and mixing, reaffirming blanqueamiento. Nonetheless, the ideologies of whiteness, blackness, and mestizaje in *Mi familia* became more complex through the construction of white women as the objects of Arcadio's sexual desire.

The Meléndez Couple: Were All Blacks Beautiful in *Mi familia*?

As I previously observed, Arcadio and Migdalia had a relatively stable marriage and, in fact, they had sex every night.[39] However, Migdalia constantly worried about her husband's possible infidelities, a theme that promulgated Puerto Rico's machista discourses by depicting men as incapable of maintaining a monogamous relationship. Despite the fact that Arcadio was never unfaithful, he was continually tempted by Lola and Nieves. For these two females, as well as for Migdalia, Arcadio was a sex symbol and an adorable man. This representation was used for comedic purposes since Arcadio—overweight, short, and in his late forties—would not generally be considered a handsome man. Conversely, the only person who found Migdalia attractive was Arcadio. No other characters referred to Migdalia as an attractive woman or characterized her as sexy.

An important characteristic of Arcadio and Migdalia was that both were overweight. Even though Migdalia was presented as happy with herself, other characters made references to her obesity and teased her. While Arcadio's fat body was characterized as adorable by other women, Migdalia's corpulence was portrayed as unattractive, particularly by those outside the nuclear family. In this fictional community, only men had control of their bodies and desires. Notwithstanding this machista-centered ideological construction, Arcadio praised his wife's body and saw her as a very sensual and attractive woman.

In *Mi familia*, the portrayal of a black, large, happy, sexually active, lower-middle-class ordinary couple can be seen as a transgression of social codes regarding Catholic morality, body constraints, and televisual whiteness. These black bodies, then, broke with the norm within the Meléndez community and with previous representations of white middle-class televisual families that had appeared on Puerto Rico's commercial television since 1954. Nevertheless, Arcadio's ongoing desire for whiteness presented a problematic terrain for racial representations and negritud.

"Whiteness" and "whitening" became synonymous with Arcadio's desire. Contrary to mulato/a characters whose constructed (textual) racial ambivalence and class allowed them to achieve whitening, Arcadio lived in a perpetual and unfulfilled longing for white female bodies. He had married a black woman who like himself was part of the same marginalized community. He never questioned his marriage to Migdalia, not only because he loved her but also because contrary to potential sexual relations with the desired white women, this racial union was socially and culturally acceptable. Nonetheless, Arcadio's ongoing sexual desire toward white women recreated his racial ambivalence about the way he was supposed to behave (as a married black man) and his innate and colonized (im)position to desire whiteness.[40]

The selection of whiteness as the object of black male desire created a disempowering and contradictory location of black reaffirmation. Migdalia's racialized body and beauty were judged by other characters and stood as an ongoing comparison to Lola and Nieves. These two female characters represented what Migdalia could never be: white, slim, and "beautiful." Informed by Puerto Rico's racial, cultural, gender, and social discourses, the narrative delimited whose bodies were desirable, who had the power to desire them, and who was in control of these desires. Nonetheless, while whiteness (through the mestizaje discourse) was the norm in this fictional community, particularly in the sexual terrain, the narratives sporadically presented black vernacular cultural elements. Through the incorporation of musical styles such as salsa and rap, the Meléndez family established a connection with black and mulatto sectors of the population in Puerto Rico and in the diaspora.

Black and Mulatto Popular Cultures

Some of *Mi familia*'s episodes included musical styles or performers that were popular within Puerto Rico's cultural arena during the 1990s. *Mi familia*'s inclusion of salsa and rap music was not a conscious decision by the Telemundo and *Mi familia* media professionals to embrace black and mulatto cultural elements per se. Instead, these musical styles were included to maximize profits and attract younger segments of the audience. Thus, salsa and rap in *Mi familia* were usually brought into the story by Willy's character.

In one of *Mi familia*'s episodes three famous Puerto Rican salsa players (Roberto Rohena, Papo Rosario, and Rafael Ithier, an original member and director of the internationally famous salsa group El Gran Combo) interacted with the Meléndez men. The following scene recreates the ways in which the Meléndezes in general and Willy in particular identified both with salsa as the *cultura del pueblo* (culture of the people) and with the racialized, class, and political characterizations of this musical style.

In this episode Willy, with Cheito's help, decides to record a single and a music video. As the three salsa performers arrive at the recording studio, Arcadio, Cheito, and Willy begin to talk with them.

Willy: Wow, this is so cool, Mister! Aren't you Roberto Rohena?
Roberto: The same.
Willy: I knew it. My grandmother talked to me about you a lot; she was a fan of yours. Listen, Roberto . . . Why don't you play some rhythms to see if I can learn from you?

Roberto: Of course!

(Roberto begins to play and dance with Willy)

(On another side of the recording studio)

Cheito: We will have to wait a little while because my buddies Papo Rosario and Rafael Ithier are going to record a song.

Arcadio: Papo Rosario? And Rafael Itheir, El Gran Combo's musical director? Willy, come here! Look who is here. Rafael Ithier and Papo Rosario!

Willy: This is so cool! El Gran Combo is my favorite.

Papo: And who is going to record a salsa?

Willy: I am the one! What is going on? Don't you see the *salsero* look that I have? Tell me, Mister Ithier.

Ithier: Yes, I believe so, the boy has a salsero look.

Willy's admission that he was an avid El Gran Combo fan identified him as a salsero listener. Willy also had the "salsero look," a reference that articulated the racial composition of many old school salsa musicians. Through Willy, the Meléndez fictional family was juxtaposed to black working-class Puerto Rican communities both on the island and in the United States. In this episode, Willy was constructed as being proud of his knowledge of Puerto Rican popular culture, of his negritud, and of his working-class family roots. It should be noted that Willy's association with black-mulatto cultural elements was present in many of *Mi familia*'s episodes. As an adolescent, Willy listened to Spanish and English rap, creating a secondary connection to current young black, mulatto, working-class, and transnational-marginalized communities. Through Willy's character in particular and the Meléndez family in general, one observed the bond between this fictional black family and some of the cultural elements associated with national and global diasporic black communities.

Although *Mi familia*'s incorporation of salsa and rap presented a space for negotiating blackness in this fictional community, the representations did not elaborate on the political origins of these musical styles. Nor did the narrative explore the contributions of black communities to the island's culture or the racial inequalities that form part of Puerto Rican society. The fact that negritud in *Mi familia* was generally defined through music and skin color created a monolithic and depoliticized construction of blackness. Even though the show had the potential to explore racial struggles and prejudice within the island's sociohistorical context, its narratives entrenched cultural and racial mestizaje discourses that symbolically annihilated them. As one of *Mi familia*'s production members indicated, the show was about a "Puerto Rican family which happened to be black." The colorless (i.e., whiteness) discourse that informs the ideology of la gran familia puertorriqueña permeated both the conceptualization and representation of the first black Puerto Rican fictional family on television.

I do not want to suggest that because *Mi familia* depicted black bodies, and that because they were almost absent in other locally produced programs, the producer and Telemundo were the only ones who carried the "burden of [black] representation."[41] This would be expecting far too much from the first show that presented a black fictional family in the situation comedy genre. Further and more complicated representations of race and blackness must be preceded by social, cultural, and political acknowledgement that racism is part of the culture. Certainly, as Arcadio Díaz-Quiñones observes, without a "de-colonization of the imaginary" changes will be difficult to accomplish.[42] Still, recent commercial transformations in Puerto Rico's television market might impede the production of more locally produced shows and the examination of racial ideologies and racist practices in the island's culture. My last encounter with *Mi familia*'s production hinted at the changes that are taking place in contemporary Puerto Rican commercial television that began, as I mentioned in the introduction, when all local stations were sold to U.S. media corporations.

The Hispanic Market: The Beginning of *Mi familia*'s End

In 1999, during one of my informal phone conversations with Judith Pizarro (*Mi familia*'s principal actress), I learned that Telemundo had decided to build a new set for *Mi familia*. Judith was very excited about the new and "beautiful" set and she persuaded me to come see it. So, there I was, visiting Telemundo on a supposedly social, casual, and fun sojourn but with notebook, pencil, and tape recorder in hand.

Mi familia's new set was indeed beautiful, but it looked Mexican. The Meléndez home resembled the rustic embellishments that are in vogue in the United States and that appropriate Mexican-styled adornments and colors. For example, new paintings on the walls featured a Mayan woman with a child, a Mexican man with a sombrero, and other images associated with Mexican culture. Judith Pizarro, Otilio Warrington "Bizcocho" (*Mi familia*'s principal actor), Gilo Rivera (the director), and Jorge Cordero (the assistant producer) surrounded me and asked me what I thought about the changes. I did not say anything, largely because I was in shock. It was evident that the station planned to export the show to other network affiliates. After all, why would they spend money on a set that included items associated with Mexican culture? However, could a comedy show like *Mi familia* survive in the U.S. Spanish-language market? How would the Mexican majority that comprises the Spanish-language television audience receive a show about a black Puerto Rican family? At that moment I thought that if the future of *Mi familia* depended on the show's success in the U.S. Spanish-language market, this was the beginning of *Mi familia*'s end. As I stood there dazed and speechless, "Bizcocho" (to fill the uncomfortable silence) remarked in an ironic tone, "yes, you know, every Puerto Rican has a Mexican within him- or herself." Everybody, including me, laughed. This tension-relieving laughter seemed to suggest that they, too, were worried.

Mi familia's opening and closing were also changed. The salsa rhythms were replaced by music that did not relate to any particular ethnic community. The new opening and closing featured the Meléndezes and some of their neighbors at different moments of their lives and inside the Meléndezes' home. In other words, besides the usual stamp at the end of the show that said "Hecho en Puerto Rico para ti" (which could be easily edited) and the familiar actors, there was no longer a direct association between the program and Puerto Rico's geographical and cultural spaces.

In a May 1999 newspaper article, Luis Roldán (Telemundo–Puerto Rico president) expressed his goal of exporting some of Puerto Rico's local programming to the network affiliates. *Mi familia* was one of the shows to be exported. However, according to Roldán, the programs in question would need to be culturally adjusted. As Roldán explained, "the programs that will be exported are not going to be exactly as the ones aired here. For example, a program like *Mi familia* could be a family in which the father is Mexican, the mother is Puerto Rican, and the neighbors are Cuban."[43]

When I read about Roldán's plans, I wondered about the incorporation of a "Mexican father." From the perspective of 1990s Puerto Rican society, it would have been more logical to include Dominicans or Cubans, not only because of the Afro diasporic connections and the actual presence of these migrant communities on the island but also because of the similarities among the Spanish Caribbean cultures. It was clear that Roldán was basing his judgment not on Puerto Rican realities but on the U.S. Spanish-language tele-vision's construction of "Hispanic" realities. Roldán was probably trying to target the U.S. Mexican majority that constitutes the Hispanic audience.[44] It was also evident that in his (and the network's) plans, race was going to be substituted with ethnicity. In other words, the new *Mi familia* was not going to depict black "Hispanics," rather it seems that the situation comedy's main theme was going to be about the cultural misunderstandings among Puerto Ricans, Cubans, and Mexicans. That, however, never transpired. For the short period of time that *Mi familia* was exported to Miami and New York City, the ethnic and racial composition of the fictional family and neighbor-hood and the themes associated with Puerto Rico's culture remained intact.[45]

In Puerto Rico, *Mi familia* continued on the air for three more years. How-ever, in October 2002 *Mi familia*'s production members and local media professionals in general witnessed a dramatic change in the island's tele-vision market. The Univision network, which in 2001 purchased the local station WLII-TV (channel 11), had four of its programs among the top-ten rated shows.[46] Although five of the top-ten programs listed on the survey were local productions broadcast on Telemundo (channel 2) and Televicentro (channel 4) and whereas one of Univision's highly rated shows was produced locally, a "nationalistic outburst" emerged.[47] People began to call local radio programs criticizing the *enlatados* (imported television programs) in gen-eral, and specifically, Univision–Puerto Rico.[48]

Even though since the mid-1970s and early 1980s, as I previously dis-cussed, local stations had been owned by U.S. media corporations, these sta-tions remained autonomous in terms of local productions, program selec-tions, and business arrangements with independent producers. Univision completely transformed Puerto Rico's commercial television environment. After buying WLII-TV, Univision executives fired most of the local manage-ment, brought people from the network to work at the station, and can-celed many of the locally produced programs.[49] Contrary to Telemundo–Puerto Rico and Televicentro, WLII-TV, now as one of Univision's affiliates, was going to rebroadcast most of the network shows.

Television professionals in Puerto Rico expressed diverse opinions about Univision's new dominance. One producer indicated that "we [Puerto Ri-cans] are a race in extinction," others categorized the situation as a "cycli-cal process," while some were surprised over the fact that Univision pro-grams that "are targeted to Mexicans" had good ratings on the island.[50] A final group questioned the validity of the audience survey, implying that Univision had purchased the survey and tampered with the results.[51] Regardless of the public outcry, the new television environment had an impact on Telemundo's locally produced programs. Some of the local shows were canceled while others, such as *Mi familia*, were rescheduled.[52] After being scheduled on the Saturday 8:30 P.M. time slot for six months, *Mi familia* was canceled in July 2003.

As I discussed throughout this chapter, it is evident that *Mi familia* was not the best show or even the most progressive program ever produced in Puerto Rico's commercial television. It is also clear that the situation comedy contained multiple problematic representations. In fact, some might be tempted to see *Mi familia* only as a further manifestation of the racial stereotypes and prejudice expressed through blackface. Still, *Mi familia* represented a black family, and that was revolutionary given the virtual absence of blacks in the history of the medium in Puerto Rico. Regardless of the fact that the Meléndez family was allegedly colorless, the audience was seeing a black Puerto Rican fictional family performed by black and mulatto mimetic actors on prime-time television. *Mi familia* created a possibility for other locally produced shows to open a space for more representations of blackness and the problematization of racism in Puerto Rico. However, based on current television trends in Puerto Rico's commercial television, those opportunities may be disappearing.

Black participation and, ultimately, the issue of black televisual visibility versus invisibility is complicated by local television's rapid submersion within the generic Hispanic market. The cultural deterritorialization that informs contemporary media globalization processes and televisual flows is having its impact on Puerto Rico.[53] And, as I mentioned in the introduction, Hispanic television is (at least as of 2004) synonymous with whiteness. Given that the majority of U.S. Hispanics consider themselves white (according to the 2000 Census, only 2.7 percent selected black as a racial categorization), should we worry about Eurocentrism and the rejections of blackness and brownness that informs Latin American and Spanish Caribbean cultures?[54] Are we going to question the white ideological normativity that characterizes the U.S. Spanish-language and Latin American televisual representations? Or will we instead continue to embrace (without question) the cultural and racial mestizajes and categorize these racial, social, historical, and cultural constructs as just hybrid, multicultural, and multiracial formations? These are just a few questions. I hope that other scholars, community activists, and media professionals will provide some answers.

In the meantime, black and mulatto Puerto Ricans, Dominicans, and Cubans (among others) who live in Puerto Rico might have to wait for the sporadic Brazilian telenovelas that are the few cultural artifacts exported from Latin America that depict some black performers. Maybe nonwhite audiences in Puerto Rico will begin to consume Black Entertainment Television (BET), Fox, and UPN. Although culturally and linguistically different, at least through the aforementioned U.S. television channels and networks, these marginal audiences and citizens will have the opportunity to see people who physically look more or less like them.

Coda

In early January 2004, I went to Puerto Rico for my annual holiday visit. The Christmas season is the time when I see my parents, family members, and some of my New York City and Puerto Rican theater friends and acquaintances. For me these *teatreros* (theater people) are another kind of family, one that, regardless of ideological differences and theater preferences, shares an inexplicable passion for doing and seeing theater.

While on the island, I met the secretary of *El colegio de actores de teatro de Puerto Rico* (the theater actors' guild), who informed me that the theater actors were joining members of *La Unión de Periodistas, Artes Gráficas y Ramas Anexas* (UPAGRA, the journalist and television technical staff union) in a protest against Univision. According to a Communication Workers of America (CWA) article, the one-day demonstration was organized to denounce the latest policy change Univision was attempting to make at its Puerto Rico station: "the use of the studio facilities for non-union production projects"[55] As one UPAGRA member indicated, this was "a step toward importing all programming and getting rid of UPAGRA altogether."[56] Simply put, the U.S. Spanish-language network Univision, which is an anti-union media corporation, wanted to implement its corporate policy in Puerto Rico and thus eliminate the only television professionals who are unionized. This was the beginning of what Marcelo Ballvé categorizes (in relation to Spanish-language networks in the United States) as the "maquiladora-style importation of programs from Latin America's big production houses."[57]

I should admit that I was hesitant about attending the demonstration. After all, how could one fight a U.S.-based conglomerate without any possible intervention from the local government? What is the purpose of denouncing the exploitation of media and television professionals when, for the FCC, the less powerful producers (i.e., the people who culturally "do" television and the individuals who work on the technical aspects of television) are presumably nonexistent? Why protest when, as Thomas Streeter writes, it is primarily the corporations and individuals who are granted licenses, own television stations, and have the lawyers and lobbyists that "*re-present* corporate interests" that are involved in the legally complex and "predefined role playing" of the FCC policy world?[58] Regardless of these discouraging realities and the likelihood that the FCC would once again ignore what the CWA has labeled as Univision's "unrelenting union-busting tactics,"[59] I decided to join the protest.

I contacted several theater friends to see if they were going to participate in the demonstration. Some of these friends had voice-overs scheduled for January 16 (the day of the rally) and so could not cancel the only (somewhat) steady and profitable job for actors and actresses in contemporary Puerto Rico. Others simply chose not to go. Although they thought that the protest was important, they were afraid that if Univision wanted to cast some local performers for a trans-Latin American telenovela or to hire any of them to host a Miami-based morning show or talk show, they could be blacklisted for being involved in a labor movement. Thus, I finally went with a teatrera from New York City who, like me, did not have anything to lose.

When we arrived in the mid-afternoon, there were approximately thirty to forty people walking in a circle in front of Univision's fence. Most of the actors from *el colegio de actores de teatro* who went to the protest had already left. The people participating in the demonstration were technical staff from the other local stations (Telemundo and Televicentro), the Commonwealth TV station (channel 6), and two journalists who joined their union colleagues. However, at least during the three hours that we walked in a circle, truck drivers and several journalists passed by waving and honking their car horns in an apparent show of solidarity. According to a *Newspaper Guild* report, UPAGRA members were joined by "the Union of Tronquistas, the Confederacy of Teachers, CWA, and the United Steel Workers."[60]

As I am writing these words, I still do not know what happened with Univision and the UPAGRA negotiations. UPAGRA's contract with Univision expired more than a year prior to January 16, 2004. I wonder if local media and television professionals will continue their fight against powerful Univision or any other media conglomerate that could affect their jobs. I also wonder if Puerto Rican audiences and consumers will demand more local representations of culture and as a result more job opportunities will materialize for the people who culturally "do" and work on television. Finally, I wonder if academics in Puerto Rico will engage in dialogues regarding the debacle that is unfolding in the island's commercial television. Truthfully, I do not have any answers. What I have are many questions and expectations.

Translating and Representing Blackness

In a September 2003 article entitled "Physical Diversity in Miss Puerto Rico Universe 2004," a journalist praised the local beauty pageant for including "diverse" women. According to the article, some women had the "ideal" physical characteristics for that kind of event: they were "tall, slim, had healthy hair and exotic features."[1] Two of the candidates were described in racial terms: one was "trigueña" and the other woman "looked more European [white, blond, and with green eyes] than Latina." The whiteness that informs Puerto Rico's Miss Universe and the fashion world was not directly addressed by the journalist. However, the use of the word *diversity* signals some type of recognition regarding gendered and racialized distinctions in Puerto Rico. Although sporadically discussed in the island's media outlets, it is evident that some members of the ethnic family (Puerto Ricans on the island and in the diaspora) are (and have been) aware of the racial hierarchies that characterize Puerto Rico's culture and society.

In Puerto Rico's commercial television, the black actors' and actresses' response to antiblack racism began to be expressed publicly during the early 1970s. During this same era some televisual cultural artifacts — directly and indirectly influenced by U.S. commercial television concepts — were designed to provide opportunities for black performers and to address the topic of individualized racial prejudice. In reference to *Mi familia*'s depiction of a black fictional family, one production member observed, "We are like monkeys. If the U.S. has a show with black people, then we have a show with blacks." Over the years, the locations of televisual blackness were somewhat transformed by the translation of television concepts, commercial ideas, and radical political rhetoric coming from or associated with U.S. media cultures and grassroots movements. The show *Soul Train*, the conceptualization of salsa music shows, a situation comedy entitled *Black Power*, and *Mi familia* hint at the televisual, social, political, economic, and cultural bridge that links Puerto Rico with the United States.

Even though there is an easily recognizable connection between the aforementioned cultural artifacts and the United States, some may question my linear analyses and claim that the televisual influences might have come from other parts of the world. Given that since its inception the medium has been located in an in-between cultural space between the United States and Latin America, I will simply ask two questions. First, in which part of Latin America were situation comedies addressing the problem of racial prejudice during the early 1970s? Second, how should one interpret the comments of *Mi familia*'s production members who noted that they were influenced by the commercial success of U.S. black-oriented situation comedies?

I am almost certain that the answer to the first query is "Nowhere." With the exception of Brazil, there has been a dearth of research in Latin American and the Spanish Caribbean televisual racial representations. Still, even in Brazil, the U.S. presence was palpable in the 1969 telenovela entitled *A cabana do Pai Tomás*, an adaptation of Harriet Beecher Stowe's *Uncle Tom's Cabin*.[2] If a Brazilianized and televisual *Uncle Tom's Cabin* had aired on TV Globo in the late 1960s, how can one question the potential U.S. impact on Puerto Rico's commercial television?

Arjun Appadurai contends that global cultural economies should be understood as "complex, overlapping, and disjunctive orders."[3] In the case of Puerto Rico, a U.S. Commonwealth whose economy, politics, and media structures directly and indirectly depend on the United States and that is "a nation on the move," a translocal, constantly in motion island-mainland community, the U.S. multiple influences are foreseeable.[4] That said, the main problem regarding Puerto Rico's televisual blackness was not the so-called imperialistic importation of U.S. concepts, ideas, cultures, and political discourses associated with black commodified cultures and grassroots movements. Rather, the key ideological issue was that the transformations of mediatized blackness were not products of local and massive sociopolitical mobilizations and protests against racism.

Indeed, this racialized adjustment provided opportunities for black performers and negotiable spaces for the representation of Afro Puerto Rican and Afro diasporic vernacular cultures. Furthermore, through the appropriation of cultural practices and politically distinct discourses associated with the civil rights and black power movements, black performers challenged the antiblack racism that characterized Puerto Rico's society and television. However, and as expected, local television and media depictions of blackness functioned as translations, and as such, they rearticulated "the interest of certain domestic constituencies over others."[5]

Lawrence Venuti argues that "translation never communicates in an untroubled fashion because the translator negotiates the linguistic and cultural differences of the foreign text by reducing them and supplying another set of cultural differences, basically domestic, drawn from the receiving language and culture to enable the foreign to be received."[6] In the case of Puerto Rico's commercial television translations of blackness, the social and class positions of blacks in both Puerto Rico and the Spanish Caribbean, and Afro Puerto Rican and Afro diasporic vernacular cultures were, in some cases, secondary or even irrelevant factors. The locally and discursively scripted scenarios that characterized Puerto Rico as a mestiza and racially equal nation in contrast to the United States (a fragmented and racist society) permeated some translations and interpretations of media blackness in Puerto Rico.

I situate performers, producers, and the television industry as the main translators of blackness on the local media stages. These translators played varying yet relevant roles in the selection of the text, concept, idea, cultural practice, or political mobilization and in the meanings inscribed in the translations. Additionally, the translators' interpretations resonated with what they considered ideologically, culturally, racially, politically, and commercially significant. Consequently, each translator created a media setting for the performativity of blackness. Either through "mimetic representation" (performing blackness via Caribbean, CubaRican, Cuban, jíbara, and accentless voices; blackface; or high levels of melanin in the body), by way of social actors ('black' performers trying to reclaim and reenact their own vision of 'blackness'), or by televisual conceptualizations (producers' and the television industry's demarcations of what kind of blackness should be televised), blackness became an unstable signifier.[7] As in all translations, the (in this case) literal and symbolic coloring inscribed in the texts, performances, and depictions was never definite. Journalists and audiences actively participated in the creation of meanings generating multiple and complex interpretations. Still, these various significations operated through Puerto Rico's racial ideologies, cultural discourses, and particular historical, social, political, and economic conditions.

For some translators la negritud served as a masquerade for political and social criticism. The translators' ethnicity and race were key discursive ele-

ments in the translating process. Regardless of the stereotypical representations, those translators who used lo negro as a mask for social criticism
and political satire and who were white members of the ethnic family were
widely received. The translators' popularity with audiences related to their
talent as performers, their satiric and political representations, and their use
of blackness as the voice of the working class. Whereas these translators challenged the island's political and class-based structures, they did not represent a threat to the racialized order. On the contrary: masking blackness reasserted the racial hierarchies in the CubaRican space and in Puerto Rico's
national imaginary. I would like to suggest that the majority of the audience accepted these translations not only because of the themes discussed
in the acts but also because the masking of blackness reaffirmed the alleged
whiteness within the mestiza nation. The audience was fully aware of the performances of blackness; therefore, the translator's whiteness (and ethnicity)
gave him or her the power to question the social, political, and class systems and even, in the case of Ramón Rivero, Puerto Rico's colonial-racial
hierarchical structures.

Donning blackface was complicated in that these depictions of blackness
became normalized media representations. Some translators used lo negro
to reproduce a performance associated with a generally known theatrical tradition (Cuban Bufo theater) while others continued with a highly successful characterization that was initiated in radio (the black voice Caribbean
maid characters). When some audience members or other translators (black
performers) criticized these representations, famous blackface actors from
a variety of historical moments and sociocultural locations became symbols for reasserting the validity of blackface. Because massive demonstrations
against blackface never took place in Puerto Rico, the majority of the audience and journalists accepted these translations of lo negro. Moreover, given
these local audiences' and journalists' apparent unawareness of the multiple
and historically specific U.S. media depictions of blacks and African Americans' political mobilizations, as well as Puerto Rican media's construction of
blackface as just another type of theatrical or media performance, the translators who donned blackface "hoped for" and actually obtained "consensus."[8]

A small group of translators (which, not coincidentally, comprised self-
identified black social and mimetic actors) positioned lo negro as an integral
part of their identities and tried — as much as it was culturally and televisually
possible — to challenge their marginality. Some of these translators appropri-

ated a foreign figure to disguise their criticism. For example, and as discussed in chapter 2, in 1975 the black actress Carmen Belén Richardson intended to use a fictional Angela Davis to question Puerto Rico's racist culture. Nonetheless, this character was too closely associated with a real and politically radical African American woman. In addition, one should consider that in the early 1970s, Richardson actively protested against antiblack racism both in television and in the society at large. Thus, reality and performance merged through her translation. Even though the character Angela Davis was created as a performative mask to question Puerto Rico's racial ideologies, the local Angela was caricatured. Therefore, the translators-performers' race, public personae, and characters saturated the ways in which audiences and journalists might have interpreted the translation of blackness.

Some of these translators' (black performers) appropriation of a political discourse associated with the United States (both the civil rights and black power movements) complicated the translating and interpreting processes. The political rhetoric used by these performers was not localized precisely because they wanted to interrogate Puerto Rico's cultural and racial hierarchies. As a result, the majority of the audiences, the industry, and journalists rejected both the translations and the translators. Protests against racism were read as imported ideological constructs that could destabilize the ethnic (island–territorial-based) family. The scripted, theatrical, and frozen-in-time scenarios wherein Puerto Rico was depicted as mestiza and racially equal and the United States was represented as segregationist and racist were fundamental discursive elements in the creation of meanings.

As mobilizations the black performers' protests were products of a particular sociohistorical moment wherein local and global alternative and grassroots movements confronted colonialism, imperialism, and racism. In the case of Puerto Rico, this "war of maneuver" remained part of cultural and academic circles without transforming local institutions.[9] I am not implying that these diverse sites of resistance were insignificant. In reality, they created multiple and contested terrains that confronted dominant racial, gender, and sexual ideological discourses. What I am trying to foreground is that these alternative movements did not transform Puerto Rico's racialized and cultural "order."[10] In the case of the island's commercial television, whereas the black performers' protests generated spaces for black actors and actresses in local telenovelas, the racialized constructions remained essentially the same: the black actresses performed the maid characters who were once embodied by white actresses in blackface. Alas, blackness remained fixated on a particular mode of representation.

For the most powerful translators (producers and the television industry), lo negro primarily signified profits. Obviously, the translators and performers who donned blackface or the black actors and actresses who played television roles were also influenced by the commercial aspect of their performances. However, the difference between these groups was power. Although some self-identified black performers and translators tried to incorporate their own vision of blackness into the creative process, their lack of power in the field of television production restricted their representations. Those who did not conform to the producers' or industry's vision were marginalized from the televisual space. Others, although fully conscious of Puerto Rico's racist practices, remained silent.

With the exception of two actors-producers who performed in blackface, the producers' and industry's translations operated through a mediatized distance between their conceptualization of lo negro and the televisual representations. In other words, the audience consumed a particular product (character or show) without being fully aware of who was in charge of the cultural creation. For example, audiences watched the self-identified black actor Otilio Warrington performing the character Arcadio in the situation comedy *Mi familia* and perhaps believed that the actor had control of the televisual construction and representation of blackness. Audiences and journalists might not have realized that, in most cases, the black performers did not have any power in the televisual translations of lo negro. The producers and industry translators selected the cultural artifact, designed the ways in which blackness was going to be constructed, and determined which performances of blackness were going to be allocated within the televisual space. In sum, the producers' and industry's translations shaped the locations of televisual blackness.

With the exception of telenovelas, some U.S. commercial television genres were modified to accommodate Puerto Rico's popular cultures and particular sociocultural conditions (i.e., variety shows, music shows, and situation comedies). After the Cuban Revolution and the disruptions of the anastomosis flows between Puerto Rico and Cuba, the U.S. media functioned as a resource for selecting a particular black representation, product, or concept. As a matter of fact, translations of blackness associated with the United States had been done since 1955. As I discussed in chapter 1, the character Lirio

Blanco was a version of the U.S. pickaninny stereotype. Furthermore, since the beginning of commercial television, the variety show had been a space for representing black musicians (together with the blackface negrito characters). However, beginning in the early 1970s, and as a result of the inclusion of blackness in U.S. commercial television, the producers and industry translators saw the United States as a testing ground for the marketability of lo negro in Puerto Rico's television.

For the most part, variety and music shows became the principal stages wherein Afro Puerto Rican and Afro diasporic vernacular cultures were represented (for example, salsa, merengue, some sporadic performances of Bomba and Plena music and dances, and poesía negroide). Any commercially successful musical performer, band, or musical style was granted a place on television. It is precisely through these televisual locations that the nation was constructed as mestiza and, to a certain extent, racially equal. Popular black and mulatto musicians *always* had a space on television and they could even sing, for example, about the oppressive condition of being black. However, it was one thing to sing about racial subjugation on television and quite another to take a direct verbal and confrontational stance that attacked television's racist culture. While these representations created negotiable spaces for the articulation of marginalized class, racial, gender, and Afro diasporic identities, they were predominantly restricted to specific television scenes. The televisual flow of images (including television commercials) depicted the locality of the inadvertently multiracial variety and music shows. The producers' and the industry's translations delimited the inclusion of racialized citizens and performers, relegating them into particular television genres.

As a result of the producers' and industry's translations of some U.S. television concepts, a few black actors and actresses were able to enter Puerto Rico's commercial television and media cultures. The few black performers who became part of the televisual space continued to work (sporadically) on television. Nonetheless, because the majority of the audience and journalists did not request more portrayals of blackness or the problematization of race in Puerto Rico, the black performers ultimately and indirectly depended on the U.S. media cultures or the producers' and industry's interest to initiate the translation of a commercially fresh product wherein blackness could possibly be depicted.

In the case of U.S. black-oriented television programs, the producers and industry translators carefully selected the televisual concept or idea for translation. For instance, whereas *Mi familia* generated cultural, racial, class, and political discursive significations completely different from those of *The Jeffersons* and *The Cosby Show*, the producers and industry translators nonetheless appropriated the idea from black situation comedies that depicted upwardly mobile African American families. In other words, 1970s U.S. black comedies such as *Good Times* and *What's Happening!!*, which constructed life in the ghetto but which also recreated "racial solidarity" among blacks, were apparently not cultural artifacts that the producers and industry desired to translate.[11] These shows had the potential to disrupt the familial and racialized order by articulating class stratification based on race or black cultural and political connections. Even in translation, U.S. black-oriented concepts or programs could destabilize television's (and the nation's) hegemonic racial stability. I would argue that this is precisely why the producers and industry translators constantly reestablished whiteness through the ideology of mestizaje ingrained in la gran familia puertorriqueña discourse. Thus, *Mi familia* was a Puerto Rican nonracial family; the glocal *Soul Train* included a blonde, white woman at the center of the show; and *Black Power* positioned class, not race, as the key element for social mobility in Puerto Rico. The performances of lo negro were always enclosed in whiteness.

It should be clear that I am not characterizing black television performers as the only translators who were (or have been) aware of Puerto Rico's racialized ideologies. That would be a ridiculous overgeneralization. Although the levels of melanin in the skin are not an indication of racial consciousness, the black performers' marginality in both television and society might have accounted for their protests against racism. As Michael Hanchard notes, racial consciousness is "the dialectical result of antagonism between two or more groups defined as races in a given society. . . . It represents the thought and practice of those individuals and groups who respond to their subordination with individual or collective action designed to counterbalance, transpose or transform situations of racial asymmetry."[12] Negros/as, blancos/as, and trigueños/as media professionals might have been sensitive to the racist casting practices that permeated the medium. However, at least in local media outlets, nonwhite performers were the ones who publicly voiced their opinions against blackface and criticized the limited opportunities for black people on television.

Antiblack racism has been a complex issue in Puerto Rican society, television, and media cultures. Nonetheless, as demonstrated by the analyses presented in the previous chapters, it is evident that the island's commercial entertainment programming (and media cultures in general) created diverse "cultural forums" wherein some of the island's political, economic, cultural, and even racial conditions were discussed.[13] The cultural artifacts and dialogues examined in this research presented some important themes that circulated in Puerto Rico's public spheres from the late 1940s to the 1990s. The U.S. colonial control and presence on the island, local political debates, the migrations of Cubans and Dominicans, and the conflicts within the Cuban diaspora were some of the issues presented in the media's (radio and television) fictionalized narratives. These mediated narrations re-articulated and re-negotiated various national realities across historical periods.

Each cultural creator with power in the field of radio and television production incorporated his or her own vision of particular social, cultural, political, and ethnic conflicts in the respective media texts. Media creators in Puerto Rico were not marionettes of the United States and the local Commonwealth government (as some scholars have led us to believe), but, rather, they were individuals who, through their creative artifacts, provided spaces for discussions regarding a multiplicity of local issues that they *personally considered relevant*. In some ways, these creative positions reflected the political, cultural, and social ideologies of those behind the conceptualization and creation of media artifacts. Simply put, there were ideological differences among Ramón Rivero's (writer and producer) *El tremendo hotel*, Manuel Montero "Membrillo" (writer) and Elín Ortíz's (producer) *Los suegros*, and Felipe San Pedro (writer) and Paquito Cordero's (producer) *Mi familia*, not only because of these cultural products' location in time but, more important, because these creative people were totally distinct individuals. This is precisely why it is imperative to examine the encoding processes, creators, and texts when examining television in particular and media cultures in general. If one only accounts for the political, legal, and economic aspects of media cultures, individual agency is simply removed. In the case of Puerto Rico, and based on the island's colonial status, everything produced locally would then be categorized only as an example of U.S. cultural and media imperialism.

Not only did entertainment programming in Puerto Rico generate "dense, rich, and complex" spaces but, in most cases, diverse individuals, groups, and communities actively engaged in dialogues about fictionalized narratives, characters, and performers.[14] One can see this dynamic participation in, for example, the audiences' selection of the fictional character Calderón (in *El tremendo hotel*) as the mayor of the fictional town Mirafanguito, the debates favoring and opposing Lucecita's Afro, and the Cuban right-wing protests against *Los suegros* and *Los suegros y los nietos*. Audiences, as social actors, produced diverse meanings and voiced their complex and sometimes contradictory opinions either by sending letters, calling a production company, standing outside a television station, or by using their own media outlets to express their points of view.

That said, one is compelled to ask, what happens when the entire televisual world represents a sociopolitical, cultural, and ethnic landscape that has no connection with the local? What are the repercussions of having "communicative spaces" that do not address national debates?[15] When the local ceases to exist and the performances of cultures have no resemblance to the struggles that comprise the national, multifarious quandaries arise. When there are no laws to restrain the importation of programs and when media professionals are at the mercy of global economic and media flows, one faces a catch-22 situation. This is precisely the future of Puerto Rico's commercial television. This is also one of the (numerous) problems of being a colony: not having any control over the island's communication systems.

Epilogue: Miss Universe Puerto Rico 2004

On the morning of October 4, 2003, I logged on to the Internet for my daily reading of Puerto Rican newspapers. Alongside the seemingly quotidian stories about increases in unemployment, crime, and debates among local politicians regarding the next elections, one subheading and photo captured my immediate attention. Twenty-eight years after the hand-picked selection of Wilnelia Merced to represent the island in the Miss World pageant, a group of connoisseurs of beauty and fashion had awarded the Miss Universe Puerto Rico crown to a twenty-two-year-old, six-foot-tall, slim, working-class, and (self-described) trigueña woman named Alba Reyes. Considering the ways in which Wilnelia Merced had been represented in local newspapers and magazines in 1975, I was curious to see how the local media and Miss Universe fans would describe this newly elected "Puerto Rican beauty."[16] As expected, Reyes's nonwhiteness became the focus of attention. However, instead of blaming the sun for Reyes's dark skin (as one journalist did when referring to Wilnelia Merced), journalists and some beauty contestant followers celebrated the election of what they categorized racially as a trigueña, morena, and black woman.

"Tall, morena, and beautiful," "racially different from other Miss Puerto Rico queens," and "a great break from the norm" were some of the comments expressed by local journalists.[17] In reference to her nonwhiteness as an impediment to winning the contest, Alba Reyes stated that "[the color of her skin] gave me more drive because I always wanted to be the first trigueña to win Miss Puerto Rico."[18] On the other hand, on the Miss Puerto Rico official Web page, the *missiologos/as* (a label adopted by beauty pageant fans in Puerto Rico) discussed and debated the selection of a nonwhite woman. Some fans, without elaborating on their aesthetic judgment, declared that Alba Reyes was not "astonishingly beautiful" and one fan even described Reyes as "very ugly." However, other missiologos/as voiced satisfaction over the choice of a "trigueña candidate," a woman who "represents the diversity of beauties that are part of the culture."[19] The cultural nationalism that informs Puerto Rico also saturates the Miss Universe Puerto Rico. Therefore, although some fans did not believe Alba Reyes deserved to be crowned, many of them nonetheless chose to support the new queen because Alba Reyes was, first and foremost, a Puerto Rican woman. Through the election of a trigueña/morena/black woman, gendered blackness seemed to be located inside the national space.

How can one understand this representation of national beauty in the global arena? Maybe Puerto Rico, influenced by what Stuart Hall categorizes as the "global fascination with ethnic and racial difference," has decided to embrace (partially) and accept the black element that for centuries has been hidden in the closet.[20] Or perhaps the local beauty and fashion worlds are being permeated by what Gilberto Blasini and L. S. Kim categorize as the "new Exotic-American identity," wherein American (U.S.) beauty "downplays certain traits of traditional Eurocentric body aesthetics while not erasing whiteness completely."[21] More important, in the United States, and indeed in the global media market, there has been a recent "Latin explosion" wherein some Puerto Ricans (for example, Jennifer López, Ricky Martín, and Mark Anthony) have played a pivotal role in the commodification of *latinidad*.[22] Within these mediated representations, Latinas in general and Jennifer López (and her butt) in particular have been constructed as both sexual and beautiful female bodies.[23] Consequently, given that in Puerto Rico black and particularly mulata women have always been considered sensual and hypersexual bodies, the translation of the U.S. "aestheticization of multiculturalism" (as with other cultural practices) would probably operate through the ideology of mestizaje.[24] In other words, the U.S. "aestheticization of multi-culturalism" and the "new Exotic-American identity" would not really alter Puerto Rico's mestizaje and its racial and cultural hierarchies. What might occur is that U.S. contemporary popular culture's alleged aesthetic attraction to racial Otherness will open momentary spaces of inclusion for the non-whites who are already part of the mestiza ethnic family.

It is too soon to speculate about the repercussions of the 2003 election of a Puerto Rican trigueña as a symbol of national beauty. Still, one should keep in mind the transitory late 1960s and early 1970s construction of black women as *exotic chic* and its partial impact in Puerto Rico. One should also take into account that in the 2000 Census only 10.8 percent of the population on the island categorized themselves as black. Equally important, one should consider the popularity of plastic surgery in today's beauty culture market. Thus, while Paul Gilroy urges us to transcend race and embrace a "planetary humanism," I firmly believe that, as Howard Winant argues, "racism must be identified by its consequences."[25] And it is precisely through the pervasive repercussions of antiblack racism and through what Fanon calls the problem of the black body presence (to which I add, the Eurocentric, patriarchal, and colonizing dilemma of the black female body presence) that beautiful Alba Reyes was apparently required to transform (make invisible) body parts that, at least in Puerto Rico (and in the Spanish Caribbean), are associated with blackness.[26]

In a February 25, 2004 article, a journalist explained to the public that Alba Reyes underwent ambulatory surgical procedures to eliminate "two facial scars" and the "age lines" around her mouth.[27] After reading this article, I visited the Miss Puerto Rico Web page to see if the missiologos/as had dis-cussed Reyes's plastic surgery. According to the Miss Puerto Rico fans, Alba Reyes was "nowhere to be found." Whereas there were some sporadic stories about Reyes in local newspapers, the articles no longer included photos of the 2004 Miss Universe candidate. The missiologos/as speculated that Reyes was out of the public eye because she underwent a plastic surgery operation to "improve" what some categorized as her "ugly nose."[28] Although some missiologos/as were appalled about Reyes's possible rhinoplasty and catego-rized the surgical procedure as a direct rejection of Puerto Rican blackness, others expressed that, in order to have an actual chance at the 2004 con-test, Reyes had to change her nose "to look more beautiful."[29] Although I was never able to confirm the allegations of the missiologos/as, there were rumors that Reyes had three plastic surgery operations: rhinoplasty, liposuction to diminish her voluptuous buttocks, and breast implants to enhance her flat chest.

Thus, should one applaud the selection of a trigueña/morena/black woman as local journalists did? Is Alba Reyes a "great break from the norm" as a journalist claimed? Or is she being surgically constructed into the norm? Besides the brown tone of her skin, which is nearly impossible to whiten, Alba Reyes's body was apparently rebuilt to accommodate European and Western ideologies of female beauty. The once common television practice of cosmetic whitening, which through the use of wigs and a light makeup foundation camouflaged the "flaws" of racial mestizaje, has the potential to become a recurrent and permanent whitening process. The Eurocentrism that has informed Puerto Rico's culture and the local and global beauty worlds has not diminished. Instead, the local beauty contest has been influenced by the recent U.S. and European beauty market infatuation with a touch of racial otherness.[30]

In both the local and global arenas, problematic manifestations of race and blackness still persist. While in Puerto Rico the translations of commodified cultures have introduced (in some instances) negotiating spaces and opportunities for the marginal Others, we should situate them within the context of the racial stratifications that comprise the national. As long as the scenarios of mestizaje and racial fairness continue to be represented on the national stage, mediated blackness will function as theatrical scenes to maintain the illusion of racial equality submerged in la gran familia puertorriqueña discourse.

Notes

INTRODUCTION

1 *Mi familia* production member, interview by the author, July 1997. All of the Spanish to English translations of newspaper and magazine articles, scripts, and interviews were done by the author. Some of the information presented in this book comes from personal and phone interviews with Puerto Rican and Cuban media professionals, family members of specific performers or scriptwriters, technical staff, and other creative people. At times, I exclude the names and professional affiliations of the interviewees, especially when dealing with the delicate topic of racism.

2 Hilario de León, "Buscan revivir personaje de Diplo," *El Nuevo Día*, January 17, 2000.

3 In 1954 two commercial stations began broadcasting in Puerto Rico: Telemundo WKAQ-TV (channel 2) and WAPA-TV (channel 4). WKAQ-Telemundo was owned by Puerto Rican entrepreneur Angel Ramos and WAPA-TV was under the ownership of Puerto Rican businessman Ramón Quiñones. Toward the end of the 1950s and the beginning of the 1960s, three stations began operations on the island: WRIK (channel 7), WIPR (channel 6, the Commonwealth television station), and WKMB (channel 11). WIPR was the first educational station in Puerto Rico and in Latin America. For more information on Puerto Rican television ownership changes, see Rodolfo B. Popelnik, "Puerto Rico," in *Encyclopedia of Television*, ed. Horace Newcomb (Chicago: Fitzroy Dearborn Publishers, 1997), 1319–21. For information on the beginnings of Puerto Rico's commercial television, see the newspaper articles, "Al llegar la televisión necesitará más asientos," *El Mundo*, March 26, 1954; "El auge de la televisión sigue en marcha," *El Mundo*, November 15, 1954; "La WKAQ-TV sigue los pasos de la WKAQ," *El Mundo*, March 26, 1954; "WKAQ comenzará transmisiones," *El Mundo*, February 12, 1954; and "WAPA-TV inauguró sus transmisiones," *El Mundo*, May 3, 1954.

4 América Rodríguez, "Creating an Audience and Remapping a Nation: A Brief History of U.S. Spanish Language Broadcasting," *Quarterly Review of Film and Television* 16, nos. 3–4 (1999): 357–75; John Sinclair, *Latin American Television: A Global View* (Oxford: Oxford University Press, 1999); John Sinclair, "From Latin Americans to Latinos: Spanish-Language Television and Its Audiences" (paper presented at the Cultural Industries and Dialogue Between Civilizations in the Americas, Montreal, Canada, April 2002); and Federico Subervi-Vélez, Charles Ramírez-Berg, Patricia Constantakis-Valdés, Chon Noriega, Diana Ríos, and Kenton T. Wilkinson, "Mass Communication and Hispanics," in *Handbook of Hispanic Cultures in the United States: Sociology*, ed. Félix Padilla (Houston: Arte Público Press, 1994), 304–57.

5 Some of the limited research on Puerto Rican television has focused on the U.S.

influence and control of the island's media outlets and the importation of the American model of commercial television. For example, Federico Suber/ vi-Vélez, Nitza Hernández-López, and Arlene Frambes-Buxeda characterize Puerto Rican television as "an excellent promoter for American products" and as a medium that "has depended on U.S. technology." These scholars primarily target television's economic, legal, and technological aspects, indirectly and directly situating the island's medium as another site of U.S. imperialistic control. On the other hand, Eliseo Colón-Zayas and Arlene Dávila examine locally produced comedies. Colón-Zayas explores *Sunshine's Café* and *No te duermas*, and Dávila analyzes *El kiosko Budweiser*, each paying special attention to the ways in which vernacular and national cultural elements, politics, and satire were incorporated into these televisual texts. Roberta Astroff, "Communication and Contemporary Colonialism: Broadcast Television in Puerto Rico," *Studies in Latin American Popular Culture*, no. XI (1987): 11–24; Eliseo Colón-Zayas, "La hora del cuerpo: recepción y consumo de la comedia en Puerto Rico," *Diá·logos*, no. 30 (1991): 65–75; Arlene Dávila, "El Kiosko Budweiser: The Making of a 'National' Television Show in Puerto Rico," *American Ethnologist* 25, no. 3 (1998): 452–71; and Federico Suber/ vi-Vélez, Nitza Hernández-López, and Arlene Frambes-Buxeda, "Mass Media in Puerto Rico," *Centro* 3, no. 1 (winter, 1990–1991): 16–37.

6 Astroff, "Communication and Contemporary Colonialism," 22.

7 Horace Newcomb and Paul Hirsch, "Television as a Cultural Forum," in *Television: The Critical View*, 5th ed., ed. Horace Newcomb (Oxford: Oxford University Press, 1994), 503–15.

8 I would like to point out that in her essay on telenovelas Ana López positions Puerto Rico as part of the Latin American and Spanish Caribbean television cultural environments. See Ana López, "Our Welcomed Guests: Telenovelas in Latin America," in *To Be Continued: Soap Operas around the World*, ed. Robert Allen (London: Routledge, 1995), 256–75.

9 Diana Taylor, *The Archive and the Repertoire: Performing Cultural Memory in the Americas* (Durham, N.C.: Duke University Press, 2003), 2.

10 See Jorge Duany, *The Puerto Rican Nation on the Move: Identities on the Island and in the United States* (Chapel Hill: University of North Carolina Press, 2002); and Nancy Morris, *Puerto Rico: Culture, Politics, and Identity* (Westport, Conn.: Praeger, 1995).

11 On the island, the Mediafax Company offers television audience measurements for a fee. Every four weeks, Mediafax provides advertising agencies and television stations with a statistical sample of TV households based on an average of 405 metered households that are equipped with approximately 660 TV set meters. The viewing audiences' shares and ratings include local commercial television channels, PBS (Puerto Rico's government-run television station), and Cable TV Operators. Audiences are categorized by age group and gender and include children (2–11), teens (12–17), men

and women (18+). Popelnik, "Puerto Rico," 1320; *TV Audience Measurements, Puerto Rico* (San Juan, Puerto Rico: Mediafax, 1999); and Telemundo-Puerto Rico media professional, interview by the author, July 1997. Due to copyright laws, I cannot include Mediafax numbers.

12 Milly Buonanno, "The Paradigm of Indigenization: Television between Global Supply and Local Consumption" (paper presented at the Radio-Television-Film Department, University of Texas, Austin, February 1998), 4. See also Milly Buonanno, *El drama televisivo: Identidad y contenidos sociales* (Barcelona, Spain: Gedisa, 1999).

13 It should be noted that since 1999 satellite television (DIRECTV-Puerto Rico, a subsidiary of DIRECTV Latin America) has been part of the local market. Although the company asserts that it has 130,000 clients on the island, there is still no actual data regarding local audiences' consumption of DIRECTV. Rodolfo Popelnik, "Television in Puerto Rico," in *Encyclopedia of Television*, 2d ed., ed. Horace Newcomb (Chicago: Fitzroy Dearborn Publishers, 2004), 1858–62. For information on the consumption of local and U.S. English-language programming, see Eliut D. Flores-Caraballo, "The Politics of Culture in Puerto Rican Television: A Macro/Micro Study of English vs. Spanish Language Television" (Ph.D. diss., University of Texas, 1991).

14 Joseph D. Straubhaar, "Beyond Media Imperialism: Assymetrical Interdependence and Cultural Proximity," *Critical Studies in Mass Communication* 8 (1991): 39–59; Joseph D. Straubhaar, "Cultural Capital, Media Choices, and Cultural Proximity in the Globalization of Television in Brazil" (paper presented at the Latin American Studies Association Conference, Chicago, 1998).

15 Elizabeth Fox and Silvio Waisbord, "Latin Politics, Global Media," in *Latin Politics, Global Media*, ed. Elizabeth Fox and Silvio Waisbord (Austin: University of Texas Press, 2002), 19.

16 For information on globalization processes and exportations of programs in Latin America, see John Sinclair, "The Globalization of Latin American Media," *NACLA*, March/April 2004, 1–6.

17 Thomas Streeter, *Selling the Air: A Critique of the Policy of Commercial Broadcasting in the United States* (Chicago: University of Chicago Press, 1996).

18 It should be clear that from 1970 to 1979 WRIK-TV was owned by United Artists. In 1979 Puerto Rican producer, writer, and actor Tommy Muñiz bought the station. Popelnik, "Puerto Rico," 1320.

19 Telemundo executives, interviews by the author, July 1997.

20 Other minor commercial stations are WPRV-TV (channel 13); WSJU-TV (channel 18); WSJN-TV (channel 24); and WRWR-TV (channel 30). Popelnik, "Television in Puerto Rico."

21 For an excellent analysis of the U.S. Hispanic market and the Mexican cultural dominance in U.S. Spanish-language television, see Arlene Dávila, *Latinos, Inc.: The Marketing and Making of a People* (Berkeley: University of California Press, 2001). See

also John Sinclair, " 'The Hollywood of Latin America': Miami as Regional Center in Television Trade," *Television and New Media* 4, no. 3 (2003): 211–29.

22 Sinclair, " 'The Hollywood,' " 221.

23 Ibid.

24 See Claudia Hernández and Andrew Paxman, *El Tigre: Emilio Azcárraga y su imperio Televisa* (Mexico City: Grijalbo, 2000); and Dávila, *Latinos, Inc.*

25 Paulo Freire, *Pedagogy of the Oppressed*, trans. Myra Bergman Ramos, rev. ed. (New York: Continuum, 1993).

26 Stuart Hall, "The Whites of Their Eyes: Racist Ideologies and the Media," in *Silver Linings: Some Strategies for the Eighties: Contributions to the Communist University of London*, ed. George Bridges and Rosalind Brunt (London: Lawrence and Wishart, 1981), 28–52.

27 Duany, *The Puerto Rican Nation*, 4.

28 Morris, *Puerto Rico*, 12.

29 Duany, *The Puerto Rican Nation*; Juan Flores, *From Bomba to Hip-Hop: Puerto Rican Culture and Latino Identity* (New York: Columbia University Press, 2000); Morris, *Puerto Rico*; and Ana Yolanda Ramos-Zayas, *National Performances: The Politics of Class, Race, and Space in Puerto Rican Chicago* (Chicago: University of Chicago Press, 2003).

30 Duany, *The Puerto Rican Nation*, 4.

31 For a holistic analysis of cultural nationalism in Puerto Rico, see Arlene Dávila, *Sponsored Identities: Cultural Politics in Puerto Rico* (Philadelphia: Temple University Press, 1997); Duany, *The Puerto Rican Nation*; and Ramos-Zayas, *National Performances*. For information on current debates regarding cultural nationalism, see Ramón Grosfoguel, "The Divorce of Nationalist Discourses from the Puerto Rican People: A Sociohistorical Perspective," in *Puerto Rican Jam: Essays on Culture and Politics*, ed. Frances Negrón-Muntaner and Ramón Grosfoguel (Minneapolis: University of Minnesota Press, 1997), 39–56; and Luis Felipe Díaz and Marc Zimmerman, eds., *Globalización, nación, postmodernidad: estudios culturales puertorriqueños* (San Juan, Puerto Rico: Ediciones LACASA, 2001).

32 See Frances Aparicio, *Listening to Salsa: Gender, Latin Popular Music, and Puerto Rican Cultures* (London: Wesleyan University Press, 1998); Dávila, *Sponsored Identities*; Lillian Guerra, *Popular Expression and National Identity in Puerto Rico: The Struggle for Self, Community, and Nation* (Gainesville: University of Florida Press, 1998); and Angel Quintero-Rivera, *Patricios y plebeyos: Burgueses, hacendados, artesanos y obreros: Las relaciones de clase en el Puerto Rico de cambio de siglo* (Río Piedras, Puerto Rico: Huracán, 1988).

33 Arcadio Díaz-Quiñones, "Tomás Blanco: racismo, historia, esclavitud," in *El prejuicio racial en Puerto Rico*, ed. Arcadio Díaz-Quiñones (Río Piedras, Puerto Rico: Huracán, 1985), 48.

34 See Juan G. Gelpi, *Literatura y paternalismo en Puerto Rico* (Río Piedras, Puerto Rico: Editorial de la Universidad de Puerto Rico, 1993); and Miriam Jiménez-Román, "Un Hombre (Negro) Del Pueblo: José Celso Barbosa and the Puerto Rican 'Race' toward Whiteness," *Centro* 8, nos. 1 and 2 (1996): 8–29.

35 Tomás Blanco, *El prejuicio racial en Puerto Rico*, ed. Arcadio Díaz-Quiñones (Río Piedras, Puerto Rico: Huracán, 1985).

36 There are ongoing debates about these intellectuals' celebration of *negritud*, primarily because of their poetry's objectification of the racial and female Other and the embedded sexism of the literary production. For more information about the 1930s intellectual debate and literary movement, see Aparicio, *Listening to Salsa*; Guerra, *Popular Expression*; Juan Guisti-Cordero, "Afropuerto Rican Cultural Studies: Beyond Cultural Negroide and Antillanismo," *Centro* 8, nos. 1 and 2 (1996): 56–77; and Vera M. Kutzinski, *Sugar's Secrets: Race and the Erotics of Cuban Nationalism* (Charlottesville: University Press of Virginia, 1993).

37 Peter Wade, *Race and Ethnicity in Latin America* (Chicago: Pluto Press, 1997).

38 Winston James, *Holding Aloft the Banner of Ethiopia: Caribbean Radicalism in Early Twentieth-Century America* (London: Verso, 1998).

39 See Edmund T. Gordon, *Disparate Diasporas: Identity and Politics in an African Nicaraguan Community* (Austin: University of Texas Press, 1998); France Winddance Twine, *Racism in a Racial Democracy: The Maintenance of White Supremacy in Brazil* (New Brunswick, N.J.: Rutgers University Press, 1998); and Peter Wade, "Race and Class: The Case of South American Blacks," *Ethnic and Racial Studies* 8, no. 2 (1985): 233–49.

40 Ella Shohat and Robert Stam, *Unthinking Eurocentrism: Multiculturalism and the Media* (London: Routledge, 1994), 322. See for example the constructions of gendered beauty and ugliness in the Colombian telenovela *Yo soy Betty la fea*. Yeidy Rivero, "The Performance and Reception of Televisual Ugliness in *Yo Soy Betty La Fea*," *Feminist Media Studies* 3, no. 1 (2003): 65–81.

41 Aparicio, *Listening to Salsa*; Blanco, *El prejuicio racial*; and Kutzinski, *Sugar's Secrets*.

42 *Bomba* and *Plena* are musical styles that originated in the island's coastal regions and in sugar plantation areas with large African populations. These styles, which became popular in Puerto Rico during the 1930s, combine African and European musical elements. Aparicio, *Listening to Salsa*, 27–44.

43 See Guerra, *Popular Expression*; and Dávila, *Sponsored Identities*.

44 Ramón Grosfoguel and Chloé S. Georas, "Latino Caribbean Diasporas in New York," in *Mambo Montage: The Latinization of New York*, ed. Agustín Laó-Montes and Arlene Dávila (New York: Columbia University Press, 2001), 97–118; Michael Omi and Howard Winant, *Racial Formation in the United States: From the 1960s to the 1990s* (London: Routledge, 1994); and Howard Winant, *Racial Conditions: Politics, Theory, Comparisons* (Minneapolis: University of Minnesota Press, 1994).

45 See Jorge Duany, "Caribbean Migration to Puerto Rico: A Comparison of Cubans and Dominicans," *International Migration Review* 26, no. 1 (1992): 46–66; Jorge Duany, "Reconstructing Racial Identity: Ethnicity, Color, and Class among Dominicans in the United States and Puerto Rico," *Latin American Perspectives* 25, no. 100 (1998): 147–72; and Duany, *The Puerto Rican Nation*. See also Yolanda Martínez-San Miguel, *Caribe Two Ways: Cultura de la migración en el Caribe insular hispánico* (San Juan, Puerto Rico: Ediciones Callejón, 2003), 151–200.

46 Mayra Santos-Febres, "Por cientos contranatura," *El Nuevo Día*, May 6, 2001. Similar results in terms of racial identification were obtained from a survey conducted in Puerto Rico between 1956 and 1957. When the respondents were asked what was the "best color to have," approximately 1 percent responded, "black." However, 76 percent stated that people, regardless of their skin color, would have the same opportunities. Michael Banton, *Ethnic and Racial Consciousness* (New York: Longman, 1997), 58–59.

47 Mayra Montero, "Suizos," *El Nuevo Día*, May 6, 2001.

48 Banton, *Ethnic*; Duany, "Reconstructing Racial Identity"; and Wade, *Race and Ethnicity*.

49 Isabelo Zenón-Cruz, *Narciso descubre su trasero* (Humacao, Puerto Rico: Furidi, 1975), 250. The origin of *negro* as a negative connotation is related to the institution of racial slavery. The term *colored people* was originally used during the Spanish colonial period to show courtesy and warmth to black and mulatto individuals. See Manuel Alvarez-Nazario, *El elemento afronegroide en el español de Puerto Rico* (San Juan, Puerto Rico: Instituto de Cultura Puertorriqueño, 1974).

50 Samuel Betances, "The Prejudice of Having No Prejudice in Puerto Rico, Part I," *The Rican*, no. 2 (1972): 41–54; Samuel Betances, "The Prejudice of Having No Prejudice in Puerto Rico, Part II," *The Rican*, no. 3 (1973): 22–37; "El prejuicio racial en el lenguaje popular," *El Nuevo Día*, October 8, 2000; Melba Ferrer, "Emancipation Fails to Abolish Racism," *San Juan Star*, March 22, 1997; Pepo García, "Alerta contra el discrimen racial," *El Nuevo Día*, January 17, 2000; Eugenio García-Cuevas, "Opinan los letrados," *El Nuevo Día*, October 8, 2000; Jorge López-Llano, "Hay discrimen en el hablar," *El Reportero*, June 16, 1982; López-Llano, "Racismo a todos los niveles," *El Reportero*, June 17, 1982; López-Llano, "Doloroso discrimen en novelas," *El Reportero*, July 2, 1982; Patricia Reyes-Vargas, "Estudiantes denuncian racismo en la UPR," *El Imparcial*, March 29, 1965; Ernesto Manuel Rivera, "Sin estadísticas para medir el discrimen racial," *El Nuevo Día*, December 18, 2001; Francisco Rodríguez-Burns, "Afro que escondemos," *Primera Hora*, January 21, 2002; Eneid Routté-Gómez, "El Negro: El blanco del racismo," *El Nuevo Día*, October 13, 2000; Mario Santana, "Oculto en el clóset el prejuicio racial," *El Nuevo Día*, March 23, 1998; Mario Santana, "Racismo que se ve y se siente cada día," *El Nuevo Día*, March 24, 1998; and Jaime Torres-Torres, "¿Dónde está el negrito bembón?," *El Nuevo Día*, October 8, 2000.

51 Jiménez-Román, "Un Hombre (Negro)," 11.

52 James C. Scott defines the public transcript as a "shorthand way of describing the open interaction between subordinates and those who dominate." He adds, "in ideological terms the public transcript will typically, by its accommodationist tone, provide convincing evidence for the hegemony of dominant values, for the hegemony of dominant discourse." Scott, *Domination and the Arts of Resistance: Hidden Transcripts* (New Haven, Connecticut: Yale University Press, 1991), 2–4. I am using Diana Taylor's concept of "scenarios," which she describes as "meaning-making paradigms that structure social environments, behaviors, and potential outcomes." Taylor, *The Archive and the Repertoire*, 28.

53 Taylor, *The Archive and the Repertoire*; and Scott, *Domination*, 4–5.

54 Newcomb and Hirsch, "Television as a Cultural Forum."

55 For an excellent examination of Puerto Ricanness versus non–Puerto Ricanness see Morris, *Puerto Rico*. For a historical analysis of Puerto Rico's debates regarding the use of Spanish and English, see Frances Negrón-Muntaner, "English Only Jamás but Spanish Only Cuidado: Language and Nationalism in Contemporary Puerto Rico," in *Puerto Rican Jam*, 257–85.

56 Duany, *The Puerto Rican Nation*.

57 Ibid., 2.

58 Arjun Appadurai, "Disjuncture and Difference in the Global Cultural Economy," in *Global Culture: Nationalism, Globalization, and Modernity*, ed. by Mike Featherstone (London: Sage, 1990), 295–310. While culturally different, see the 1980s public debates regarding the importation of *Dynasty* in Norway. As Jostein Gripsrud contends, media imports and the controversies around them can actually illuminate people's participation and desire for multiple cultures, "realities," and political debates. Gripsrud, *The Dynasty Years: Hollywood Television and Critical Media Studies* (London: Routledge, 1995).

59 Nancy Morris, "The Myth of Unadulterated Culture Meets the Threat of Imported Media," *Media, Culture, and Society* 24, no. 2 (2002): 279.

60 José Luis González, *El país de cuatro pisos y otros ensayos* (Río Piedras, Puerto Rico: Huracán, 1980).

61 Cesar Salgado, "Cubarican: efectos de la capilaridad colonial" (paper presented at the Second Cuban Research Institute Conference on Cuban and Cuban-American Studies, Miami, Florida, 1999).

1. CARIBBEAN NEGRITOS

In this chapter I use the actor's artistic name (Ramón Rivero) instead of his real name (Ramón Ortíz del Rivero).

1 Black voice and blackface were also part of Cuba's radio and television before the 1959 Cuban Revolution. Since 1938, the comedy sketches of *Chicharito y Sopeira* included

a black voice character (Chicharito) and a Galician character (Sopeira). In 1950, with the arrival of television in Cuba, Alberto Garrido and Federico Piñeiro (the actors who performed the radio characters Chicharito and Sopeira) had their own prime-time show on CMQ-TV. Mayra Cue-Sierra, e-mail to author, March 2001. Although several articles and books address the theme of blackface in Cuba's Bufo comedy, there is no research regarding black voice and blackface in pre-revolutionary Cuban radio and television.

2 It should be noted that race represented a contested terrain during Cuba's fight for independence. For more information on race in pre- and post-independence Cuba and the development of Cuba's nationhood, see Darien Davis, "Criollo or Mulatto? Cultural Identity in Cuba, 1930–1960," in *Ethnicity, Race, and Nationalism in the Caribbean*, ed. Juan Manuel Carrión (Río Piedras, Puerto Rico: University of Puerto Rico, 1997), 69–96; Alejandro De la Fuente, *A Nation for All: Race, Inequality, and Politics in Twentieth-Century Cuba* (Chapel Hill: University of North Carolina Press, 2001); Ada Ferrer, *Insurgent Cuba: Race, Nation, and Revolution, 1868–1898* (Chapel Hill: University of North Carolina Press, 1999); Aline Helg, *Our Rightful Share: The Afro-Cuban Struggle for Equality, 1886–1912* (Chapel Hill: University of North Carolina Press, 1995); Pedro Pérez-Sarduy and Jean Stubbs, eds., *Afro-Cuban Voices: On Race and Identity in Contemporary Cuba* (Gainesville: University Press of Florida, 2000); and Curtis Stoke, "Race and Revolution in Cuba," *Race and Reason* 3 (1996–97): 55–61.

3 See "Y amigos, esta es mamá Dolores," *El Mundo*, July 26, 1949; "Mona Marti es negra Balbina en la novela Sierra Negra," *El Mundo*, July 16, 1950; El Barón De Cardi, "Mona Marti ejerce 'El derecho de nacer' de mamá Dolores," *El Mundo*, March 7, 1959; and "Todos tenemos algún color: Mona Martí," *Bohemia*, June 18–24, 1973, 43.

4 Nora Mazziotti, *La industria de la telenovela: La producción de ficción en América Latina* (Buenos Aires: Paidós, 1996), 30.

5 Although telenovela production began in Puerto Rico in 1958, there is no research on the history of this genre or the island's commercial television.

6 Mayra Cue-Sierra, "Nace la telenovela de continuidad en América Latina," *Cubarte*, September 19, 2003; María Inés Mendoza, "La telenovela venezolana: De artesanal a industrial," *Diá·logos*, no. 44 (1996): 23–42; Ana López, "Our Welcomed Guests"; Jesús Martín-Barbero, "Memory and Form in the Latin American Soap Opera," in *To Be Continued*, 276–84; Jesús Martín-Barbero and Sonia Muñoz, eds., *Televisión y melodrama: Género y lecturas de la telenovela en Colombia* (Bogotá: Tercer Mundo, 1992); Nora Mazziotti, ed., *El espectáculo de la pasión: Las telenovelas latinoamericanas* (Buenos Aires: Ediciones Colihue, 1995); and Mazziotti, *La industria de la telenovela*.

7 Martín-Barbero, "Memory and Form," 182.

8 Raúl Nacer, interview by author, December 2000. Raúl Nacer was a Cuban media

professional who began working in Puerto Rican commercial media (radio and advertising) in 1951. In addition, Nacer was the director of most of the locally produced telenovelas in Puerto Rico during the late 1950s, 1960s, and 1970s. Unfortunately none of the radionovela and telenovela script adaptations are available. See also "Cuba y Puerto Rico Son . . . ," *Bohemia* 43, no. 13 (March 26, 1950): 54.

9 This construction was present in the highly popular radionovela and subsequent telenovela *El derecho de nacer*. The script, written by the Cuban scriptwriter Félix Caignet, centers on Albertico Limonta, the illegitimate son of María Helena del Junco, the daughter of the inhumane and rich Rafael del Junco. Albertico was raised by mamá Dolores, a black woman who, afraid that Rafael del Junco might kill his illegitimate grandson, kidnapped the child and raised him as her own son. In this cultural product, the black, good, and sacrificing mamá Dolores was constructed as the heroine. However, in sacrificing to raise Albertico, mamá Dolores gave up having a life of her own. I would like to point out that even though there are multiple studies on the radionovela and telenovela genre, the commercial perspective, and its popularity in Latin America, there are no textual analyses available on early radionovelas and telenovelas. For a thematic description of *El derecho de nacer*, see Mayra Cue-Sierra, "El derecho de nacer," *Cubarte*, September 25, 2003; and Joel Zito Araújo, *A negação do Brasil: O negro na telenovela brasileira* (Sao Paolo, Brazil: Editora Senac, 2000). See also Mayra Cue-Sierra, "Historias inéditas," *Cubarte*, September 11, 2003.

10 See "100 Estrellas que iluminaron el siglo," *Teve Guía*, December 2000; Annie Alfaro, "Aquel tiempo del teatro Bufo," *El Nuevo Día*, July 2, 1989; Norma Borges, "Diplo," *El Mundo*, May 18, 1985; Eliseo Colón-Zayas, "La hora del cuerpo: recepción y consumo de la comedia en Puerto Rico," *Diá·logos*, no. 30 (1991): 65–75; Jorge Felices, "Homenaje esta noche a la farándula bohemia," *El Mundo*, December 26, 1943; "La historia de Diplo, favorito de los soldados portorriqueños," *El Mundo*, October 10, 1944; Lillian Rivas, "Diplo y su risa en nuestra memoria," *El Mundo*, May 27, 1990; and Gloria Villar, " 'Diplo' debutará en Nueva York el día 21," *El Mundo*, November 9, 1947.

11 "Actores cubanos no cruzan piquete," *Bohemia* 43, no. 45 (November 18, 1951), 39. Angel Ramos was also the owner of *El Mundo* newspaper, and in 1954, as I indicated in the introduction, he established WKAQ-Telemundo, channel 2.

12 "PIP rinde homenaje póstumo actor Diplo," *El Imparcial*, August 28, 1956.

13 Colón-Zayas, "La hora del cuerpo."

14 Homi K. Bhabha, *The Location of Culture* (London: Routledge, 1994), 70.

15 Salgado, "Cubarican."

16 There is only one existing clip from the 1956 show *La farándula Corona*. Telemundo-Puerto Rico burned many of the 1950s, 1960s, and 1970s shows due to "lack of space."

17 Salgado, "Cubarican."

18　Ibid., 3–4, 7.

19　Ibid., 8.

20　Nancy Raquel Mirabal, " 'No Country But the One We Must Fight For': The Emergence of an Antillean Nation and Community in New York City," in *Mambo Montage: The Latinization of New York*, ed. Agustín Laó-Montes and Arlene Dávila (New York: Columbia University Press, 2001), 57–72; and Virginia Sánchez-Korrol, *From Colonia to Community: The History of Puerto Ricans in New York City* (Los Angeles: University of California Press, 1994).

21　William Rosa, "La 'Confederación de las antillas' y la novela caribeña del siglo XIX," *Caribbean Studies* 22, nos. 3–4 (1989): 1–11.

22　Mirabal, "No Country"; Salgado, "Cubarican"; Juan Angel Silén, *Historia de la nación puertorriqueña* (Río Piedras, Puerto Rico: Editorial Edil, 1980).

23　Sánchez-Korrol, *From Colonia to Community*, 12.

24　Jorge Ibarra, *Prologue to a Revolution: Cuba, 1898–1958*, trans. Marjorie Moore (London: Lynne Rienner, 1998).

25　Jorge Duany, "Popular Music in Puerto Rico: Toward an Anthropology of Salsa," *Latin American Music Review* 5, no. 2 (1984): 186–216; Juan Guisti-Cordero, "Afropuerto Rican Cultural Studies: Beyond Cultural Negroide and Antillanismo," *Centro* 8, nos. 1 and 2 (1996): 56–77; José Luis González, *El país de cuatro pisos y otros ensayos*; Angel Quintero-Rivera, *Salsa, sabor y control: Sociología de la música tropical* (Madrid: Siglo veintiuno, 1998); and Silvio Torres-Saillant, *Caribbean Poetics: Toward an Aesthetic of West Indian Literature* (Cambridge: Cambridge University Press, 1997).

26　José Luis Torregrosa, *Historia de la radio en Puerto Rico* (Hato Rey, Puerto Rico: Esmaco, 1993).

27　Ibid., 35–40.

28　For an excellent analysis of Puerto Rican composers, musicians, and musical styles, see Quintero-Rivera, *Salsa, sabor y control*.

29　As Peter Wade observes through recordings and commercial radio, Cuban music became highly popular in Colombia during the 1920s and 1930s. Peter Wade, *Music, Race, and Nation: Música Tropical in Colombia* (Chicago: University of Chicago Press, 2000). Also see Juan Otero-Garabís, *Nación y ritmo: Descargas desde el caribe* (San Juan, Puerto Rico: Ediciones Callejón, 2000).

30　Fátima Fernández, "Algo más sobre los orígenes de la televisión latinoamericana," *Diá•Logos*, no. 18 (1987): 33–45. For information on the predominance of Cuban media professionals in advertising, both in Puerto Rico and in the U.S. Spanish-language market, see Arlene Dávila, *Latinos, Inc.: The Marketing and Making of a People* (Berkeley: University of California Press, 2001).

31　"Lo cubano en las ondas," *Bohemia* 43, no. 27 (May 27, 1951), 52.

32 Harold Hull, "Cuba marcha al frente de América Latina en TV," *El Mundo*, February 12, 1954. See also "Agencia de publicidad entrena a sus expertos," *El Mundo*, March 26, 1954.

33 Alicia Bibiloni, interview by author, May 2001; Paquito Cordero, interview by author, July 1997; Raúl Nacer, interview by author, December 2000; Angel F. Rivera, interview by author, December 2000; Luis Antonio Rivera, interview by author, December 2000; Felipe San Pedro, interview by author, July 1997.

34 For an impressive historical examination of Cuban Bufo theater, see the work of Rine Leal. Rine Leal, *Breve historia del teatro cubano* (Havana: Editorial Letras Cubanas, 1980); Rine Leal, *La selva oscura: de los Bufos a la neocolonia* (Havana: Editorial Arte y Literatura, 1982); Rine Leal, "Marginalismo y escena nacional," *Revista Tablas* 1 (January–May 1982): 13–22; Rine Leal, *Teatro del siglo XIX*, vol. 1 (Havana: Editorial Letras Cubanas, 1986); Rine Leal, *Teatro mambí* (Havana: Editorial Letras Cubanas, 1978). Also see Magaly Muguercia, "El 'teatro de arte' en Cuba entre 1936 y 1950," *Revista Tablas* 4 (1984): 2–15; and Eduardo Robreno, *Historia del teatro popular cubano*, vol 74: *Cuadernos de historia habanera* (Havana: Oficina del Historiador de la Ciudad de la Habana, 1961).

35 Leal, *Breve historia*, 30.

36 Laurie Aleen Frederik, "The Contestation of Cuba's Public Sphere in National Theatre and the Transformation from Teatro Bufo to Teatro Nuevo," *Gestos* 31 (2001): 65–98; and Leal, *Teatro del siglo XIX*.

37 Jill Lane, "Blackface Nationalism, Cuba 1840–1868," *Theatre Journal* 50, no. 1 (1998), 28.

38 Leal, *Breve historia*; Leal, *Teatro del siglo XIX*; Robin D. Moore, *Nationalizing Blackness: Afrocubanismo and Artistic Revolution in Havana, 1920–1940* (Pittsburgh: University of Pittsburgh Press, 1997).

39 Leal, *Breve historia*; Moore, *Nationalizing Blackness*; and Lane, "Blackface Nationalism."

40 Frederik, "The Contestation," 81.

41 Eric Lott, *Love and Theft: Blackface Minstrelsy and the American Working Class* (Oxford: Oxford University Press, 1995); David R. Roediger, *The Wages of Whiteness: Race and the Making of the American Working Class* (New York: Verso, 1991); Michael Rogin, *Blackface, White Noise: Jewish Immigrants in the Hollywood Melting Pot* (Los Angeles: University of California Press, 1996); and Werner Sollors, *Beyond Ethnicity: Consent and Descent in American Culture* (New York: Oxford University Press, 1986).

42 Lott, *Love and Theft*, 8.

43 Rogin, *Blackface, White Noise*, 45–48.

44 For information on Cuban Bufo audiences, see Lane, "Blackface Nationalism," n. 26, 35.

45 Moore, *Nationalizing Blackness*. After 1868 and the first performance of *Los Bu-fos Habaneros* group, multiple companies began to perform in various parts of the island. For information on Bufo companies, see Frederik, "The Contestation," 76.

46 Leal, "Marginalismo." Bufo theater is still part of contemporary Cuba. In addition, even though there were radical social transformations after the 1959 Cuban Revolution that benefited Afro Cubans, black performers are almost completely absent from Cuba's stages and television. See Alden Knight, "Tackling Racism in Performing Arts and the Media," in *Afro-Cuban Voices*, 108–17.

47 Frederik, "The Contestation," 75.

48 Ibid.

49 It should be clear that there were various representations of negritos in Cuban Bufo. For more information on the negrito and other Bufo types, see Moore, *Nationalizing Blackness*, 46–48.

50 Frederik, "The Contestation," 78. For a textual examination of the negrito catedrático, see Lane, "Blackface Nationalism."

51 Frederik, "The Contestation," 79–81.

52 Angelina Morfi, *Historia crítica de un siglo de teatro puertorriqueño* (Madrid: Manuel Pareja, 1980), 109.

53 Ibid., 110.

54 Guerra, *Popular Expression*, 66.

55 Quintero-Rivera, *Conflictos de clase y política*, 31–32.

56 Morfi, *Historia crítica*, 113–31.

57 The influence of Bufo comedy can be observed in the plays of Rafael Escalona, Eleuterio Derkes, Sotero Figueroa, and Manuel Alonzo Pizarro. However, one of the most important plays in the history of Puerto Rican theater during the nineteenth century that criticized racial prejudice and mestizaje is Alejandro Tapia's *La cuarterona*. Although the play condemns racism, the narrative is set in Cuba. *La cuarterona* is part of the romantic literary period that influenced many nineteenth-century Spanish Caribbean and Latin American writers.

58 Quintero-Rivera, *Conflictos de clase y política*, 70–75.

59 Ibid. For an analysis of Puerto Rico's politics during the early twentieth century, see Grosfoguel, "The Divorce of Nationalist Discourses"; Mariano Negrón-Portillo, "Puerto Rico: Surviving Colonialism and Nationalism," in *Puerto Rican Jam*, 39–56; and Quintero-Rivera, *Conflictos de clase y política*.

60 Silén, *Historia de la nación*, 249.

61 Carlos Rodríguez-Fraticelli, "Pedro Albizu Campos: Strategies of Struggle and Strategic Struggles," *Centro* 4, no. 1 (1991–1992): 25–33. See also Amílcar Tirado-Avilés, "La forja de un líder: Pedro Albizu Campos, 1924–1930," *Centro* 4, no. 1 (1991–92): 13–23.

62   "Pueblos Hispanos," in J.B. Mathews Papers, Duke University, Durham, North Carolina, 1943.

63   Rodríguez-Fraticelli, "Pedro Albizu Campos," 29–30.

64   For information on Puerto Rican migrations to the United States, see Duany, *The Puerto Rican Nation*; and Sánchez-Korrol, *From Colonia to Community*.

65   Frank Bonilla and Ricardo Campos assert that this economic transformation changed the social organization of production and converted the island into a "consumer market for U.S. goods." Although U.S. companies have been part of the island's economy since the nineteenth century, from 1949 to 1954, many more U.S. industries took advantage of Operation Bootstrap incentives and expanded their markets into Puerto Rico. See Frank Bonilla and Ricardo Campos, "Industrialization and Migration: Some Effects on the Puerto Rican Working Class," *Latin American Perspectives* II, no. 10 (summer 1976), cited in Luis Alberto Hernández, "The Origins of the Consumer Culture in Puerto Rico: The Pre-Television Years (1898–1954)," *Centro* 3, no. 1 (winter 1990–1991): 38–54.

66   Duany, *The Puerto Rican Nation*, 126. Also see Morris, *Puerto Rico*.

67   Description in the 1935 *La Farándula Bohemia*'s flyer. Fundación Ramón Rivero, San Juan, Puerto Rico.

68   Ferrer, *Insurgent Cuba*, 210–11, n. 63.

69   For example, the play *De naranjito a naranjales (Unión, Unión, Unión)* narrates the expulsion of Luis Muñoz Marín from the Liberal Party.

70   *Diplo*, WIPR-TV (1980).

71   Bibiloni, interview.

72   Gloria Villar, "Mano Meco el de las carcajadas y Rivera Pérez el serio," *El Mundo*, February 4, 1951.

73   José Arnaldo Meyners, "Diplo: una personalidad artística en ascenso," *El Mundo*, July 1, 1945. See also Enver Azizi, "Diplo," *El Mundo*, February 4, 1946; and Alfredo Matilla, "La buena risa," *El Mundo*, May 14, 1950.

74   "Noticias," *El Mundo*, November 18, 1950. There is no information in Puerto Rico regarding the Venezuelan adaptation of *El tremendo hotel*.

75   In Puerto Rico, as in other Latin American countries, local television productions followed the U.S. "broker system" model. On some occasions advertising agencies adapted a specific U.S. program to Puerto Rican culture and hired local talent, while on others, Puerto Rican actors-producers sold program ideas to advertisers who were developing shows with one specific sponsor in mind. The actors-producers' primary strategy was to create a generic program that would incorporate the sponsor into the show's title. Thus, many of the programs produced locally during Puerto Rican television's early years were designed, performed, directed, and sold by a group of actors who took advantage of the medium as an unstructured enterprise.

During its first year, Telemundo (WKAQ-TV) did not have a sales department. Instead, the station's management dealt primarily with the technical aspects of transmissions without yet envisioning the financial opportunities of producing its own programming.

76 Telemundo began its transmission in 1954 with programming scheduled from 4:30 P.M. to 10:30 P.M., airing a combination of local and imported shows. The imported U.S. programs included *Public Prosecutor*, *Perry Como*, and *Victory at Sea*, while locally produced programs included *Buscando estrellas Coca Cola*, *Mímicas Del Monte*, and *Gran show Libby's*. In addition, Mexican and U.S. movies were part of Telemundo's programming. During television's early formative period, U.S. programs were incorporated primarily because local program production was not yet ready for implementation. Telemundo's locally produced prime-time programming integrated some shows that were indigenous versions of U.S. programs and others that reproduced U.S. genres or concepts. Also, other shows were based on scripts that originated in Puerto Rico and Cuba.

77 "Reconocen labor de Diplo," *El Mundo*, November 15, 1954.

78 Gladys M. Jiménez-Muñoz, "Siomara mi hejmana: Diplo y el travestismo racial en el Puerto Rico de los años cincuenta," *Bordes* 2 (1995): 15–27.

79 There are no copies available of *Una gallega en la Habana* in Puerto Rico.

80 "Acabó de filmar la película 'Una gallega en la Habana,'" *El Mundo*, February 21, 1955; Wilfredo Braschi, "Diplo filmará cinta con Catita en Cuba," *El Mundo*, December 4, 1954; Dario Carlo, "Diplo vuelve tras de filmar cinta," *El Mundo*, February 24, 1955; "Diplo y Pinito en la Habana," *El Mundo*, February 7, 1955; and Malén Rojas Daporta, "Diplo es productor de películas cortas," *El Mundo*, November 12, 1955. See also "La taberna despide hoy a Calderón," *El Mundo*, January 17, 1955.

81 Rivero died in 1956; thus, his attempt to cross over into the U.S. market was never realized. However, according to Bibiloni, Rivero was fully aware of the fact that in Hollywood it was impossible to perform in blackface. The movie entitled *Wherever You Go* was never produced.

82 One can also assume that, like other followers of the Nationalist Party, Rivero and Torregrosa joined the Pro-Independence Party (founded in 1946) and supported its nonviolence philosophy and its political electoral position.

83 Bibiloni, interview.

84 My examination of *El tremendo hotel* comes from a textual analysis of the show's scripts and six radio recordings.

85 *El tremendo hotel* had numerous regular characters over the years. However, the ones who remained part of the show since its first episode were Doña Polita, Don Nepo, and Calderón.

86 Sylvia Alvarez-Curbelo and María Elena Rodríguez-Castro, *Del nacionalismo al*

populismo: Cultura y política en Puerto Rico (Río Piedras, Puerto Rico: Huracán, 1993), cited in Dávila, *Sponsored Identities*, 29.

87 See the introductory chapter's discussion of the 1930s intellectual debate.

88 I refer to Spaniards (plural) because in the early 1950s *El tremendo hotel* also included a gallega character named Rosiña.

89 This black voice character was created by Mona Marti, the same actress who first performed the Caribbean negras in locally produced radionovelas, and later, in tele-novelas. Although mamá Yoyo was included in several episodes of both *El tremendo hotel* and *La taberna India*, the character was not a regular part of these narratives. According to Alicia Bibiloni, Ramón Rivero included Mona Marti as mamá Yoyo in *El tremendo hotel* to take advantage of the actress's huge popularity as mamá Dolores in the local adaptation of the Cuban radionovela *El derecho de nacer*. None of the six available radio recordings of *El tremendo hotel* have the voice of mamá Yoyo. Bibiloni, interview. Also see n. 3.

90 According to Nira Yuval-Davis and Floya Anthias, women are an integral part of nationalistic discourses, not only in terms of culture but also regarding the future population of the nation. For information on national discourses and ideologies of gender, see Doris Sommer, *Foundational Fictions: The National Romances of Latin America* (Berkeley: University of California Press, 1991); and Nira Yuval-Davis and Floya Anthias, *Woman-Nation-State* (New York: St. Martin's Press, 1989). For a holis-tic interpretation of literature, music, and the nation in 1930s Puerto Rico, see Frances Aparicio, *Listening to Salsa*.

91 Both Mr. Sandwich and Ruth, la americana, were constructed as white Americans. Besides the fact that in Puerto Rico's cultural imaginary Americanness is intercon-nected to whiteness, the local members of the hotel made references to their white skin by calling them *jinchos* (a vernacular word that is used to describe individuals with extremely pale or sickly white skin).

92 Michele Hilmes, *Radio Voices: American Broadcasting, 1922–1952* (Minneapolis: Uni-versity of Minnesota Press, 1997).

93 See the introduction's discussion on Puerto Rico's racial categorizations.

94 Stephen Berrey, "'Bad Negroes,' 'Troublemakers,' and 'Outside Agitators': The Criminalization of Black Resistance and Civil Rights Activism" (ch. 4, Ph.D. diss., University of Texas, n.d.).

95 Ibid.

96 See Anibal Quijano's discussion of the "coloniality of power." Anibal Quijano, "The Colonial Nature of Power and Latin America's Cultural Experience," in *Sociology in Latin America*, ed. Roberto Briceño-León and Heinz Sonntag (Colonia Tovar, Vene-zuela: ISA, 1997), 27–38.

97 The audience participated in the candidate's selection by sending empty Sello Rojo

rice bags. It is not clear whether Rivero or the sponsors came up with this commercial idea. The inaugural celebration included a parade in Santurce and a special thirty-minute show during which the sponsor donated $150 to El Fanguito. "Vote por su candidato," *El Mundo*, February 5, 1951.

98 Correa Cotto was a real criminal who was constantly escaping prison and eluding the authorities.

99 According to Juan Silén, the Pro-Independence Party, which wanted to obtain independence through cordial relations with the United States, was influenced by U.S. Cold War rhetoric. Silén, *Historia de la nación*, 376.

100 It should be noted that *El tremendo hotel* frequently included public individuals as guests of the hotel. For example, political figures such as Felisa Rincón (the mayor of San Juan) and composers and musicians such as Sylvia Rexach, Noel Estrada, and Elsa Rivera Salgado visited the hotel.

101 Abelardo Díaz-Alfaro, "Homenaje a Ramón Ortiz Del Rivero," *El Reportero*, August 24, 1981.

102 The main difference in physical appearance between Diplomacia and Calderón was the costume. Diplomacia dressed in worn black pants, a white shirt, a checkered vest, black shoes, and a sailor's hat. Calderón dressed in a white blazer, black pants, and a little white hat. My descriptions of Diplomacia and Calderón are based on the photos provided by Rivero's family.

103 For a discussion of the jíbaro as the emblem of Puerto Rican identity during the 1950s, see Dávila, *Sponsored Identities*.

104 Ibid.

105 Cordero-Avila, "José Luis Torregrosa"; Meyners, "Diplo: una personalidad"; and 1956 newsreel provided by Rivero's family.

106 Patricia Reyes Vargas, "Diplo, un gran actor y un gran corazón," *El Imparcial*, September 1, 1956; Patricia Reyes Vargas and Harold Lidin, "50,000 asisten a entierro de Diplo," *El Imparcial*, August 27, 1956; and Malén Rojas Daporta and Juan Manuel Ocasio, "Millares asisten al sepelio," *El Mundo*, August 27, 1956.

107 Tony Mojena, *Telemundo: 40 años de recuerdo* (San Juan, Puerto Rico, television special, 1994).

108 Paquito Cordero, interview by author, July 1997.

109 Doroteo appeared in Paquito Cordero's *El show de las 12*. Mike Saéz, "El Negrito Doroteo," *Teve Guía*, January 13, 1973, 74–75. *El show de las 12* is a noon variety show that includes music, comedy, and interview segments. It has been one of the longest-running programs in the history of Puerto Rico's commercial television. Paquito Cordero became one of the most prolific and successful producers in Puerto Rico's commercial television. Coming from a middle-class family, Cordero began working in radio during the 1950s, and started his television career in 1954. His movement

from radio to television was fairly smooth, not only because there were plenty of opportunities in this new medium in 1954, but also because Cordero is the nephew of Fernando and Mapi Cortéz, two famous Puerto Rican actors who worked in Mexican movies and television for many years. Working in television during the mid-1950s, Cordero had a chance to write scripts and function as the artistic director while also continuing his acting career. In 1960 he founded Paquito Cordero Teleproducciones. In addition, during the 1970s, through his Hit Parade record company, Cordero served as a manager for singers and produced variety shows in Puerto Rican nightclubs and in New York City. Cordero Teleproducciones became a family business involving Cordero's brother, sister, son, daughter, in-laws, and some family friends in various aspects of production. During his career Cordero has produced movies, television sitcoms, comedies, and variety shows. His variety shows were exported to Latin America during the 1970s and some of his shows were also broadcast on the East Coast's U.S. Spanish-language television stations, particularly during the 1970s and early 1980s.

110 José A. Cobas and Jorge Duany, *Cubans in Puerto Rico: Ethnic Economy and Cultural Identity* (Gainesville: University Press of Florida, 1997), 1.

111 Ibid.

112 Ibid., 26.

113 Ibid., 2.

114 Only a few tapes of the 1950s *El colegio de la alegría* are available.

115 For information on Hollywood's black stereotypes, see Donald Bogle, *Toms, Coons, Mulattoes, Mammies, and Bucks: An Interpretive History of Blacks in American Films*, 3d ed. (New York: Continuum, 1995).

116 The character created a typecast for Carmen Belén Richardson, because whenever she was hired to perform comedies, people would ask her to open her eyes like Lirio Blanco used to do. Rubén Marrero, "Su error fue abrir los ojos demasiado," *Vea*, August 15, 1976, 66–68. See also Migdalia Santiago-Vidal, "Carmen Belén Richardson," *El Mundo*, August 4, 1985.

117 Aparicio, *Listening to Salsa*.

118 Ibid., 35.

119 Television programming section (1954–1955), *El Mundo* newspaper. See, in particular, "El Gran Show Libby's irá al aire por radio y televisión," March 26, 1954; "Gran programa musical se inicia mañana en Telemundo," November 29, 1954; "India presenta nuevo programa," August 2, 1954; "Mañana cantará guajiras el trovador Portabales," January 31, 1955; and "Mapy y Fernando Cortés actuarán por Telemundo," *El Mundo*, March 26, 1954.

120 These producers included Ramón Rivero, Tommy Muñiz, and after the 1960s, Paquito Cordero.

121 José Esteban Muñoz, *Disidentifications: Queers of Color and Performance of Politics* (Minneapolis: University of Minnesota Press, 1999), 31.

122 Jiménez-Muñoz, "Siomanra mi hejmana."

2. BRINGING THE SOUL

1 "Stokely's Castroite Links," *Human Events*, March 18, 1967, 3–4.

2 Ibid., 4.

3 For an impressive analysis of the Fair Play for Cuba Committee (FPCC), Robert F. Williams, and the "Afro-Cuban-American Solidarities," see Timothy B. Tyson, *Radio Free Dixie: Robert F. Williams and the Roots of Black Power* (Chapel Hill: University of North Carolina Press, 1999); and Van Gosse, *Where the Boys Are: Cuba, Cold War America, and the Making of a New Left* (London: Verso, 1993).

4 I would like to emphasize that repression against pro-independence advocates continued during the 1960s and 1970s. For an examination of Puerto Rico's politics, see Morris, *Puerto Rico*.

5 Irving Beinin, "Students Strike in Puerto Rico," *Guardian*, May 4, 1968, 10; Irving Beinin, "Puerto Ricans Plan Centennial Action," *Guardian*, May 25, 1968, 18; Irving Beinin, "MPI Looks to Workers," *Guardian*, June 1, 1968, 15; Juan Angel Silén, *De la guerrilla cívica a la nación dividida* (Río Piedras, Puerto Rico: Ediciones Librería Internacional, 1972); Silén, *Historia de la nación*; and Constance Ullman, "Puerto Ricans Mark 100-Years Fight for Freedom," *Guardian*, October 5, 1968. It should be noted that the FBI was monitoring these organizations and that right-wing newspapers were publishing stories about Puerto Rico's pro-independence movement and its association with Cuban and U.S. communist groups. For a sense of the vast anticommunist efforts in the United States, see the J. B. Mathews Papers, Duke University, Durham, North Carolina.

6 See Iris Morales, "Palante, Siempre Palante: The Young Lords," in *The Puerto Rican Movement: Voices from the Diaspora*, ed. Andrés Torres and José A. Velázquez (Philadelphia: Temple University Press, 1998), 210–27; Roberto Rodríguez-Morazzani, "Puerto Rican Political Generations in New York: Pioneros, Young Turks, and Radicals," *Centro* 4, no. 1 (1992): 96–116; Basilio Serrano, " 'Rifle, Cañón, y Escopeta': A Chronicle of the Puerto Rican Student Union," in Torres and Velázquez, *The Puerto Rican Movement*, 125–43; and Komozi Woodard, *A Nation within a Nation: Amiri Baraka (Leroi Jones) and Black Power Politics* (Chapel Hill: University of North Carolina Press, 1999).

7 Duany, *The Puerto Rican Nation*; Grosfoguel and Georas, "Latino Caribbean Diasporas in New York," in Laó-Montes and Arlene Dávila, *Mambo Montage*, 97–118; and Sánchez-Korrol, *From Colonia*.

8 The Young Lords Party and Michael Abramson, *Palante: Young Lords Party* (New York: McGraw-Hill, 1971).

9 Ibid. Also see James Early, "An African American-Puerto Rican Connection: An Auto-Bio-Memory Sketch of Political Development and Activism"; and Torres and Velázquez, *The Puerto Rican Movement*, 316–28.

10 See Joseph P. Fried, "East Harlem Youths Explain Garbage-Dumping Demonstration," *New York Times*, August 19, 1969; and José Yglesias, "Right on with the Young Lords," *New York Times*, June 7, 1970.

11 Agustín Laó-Montes, "Niuyol: Urban Regime, Latino Social Movements, Ideologies of Latinidad," in Laó-Montes and Arlene Dávila, *Mambo Montage*, 119–58; Jennifer A. Nelson, "Abortion under Community Control: Feminism, Nationalism, and the Politics of Reproduction among New York City's Young Lords," *Journal of Women's History* 13, no. 1 (2001): 157–80; and The Young Lords Party and Abramson, *Palante*. For an examination of the Puerto Rican community in Chicago; its involvement in political, social, and cultural mobilizations; and its community leaders' appropriation of Puerto Rico's radical nationalism, see Ramos-Zayas, *National Performances*.

12 Rodríguez-Morazzani, "Puerto Rican Political Generations."

13 Lillian Jiménez, "From the Margin to the Center: Puerto Rican Cinema in New York," in *Latin Looks: Images of Latinas and Latinos in the U.S. Media*, ed. Clara Rodríguez (Boulder, Colo.: Westview Press, 1997), 188–99; and Chon Noriega, *Shot in America: Television, the State, and the Rise of Chicano Cinema* (Minneapolis: University of Minnesota Press, 2000). Also see Aída Barrera, *Looking for Carrascolendas: From a Child's World to Award-Winning Television* (Austin: University of Texas Press, 2001). While *Carrascolendas* was a children's program and was not a Chicano or Boricua co-production, it is worth mentioning that Aída Barrera, the show's producer, hired many Latino media professionals and incorporated Puerto Rican, Cuban, and Mexican cultures into the shows.

14 See the work of Peter X. Feng, *Identities in Motion: Asian American Film and Video* (Durham, N.C.: Duke University Press, 2002); Michelle Raheja, "Screening Identity: Beads, Buckskin, and Redface in Autobiography and Film" (Ph.D. diss., University of Chicago, 2001); and Renee Tajima, "Moving the Image: Asian American Independent Filmmaking, 1970–1990," in *Moving the Image: Asian Pacific American Media Arts*, ed. Russell Leong (Los Angeles: UCLA Asian American Studies Center and Visual Communications, 1991), 10–33.

15 Marie Ramos-Rosado, *La mujer negra en la literatura puertorriqueña* (Río Piedras, Puerto Rico: Editorial de la Universidad de Puerto Rico, 1999); Ana Lydia Vega, "La felicidad, ja, ja, ja, ja y la universidad," *El Mundo*, September 23, 1990, 121; and Arlene Torres, "La gran familia puertorriqueña 'Ej Prieta De Belda' (the Great Puerto Rican Family Is Really Black)," in *Blackness in Latin America and the Caribbean: Social Dynamics and Cultural Transformations*, ed. Arlene Torres and Norman E. Whitten (Bloomington: Indiana University Press, 1998), 285–306.

16 See Isabelo Zenón Cruz's seminal book, *Narciso descubre su trasero*. For information on the formation of Sylvia del Villard's group, Taller Afro-Boricua, el Coquí, see Clara Cuevas, "Taller folklórico Afro-Boricua se inaugura en Viejo San Juan," *El Mundo*, May 14, 1968; and Sylvia del Villard, "Folklore afro-boricua," *El Mundo*, June 19, 1968. Within the 1960s–1970s popular culture terrain, salsa emerged as a commodified location for the representation and negotiation of class and race struggles in both New York City and Puerto Rico. Also, during the 1970s in New York, the still community-centered and culturally hybrid hip-hop culture re-articulated the economic and racial alienation of African American, Puerto Rican, and Afro-Caribbean youth. For information about rap, see Juan Flores, *From Bomba to Hip-Hop*; Raquel Z. Rivera, *New York Ricans from the Hip Hop Zone* (New York: Palgrave MacMillan, 2003); and Tricia Rose, *Black Noise: Rap Music and Black Culture in Contemporary America* (London: Wesleyan University Press, 1994). See also Jossianna Arroyo, "Raíces o/a duplicidad de los imaginarios raciales en Puerto Rico" (paper presented at the Latin American Studies Association conference, Houston, Texas, 2003).

17 For a critical analysis on the representation of African Americans in U.S. commercial television, see Kristal Brent Zook, *Color by Fox: The Fox Network and the Revolution in Black Television* (New York: Oxford University Press, 1999); John Downing, " 'The Cosby Show' and American Racial Discourse," in *Discourse and Discrimination*, ed. Geneva Smitherman-Donaldson and Teun Van Dijk (Detroit: Wayne State University Press, 1988), 46–73; John Fiske, *Media Matters: Race and Gender in U.S. Politics* (Minneapolis: University of Minnesota Press, 1996); Herman Gray, *Watching Race: Television and the Struggle for "Blackness"* (Minneapolis: University of Minnesota Press, 1995); Herman Gray, "Remembering Civil Rights: Television, Memory, and the 1960s," in *The Revolution Wasn't Televised*, ed. Michael Curtin and Lynn Spigel (London: Routledge, 1997), 349–58; Bambi L. Haggins, "Why 'Beulah' and 'Andy' Still Play Today: Minstrelsy in the New Millennium," *Emergences* 11, no. 2 (2001): 249–67; and Beretta E. Smith-Shomade, *Shaded Lives: African American Women and Television* (New Brunswick, N.J.: Rutgers University Press, 2002).

18 I am drawing from Frantz Fanon's theories on the fixation of "blackness" and the invisibility of the "black" self. See Frantz Fanon, *Black Skin, White Masks*, trans. Charles Lam Markmann (New York: Grove Weidenfeld, 1967).

19 For information on Lucecita's career during the 1960s and a detailed and impressive documentation of la nueva ola movement in Puerto Rico, see Javier Santiago, *La nueva ola portoricensis* (San Juan, Puerto Rico: Editorial del patio, 1994); and Lucecita's folders, Fundación Nacional para la Cultura Popular, San Juan, Puerto Rico.

20 Mario Previdi, "Lucecita impone el 'African look,' " *Teve Guía*, June 13, 1970, 15–17; and Javier Santiago, "La historia detrás de un Afro," *El Nuevo Día*, October 15, 2000. In addition to having her segment in *El show de las 12*, Lucecita had her own variety

show entitled *El show de Lucecita*. Produced by Paquito Cordero, *El show de Lucecita* aired on Sundays from 8:00–8:30 P.M.

21 Santiago, *La nueva ola*.

22 Ibid, 127.

23 Previdi, "Lucecita impone."

24 Magali García Ramis, "La transformación de Lucecita," *Avance*, August 6, 1973, 21–25.

25 Santiago, "La historia," 129.

26 "Lucecita no quiere quitarse el Afro," *Teve Guía*, June 13, 1970, 13–16.

27 "Derrotan el 'Afro' de Lucecita," *Vea*, May 8, 1970, 46–47.

28 "Lucecita no quiere."

29 Santiago, "La historia."

30 "Lucecita," *San Juan Weekly*, October 3, 1970, front page.

31 Tite Curet-Alonso, "¿Declaran la guerra a Lucecita Benítez?," *Vea*, October 15, 1972, 86–89; "De nuevo lo de antes," *El Nuevo Día*, October 23, 1972.

32 Tomás Figueroa and Quality Sound, Inc., *Raza Pura*, 1973.

33 María O. Olán, "No estoy en contra de nada, ni de nadie . . . sino a favor de algo," *El Mundo*, September 9, 1973. See also "Lucecita explica porque estuvo retirada por un año," *Vea*, August 12, 1973, 48–49.

34 Judith Butler, "Performative Acts and Gender Constitution: An Essay in Phenomenology and Feminist Theory," in *Performing Feminism: Feminist Critical Theory and Theatre*, ed. Sue-Ellen Case (Baltimore: Johns Hopkins University Press, 1990), 279.

35 Rosendo Rosell, *Diario las Américas*, May 24, 1973; and William Tavárez, "Se define como ejemplo vivo de la liberación femenina," *El Caribe*, May 9, 1973.

36 García Ramis, "La transformación," 22.

37 For an excellent analysis of the emergence of the gay and lesbian movement in Puerto Rico and its connections to the U.S. gay and feminist movement, see Frances Negrón-Muntaner, "Echoing Stonewall and Other Dilemmas: The Organizational Beginnings of a Gay and Lesbian Agenda in Puerto Rico, 1972–1977," *Centro* 4, no. 1 (1991–1992): 77–95. Also see Lawrence La Fountain-Stokes, "1898 and the History of a Queer Puerto Rican Century: Gay Lives, Island Debates, and Diasporic Experience," *Centro* 11, no. 1 (1999): 91–109.

38 Malín Falú, interview by author, November 2001.

39 Robin D. G. Kelley, *Yo' Mama's Disfunktional!: Fighting the Culture Wars in Urban America* (Boston: Beacon Press, 1997).

40 For an anthropological examination of contemporary hair straightening practices in some beauty salons in Puerto Rico and the ongoing negotiation of Afro Puerto Rican women regarding Eurocentric discourses of beauty, see Isar Godreau, "Peinando diferencias, bregas de pertenencia: El alisado y el llamado 'pelo malo,'" *Caribbean Studies* 30, no. 1 (2002): 82–133.

41 Maxine Leeds Craig, *Ain't I a Beauty Queen: Black Women, Beauty, and the Politics of Race* (Oxford: Oxford University Press, 2002), 107.

42 Ibid.

43 Robin D. G. Kelley, "Nap Time: Historicizing the Afro," *Fashion Theory* 1, no. 4 (1997), 347.

44 For example, according to Alejandro de la Fuente, after Stokely Carmichael and other African Americans involved in the black power movement visited Cuba, "some Afro-Cubans adopted at least some of the external symbols that these militants displayed—such as the Afro hairstyle." Although this description characterizes the Afro as an "external symbol," it would be interesting to examine the ways in which Afro Cubans translated the hairstyle. De la Fuente, *A Nation for All*, 302.

45 Interview by author, May 2001.

46 See www.lucecita.com.

47 BMG Entertainment, *Lucecita Benítez en vivo desde el Carnegie Hall* (New York: BMG, 2000).

48 Rosario Goyco-Carmoega, "Afirman no hay discriminación racial en TV isla," *El Mundo*, August 5, 1971.

49 Ibid.

50 Manuel Silva-Casanova, "Yo tengo un amigo negro," *Avance*, May 14, 1973, 55–58.

51 By the early 1970s there were primarily two black comedic actors in Puerto Rico, Carmen Belén Richardson and Otilio Warrington "Bizcocho."

52 Roland Robertson, "Glocalization: Time-Space and Homogeneity-Heterogeneity," in *Global Modernities*, ed. Mike Featherstone, Scott Lash, and Roland Robertson (Thousand Oaks, Calif.: Sage, 1995), 25–44.

53 *Soul Train* had five two-minute segments during which the hosts interviewed the soul singers. After *Soul Train*'s sudden success, the show was extended to 2:00 P.M. However, Falú left after a year, leaving Myles as the only host. Finally, due to its low ratings, the hybrid *Soul Train* was transformed to a one-hour show and then cancelled later in 1974. See Elsa Fernández-Miralles, "Soul Train," *Vea*, April 21, 1974, 10–12; and Elsa Fernández-Miralles, "70 Millones de personas ven Soul Train," *Vea*, July 8, 1974, 78–81.

54 Iván Frontera, "Don Cornelius visita Soul Train en P.R.," *Teve Guía*, April 27, 1974, 72–75.

55 For information on the local version of *Soul Train* and the ways in which soul music and performers were described in some local newspapers and television magazines, see "Carol Myles y Jay en Puerto Rico," *El Mundo*, July 29, 1973; "Concierto Roberta Flack, atractivos del Flamboyán," *El Mundo*, April 21, 1973; "Día de reyes por el canal 4," *El Mundo*, January 6, 1973; "Malín," *Angela Luisa*, February 1973, 87; Rubita Cervoni, "Revista Jet y Ebony cubrirán 'El Flamboyán,'" *El Mundo*, October 14, 1973; Maria O. Olán, "Malín Falú: La música no tiene color," *El Mundo*, August 26,

1973; and Brenda S. Vega, "Música 'Soul' tiene seguidores en la isla," *El Mundo*, July 20, 1973.

56 Falú, interview. Malín Falú had been active in Afro Puerto Rican cultural movements since 1969 when she joined Sylvia del Villard's theater company. In the mid-1970s, Falú migrated to New York City and became one of the most important figures in the Spanish-language radio market on the U.S. East Coast. See "Malín Falú," *Angela Luisa*, October 1973, 73.

57 Based on an *El Nuevo Día* article, in the 1970s Tommy Muñiz produced a show entitled *La familia Brinn* that centered on the Brinn family, a real black family and musical group. It is not clear whether the program was a comedy or a variety show because the newspaper article does not specify the genre. See Nancy Piñero Vega, "Dinga y mandinga televisiva," *El Nuevo Día*, October 13, 2000.

58 Channel 7's noon show was entitled *El batey de la alegría* and was produced by Alberto González and his production company, Bayaney. In 1973, González (a Cuban immigrant) produced and wrote shows such as *Black Power*, *Dímelo cantando*, *Machuchal*, and *A ese yo lo vi nacer* for channel 7. See "Alberto González tre malas intenciones," *Bohemia*, March 5–11, 1973, 20.

59 "Machuchal regresa a la TV," *Teve Guía*, March 10, 1973, 85–86.

60 Unfortunately no television clips are available for this show.

61 "'Black Power' ridiculiza los prejuicios raciales," *Vea*, November 25, 1973, 32–34.

62 *Black Power* aired on Fridays from 7:30 P.M. to 8:00 P.M. on channel 7. No television clips are available. See "A Gilda Haddock le gusta tanto el drama como la comedia," *Teve Guía*, November 3, 1973, 17–18.

63 Mark Anthony Neal, *What the Music Said: Black Popular Music and Black Public Culture* (London: Routledge, 1999), 98–99.

64 Fernández-Miralles, "Soul Train." The program was substituted with the U.S. *Soul Train*.

65 In addition, in March 1973 two Afro Puerto Rican musicians produced a pilot for Telemundo (channel 2) entitled *Sabor sepia*. Based on a brief description of the show, *Sabor Sepia*'s main objective was to create a space for Afro Puerto Rican and African rhythms. See "Programa piloto," *El Nuevo Día*, March 26, 1973.

66 "Presentarán programa música salsa en TV," *El Mundo*, October 7, 1973.

67 Salsa music became highly popular in Puerto Rico during the 1960s and 1970s. More important, many of the salsa lyrics directly addressed issues of race and blackness. For a critical examination of salsa see Duany, "Popular Music"; Aparicio, *Listening to Salsa*; Quintero-Rivera, *Salsa, sabor y control*; Lisa Sánchez-González, "Reclaiming Salsa," *Cultural Studies* 13, no. 2 (April 1999): 237–50. See also Jaime Torres-Torres, "¿Dónde está el negrito bembón?," *El Nuevo Día*, October 8, 2000.

68 The first locally produced situation comedy in Puerto Rico was the 1954 *Mapy y Papi*, an adaptation of the U.S. sitcom *I Love Lucy*. The translation and adaptation

of *I Love Lucy*'s scripts were done in Cuba and then both the concept and the scripts were adapted to Puerto Rican culture.

69 "Esther Palés se enamoró de El hijo de Angela María," *Teve Guía*, February 24, 1973, 72–75; and Gloria Villar, "El hijo de Angela María," *Teve Guía*, August 25, 1973, 84–88.

70 It should be noted that earlier, locally produced telenovelas had been exported to Latin America. However, for *El hijo de Angela María* Telemundo recorded the product on videotape and film for the purpose of exportation. *El hijo de Angela María* was written by Enrique Jarnés, a Spanish television scriptwriter who resided in Venezuela.

71 The original name of the character was Chanita. However, in Puerto Rico's popular culture, the character is known as Chianita.

72 "Esther Palés se enamoró"; "Mona Marti retorna a El derecho de nacer," *Teve Guía*, June 9, 1973, 1–11; "El hijo de Angela María," *Teve Guía*, August 25, 1973, 84–88; Elsa Fernández-Miralles, "Mona Marti hará un papel de negra por tercera vez," *Vea*, February 25, 1973, 74–76; and Belén Ríos, " 'Mamá Dolores' no se parece a Panchita," *Vea*, July 8, 1973, 70–72. See also Roberto Barreto, "Mamá Inés: The Next Generation," *Claridad*, January 9–15, 1998.

73 " 'Chianita' se casará con Hugo Leonel Vaccaro," *Vea*, July 9, 1973, 60–63.

74 See the introduction for a discussion of racial mestizaje.

75 "El personaje de Angela Meyer da nota pintoresca a El hijo de Angela María," *Teve Guía*, May 26, 1973, 42–43; Raquel Rey, " 'Para una actriz verdadera no hay papeles secundarios' dice Angela Meyer," *Teve Guía*, May 26, 1973, 16–18; " 'Chianita' se casará"; and Belén Ríos, " 'Chianita' nació por casualidad," *Vea*, July 8, 1973, 67–69.

76 Silva-Casanova, "Yo tengo," 57.

77 Ibid., 58.

78 Other media professionals also might have been offended by the use of blackface. For example, Otilio Warrington "Bizcocho" and Victor Santos (two black male television figures) condemned Chianita's character and the racism that permeated Puerto Rico's commercial television. However, for the most part, television magazines and newspapers focused on del Villard's and Richardson's reactions. See "¿Qué cosa es ser cómico?" *Vea*, July 8, 1973, 28–31; and Raquel Rey, "Sylvia del Villard ataca a los 'negros pintados,' " *Teve Guía*, May 13, 1973, 74–76.

79 Rey, "Para una actriz."

80 Ibid., 17.

81 "Angela Meyer vs. Sylvia del Villard," *Teve Guía*, August 3, 1974, 15–17. See also "Sylvia del Villard dice 'o comemos todos o no come nadie,' " *Teve Guía*, August 31, 1974, 14–16.

82 "Angela Meyer vs. Sylvia del Villard," 16.

83 Ibid. "Angela Meyer vs. Sylvia del Villard," *Teve Guía, Televita dice*, August 10, 1974, 27–29.

84 For information on Chianita's character and black performers' protests, see Jorge López-Llanos, "Sylvia arremete contral el prejuicio," *El Reportero*, July 6, 1982; Rubén Marrero, "Hay que 'tirar' la cosa en broma," *Vea*, January 11, 1976, 38–39; Migdalia Santiago-Vidal, "¿Qué esconde Angela Meyer detrás de Chianita?" *El Mundo*, March 10, 1985; and Pedro Zervigón, "Sylvia del Villard y la dignidad de su negritud," *El Nuevo Día*, February 9, 1990.

85 See Cobas and Duany, *Cubans in Puerto Rico*, 75–78.

86 Francisco Vergara, "Chianita es más boricua que el maví," *El Nuevo Día*, November 20, 1974.

87 Zervigón, "Sylvia del Villard."

88 When Angela Meyer (together with actress Camille Carrión) founded their theater and television production company (Producciones Meca) in the mid-1980s, they provided a space for black performers. In addition, the black characters in Meca's telenovela productions were represented as middle-class and educated individuals. For more information on Meyer's career, see Jorge Luis Burgos, "Resucita 'Chianita,'" *El Vocero*, August 18, 2001.

89 The title of this section is taken from "Escogen mulata entre dos mil bellezas para competir en Inglaterra," which appeared in *Teve Guía*, July 3, 1975, 11. I am using the racial categorizations used by local newspapers and television magazines.

90 See Aparicio, *Listening to Salsa*; Kutzinski, *Sugar's Secrets*; Shohat and Stam, *Unthinking Eurocentrisim*; and Wade, *Music, Race, and Nation*.

91 Ben Arogundade, *Black Beauty: A History and a Celebration* (New York: Thunder's Mouth Press, 2000).

92 For information on African American beauty pageants, see Leeds Craig, *Ain't I a Beauty*.

93 Kelley, "Nap Time."

94 Kelley, *Yo' Mama's*.

95 Amaury Ayala, phone interview by author, August 2002.

96 Falú, interview.

97 Ayala, interview.

98 Angela Luisa Torregrosa, "Miss Mundo 1976," *Angela Luisa*, January 1976, 16.

99 For information on Wilnelia Merced, see Samuel Badillo, "Miss Mundo y los tahúres," *El Nuevo Día*, November 26, 1975; Bartolomé Brignoni, "Cálido recibimiento para reina de belleza," *El Mundo*, November 27, 1975; Rissig Elwood-Licha, "Exhausta, mareada y feliz," *El Nuevo Día*, November 27, 1975; Nydita S. Rodríguez, "Alrededor del mundo con Miss Mundo," *El Nuevo Día*, October 19, 1976; Lydia Mercedes Silvestry de Basaldua, "Los apostadores vs. Wilnelia," *El Nuevo Día*, Novem-

ber 24, 1975; and Sucre Vásquez, "De su pueblo con amor," *El Nuevo Día*, November 27, 1975.

100 Antonio Martorrel, "Ensayo de una mirada: La estética caribeña," cited in Godreau, "Peinando," 97–98.

101 Brignoni, "Cálido."

102 Badillo, "Miss Mundo."

103 Vásquez, "De su pueblo."

104 Patricia Vargas, "Primer encuentro con la soberana," *El Nuevo Día*, October 4, 2003. For information on racist practices in Puerto Rico's beauty pageant industry, see Kelvin Rodríguez, "¿Racismo en los certamenes?" *El Nuevo Día*, January 15, 1997; and Patricia Vargas, "Majestad negra," *El Nuevo Día*, October 10, 2000.

105 Ayala, interview; "Ebony Fashion Fair Show en Puerto Rico," *El Nuevo Día*, December 13, 1977. Some of these internationally renowned black models included Elba Monge, Carmen Salamán, and Benita Stanley. Furthermore, after Wilnelia Merced won Miss World, she worked as a model in Puerto Rico, the United States, and Europe.

106 1980s white Puerto Rican model, interview by author, May 2001.

107 Colleen Ballerino Cohen, Richard Wilk, and Beverly Stoeltje, *Beauty Queen on the Global Stage: Gender, Contests, and Power* (New York: Routledge, 1996).

108 Scott, *Domination*, 4.

109 Ibid., 208.

110 Torres, "La gran familia," 299.

111 See De la Fuente, *A Nation for All*; Tyson, *Radio Free Dixie*; and Gosse, *Where the Boys Are*.

112 Michael George Hanchard, *Orpheus and Power: The Movimiento Negro of Rio De Janeiro and Sao Paulo, Brazil, 1945–1988* (Princeton, N.J.: Princeton University Press, 1994); and Howard Winant, *Racial Conditions: Politics, Theory, Comparisons* (Minneapolis: University of Minnesota Press, 1994).

113 Produced by Tommy Muñiz, *Esto no tiene nombre* began airing in 1969 on WAPA-TV, channel 4 in prime time (9:00 P.M. to 10:00 P.M.).

114 Isabel Cintrón, "El artista negro está muy limitado en Puerto Rico," *El Mundo*, November 9, 1975.

115 Duany, *The Puerto Rican Nation*, 27–28.

116 Ibid., 27.

117 For information on the integration of Cuban immigrants in Puerto Rico's economic structure, see Jorge Duany, "Two Wings of the Same Bird? Contemporary Puerto Rican Attitudes toward Cuban Immigrants," *Cuban Studies* 30 (1999): 26–51. See also Martínez-San Miguel, *Caribe Two Ways*, 103–50.

3. THE CUBARICAN SPACE REVISITED

1 For information regarding Puerto Rico's commercial television ownership, see Popelnik, "Puerto Rico."

2 Telemundo media professional, interview by author, July 1997.

3 Emilio Huyke, Tommy Muñiz, Ramón Rivero, and José Luis Torresgrosa were some of the Puerto Rican scriptwriters who actively participated in the beginning stages of Puerto Rican television. Prior to the television era, these individuals worked in radio.

4 Media professional, interview by author, May 2000.

5 *Casos y cosas de casa*, written by Alberto Cuevas, was one of the scripts originally written for Cuban television. Cubans also dominated the area of advertising in Puerto Rico and in the U.S. Spanish-language market. For an in-depth analysis of U.S. Spanish-language advertising agencies, see Dávila, *Latinos, Inc.*

6 Felipe San Pedro was born into an upper-class Cuban family. Although he studied in the "best private schools in Havana," he did not pursue a bachelor's degree due to professional opportunities in Cuban commercial radio. San Pedro began working as a radio scriptwriter in 1948 and was able to adapt his skills to television. He worked for the Cuban television station CMQ and wrote one of the most successful situation comedies in Cuba's commercial television (*Fifita y Willi*). In 1959, as did many upper-middle-class Cubans, San Pedro left Cuba and migrated to Spain, then later to Venezuela. From the 1960s to the 1970s he wrote comedies for Venezuelan, Mexican, and Puerto Rican television. In 1973 he migrated to Puerto Rico and worked exclusively for Paquito Cordero. During the 1980s the Cordero–San Pedro team had two major hits for Telemundo, the situation comedies *En casa de Juanma y Wiwi* and *La pensión de doña Tere*. In the 1990s, he wrote the situation comedy *Mi familia*. Felipe San Pedro, interview by author, July 1997.

7 In contrast to most Cuban media professionals who left Cuba in the early 1960s, Manuel Montero "Membrillo" migrated in 1973. Born into a working-class Spanish immigrant family, Montero began his professional scriptwriting career in 1953 at Radio Progreso. While Montero wrote some comedy sketches for Cuban television (specifically, for Cuban comedian Guillermo Alvarez Guedes), he devoted most of his professional work to radio, in addition to writing satiric columns for the humorous newspaper *Zigzag*. After the triumph of the Cuban Revolution and the closing of *Zizag* (due to government censorship), Montero worked at the government newspaper *Pa' lante y Pa' lante* and for the post-1959 government-monitored Radio Progreso. Due to ongoing censorship of his radio scripts and newspaper columns, the loss of his job at *Pa' lante y Pa' lante*, and the subsequent failure to find any work in Cuba, Montero and his family left the island in 1973. Because Montero's wife had family members in Puerto Rico, and given that one of his daughters was able to migrate (via Mexico) and move to Puerto Rico in 1970, the Montero family decided to make Puerto Rico their new home and country. In Puerto Rico, Manuel

Montero "Membrillo" worked as a journalist for television magazines in addition to writing numerous situation comedies and the comedy sketches in variety shows and noon programs. Some of his highly successful scripts include *El cuartel de la risa*; *Los angelitos*; *Los suegros y los nietos* (a spin-off of *Los suegros*); *Alegría del medio día*; *Super show Goya*; *Altagracia, empleada doméstica*; and *La familia política*. Montero died in 1994. Olga Montero (Manuel Montero's widow), interview by author, May 2001.

8 Puerto Rican media professional, interview by author, November 2003.

9 Mayra Cue-Sierra, "TV in Cuba: The Untold Story," in *Encyclopedia of Television*, 2d ed., ed. Horace Newcomb (Chicago: Fitzroy Dearborn Publishers, 2004), 635–37. See also the articles "Televisión en octubre," *Bohemia* 42, no. 13 (March 26, 1950), 53; "Televisión en 1950," *Bohemia* 42, no. 21 (May 21, 1950), 92; and "Televisión," *Bohemia* 42, no. 15 (April 9, 1950), 56.

10 Hernández and Paxman, *El Tigre*, 136–37.

11 For information on television's technological changes, see Popelnik, "Puerto Rico."

12 Telemundo media professional, interview by author, July 1997.

13 See ch. 1, n. 75.

14 Paquito Cordero, interview.

15 Cabrera worked for Puerto Rico's government radio and television stations (WIPR) from 1962 to 1972.

16 Pablo Cabrera, phone interview by author, September 2000.

17 Pierre Bourdieu, *The Field of Cultural Production*, trans. Randal Johnson (New York: Columbia University Press, 1993).

18 Casa Cuba is a Cuban club in Isla Verde, one of the most exclusive neighborhoods in San Juan's metropolitan area.

19 Among these Puerto Rican performers are Awilda Carbia and her character Dulce María, José Miguel Agrelot and his character Pancho Matanzas, the actor and scriptwriter Raymond Arrieta, Cuban actors and scriptwriters such as Cary Oliver and her character Caridad, Manuel Montero "Membrillo" and his character Ñico Fernández, and Felipe San Pedro.

20 Benedict Anderson, *Imagined Communities: Reflections on the Origin and Spread of Nationalism* (London: Verso, 1991).

21 My examination of *Los suegros* comes from a textual analysis of some of the show's scripts from 1981 to 1991. Because *Los suegros* lasted ten years, and because reruns are nonexistent in Puerto Rico, the situation comedy had multiple transformations in each year's fifty-two episodes. However, the older generation of Puerto Ricans and Cubans remained part of *Los suegros* narratives throughout the show's duration. Furthermore, while the situation comedy was broadcast on WAPA-TV for ten years, the first episodes of *Los suegros* were aired on channel 11.

22 David Marc, *Comic Visions: Television Comedy and American Culture* (Oxford: Blackwell Publishers, 1997). For an examination of the U.S. situation comedy genre and the articulation of cultural, social, political, and racial discourses in specific historical periods, see Brent Zook, *Color by Fox*; Vincent Brook, *Something Ain't Kosher Here: The Rise of the "Jewish" Sitcom* (New Brunswick, N.J.: Rutgers University Press, 2003); Downing, " 'The Cosby Show' "; Gray, *Watching Race*; Darrell Y. Hamamoto, *Nervous Laughter: Television Situation Comedy and Liberal Democratic Ideology* (New York: Praeger, 1989); Horace Newcomb, *TV: The Most Popular Art* (New York: Anchor Books, 1974); Smith-Shomade, *Shaded Lives*; Lynn Spigel, *Make Room for TV: Television and the Family Ideal in Postwar America* (Chicago: University of Chicago Press, 1992); and Ella Taylor, *Prime-Time Families: Television Culture in Postwar America* (Berkeley: University of California Press, 1989).

23 Aparicio, *Listening to Salsa*, 151.

24 According to Ramón Grosfoguel, Francisco Rivera Batis, and Carlos Santiago, Puerto Rico's lower class managed to endure this economic situation through federal assistance programs. In addition, similar to previous decades, massive migrations to the United States were instrumental in relieving the pressure of Puerto Rico's difficult economic situation. However, in contrast to the 1940s–1950s migration, the 1980s exodus primarily comprised professionals. Although there are no data regarding Puerto Rico's *fuga de cerebros* (brain drain), an estimate based on the 1990 U.S. Census shows that approximately 100,000 professionals migrated to the United States during the 1980s. See Olga Carrasco, "Incesante fuga de talento boricua," *El Nuevo Día*, June 7, 1999; Grosfoguel, "The Divorce"; and Francisco Rivera-Batiz and Carlos E. Santiago, *Island Paradox: Puerto Rico in the 1990s* (New York: Russell Sage Foundation, 1996).

25 In terms of class and education, the Fernández family seemed to be part of the second Cuban migration (1965–1973). According to José Cobas and Jorge Duany, the occupations of most Cubans who migrated to the U.S. (and later to Puerto Rico) between the aforementioned years were related to sales and manual labor. Cobas and Duany, *Cubans in Puerto Rico*, 47.

26 Ibid., 171–75.

27 Ibid., 173.

28 Ibid.

29 Ibid., 48.

30 For an examination of the repression of homosexuality in revolutionary Cuba, see Ian Lumsden, *Machos, Maricones, and Gays: Cuba and Homosexuality* (Philadelphia: Temple University Press, 1996).

31 According to Ana López, many films produced by the first generation of Cuban American filmmakers mythologize pre-1959 Cuban society. For an examination of

Cuban American filmmakers and their cultural products, see Ana López, "Greater Cuba," in *The Ethnic Eye: Latino Media Arts*, ed. Chon Noriega and Ana López (Minneapolis: University of Minnesota Press, 1996), 3–21.

32 *La Crónica* was founded in 1977 and, according to José Cobas and Jorge Duany, this newspaper controlled the Cuban community's public opinion in Puerto Rico's public sphere. Cobas and Duany, *Cubans in Puerto Rico*, 187–91. The success of *Los suegros* prompted a spin-off entitled *Los suegros y los nietos*. Although only a few of *Los suegros y los nietos* scripts are available, it seems that the conflict in the new situation comedy focused on the older Cubans' and Puerto Ricans' struggles regarding how to raise their grandchildren.

33 Ibid., 191.

34 Montero, interview.

35 Most of Montero's family remained in Cuba. Montero, interview.

36 See n. 7.

37 Montero, interview.

38 E-mail communication, Luis Antonio Rivera, July 2003. Luis Antonio Rivera played the part of Tito in *Los suegros* in addition to being the artistic director.

39 Manuel Montero "Membrillo" used other comedy shows to question the oppressive conditions for Dominicans in Puerto Rico. For example, the 1980s and early 1990s comedy segments on the WAPA-TV (channel 4) noon show entitled *Altagracia, empleada doméstica* (Altagracia, domestic worker), created by Puerto Rican producer Luis Vigoreaux Jr., centered on the life of Altagracia, a Dominican woman who, as the title indicates, worked as a maid. Depicted as a white, young, and hard-working woman, Altagracia was in charge of maintaining order in Don Luisito's house. Her boyfriend Tato, a Puerto Rican working-class mulatto man who worked as a tow truck driver, adored Altagracia and completely supported her. While the comedy segment mainly dealt with order, confusion, and the restoration of order caused by Altagracia, Tato, Don Luisito, Guille (Altagracia's best friend), and other sporadic characters, the text also incorporated references to Dominicans and the poverty-stricken conditions in the Dominican Republic. For example, through Altagracia's dialogues about her family in the Dominican Republic, by addressing the deportation of one of Altagracia's nephews, and by incorporating news stories about Dominicans' deaths in their efforts to migrate to Puerto Rico, the texts problematized the inhumane conditions that permeated the lives of Dominicans in both Puerto Rico and the Dominican Republic.

40 Duany, *The Puerto Rican Nation*, 27.

41 Ibid.

42 *Mi familia* media professional, interview by author, July 1997.

4. *MI FAMILIA*

1 From September 1994 to June 2002, *Mi familia* was broadcast on Tuesdays at 8:30 P.M. and the show was always on the top-ten or top-twenty rating list.

2 Interview by author, July 1997.

3 Interview by author, July 1997.

4 The most famous blackface character in the post Chianita era was Pirulo el colo-rao. Performed by a highly successful young Puerto Rican comedian (Raymond Arrieta), the character appeared in the early 1990s prime-time comedy show *Que vacilón* (WAPA-TV, channel 4). Dressed in a shiny red outfit, tennis shoes, and a curly red clownish wig, Pirulo el colorao opened his sketches by leading the live studio audience in screaming "*¿Y tu abuela, dónde está?*" (Where is your grandmother?), a phrase that is part of the island's vernacular culture and that comes from Fortunato Vizcarrondo's 1942 poem *Y tu aguela a onde ejtá*. The poem describes a black person's response to being called negro. The poem's narrator explains that his mother is in the living room (in other words, the narrator acknowledges his blackness) while the white person's grandmother is kept out of sight because she is black ("you are afraid that people will meet your mother's mother"). Responding to the antiblack racism that characterizes Puerto Rico's society, the narrator dismantles the process of whitening and the dynamics of racial mixing. Therefore, by beginning the sketches with this phrase and by donning blackface, Arrieta (a white, blue-eyed man) *apparently* wanted to demonstrate that everybody in Puerto Rico has something black in them. In other words, even though some Puerto Ricans might look white, in reality lo negro is within every Puerto Rican's (and the nation's) body.

5 Marjorie Aponte Gómez, "¿Y la risa tiene color?," *El Nuevo Día*, October 12, 2000.

6 Ibid.

7 See Rafael F. Franco, "A Baby's Factory?" *San Juan Star*, April 23, 1998; and C. J. García, "El regalo de Tito," *El Nuevo Día*, October 3, 1999.

8 Kelvin Santiago-Valles, "Policing the Crisis in the Whitest of All the Antilles," *Centro* 8, nos. 1 and 2 (spring 1996): 42–57.

9 "Confusion over the Puerto Rican Vote," *New York Times*, December 25, 1998.

10 Grosfoguel, "The Divorce over Nationalist Discourses," 68.

11 See Morris, *Puerto Rico*.

12 For information on English and Spanish-language debates in Puerto Rico, see Frances Negrón-Muntaner, "English Only Jamás but Spanish Only Cuidado: Language and Nationalism in Contemporary Puerto Rico," in *Puerto Rican Jam*, 257–85.

13 I performed a participant observation of *Mi familia*'s production process during the summers of 1997 and 1998. My textual analysis of *Mi familia* is based on the scripts written and produced between 1994 and 1999.

14 Because of the potential for controversy over the participants' answers, their names and professional affiliations have been omitted.

15 Unless indicated, Telemundo refers to the network station in Puerto Rico (WKAQ-channel 2).

16 Paquito Cordero, interview by author, July 1997.

17 Sonia Cordero, "Televisión," *El Vocero*, September 11, 1994; Todd Michael Jamison, "Blacks Break P.R. Television Comedy Barrier," *San Juan Star*, September 19, 1994; and Angela Luisa Torregrosa, "Teve cuñas," *El Nuevo Día*, September 11, 1994.

18 Melba Brugueras, "TV Día," *El Nuevo Día*, November 15, 1998.

19 Eileen Rivera-Esquilín, "Judith Pizarro . . . Entre el drama y la comedia," *El Vocero*, December 17, 1997.

20 Otilio Warrington "Bizcocho" is one of the most famous comedians on Puerto Rican television. He began his television career during the early 1970s and has participated in numerous locally produced sitcoms, variety shows, and comedies.

21 Each *Mi familia* product integration was sold in a package that included two thirty-second ads. As part of this arrangement, Cordero received approximately $1,500 per integration. This amount was divided between Cordero Teleproducciones and the actor or actress who appeared in the commercial. However, the actors received no more than half the salary they would have received for being cast as talent in a television commercial. In addition, neither *Mi familia*'s director nor the scriptwriter who served as copywriter for the ads received earnings from advertising. There are no unions for actors, directors, or writers in Puerto Rico; therefore, the creative community is not protected from financial exploitation by advertising agencies and local producers. Although several attempts have been made to organize unions for the creative community, they have all failed because of a lack of support from television stations and independent producers.

22 For information on the whiteness that characterizes Puerto Rico and U.S. Spanish-language advertising industries, see Dávila, *Sponsored Identities*; Dávila, *Latinos, Inc.*; and Rafael Lama Bonilla, "Racismo publicitario," *El Nuevo Día*, October 13, 2000.

23 Every program broadcast on Telemundo has a categorization that specifies whether a particular show is suitable for children.

24 See ch. 3, n. 6.

25 *Mi familia*'s production was accomplished with minimal financial and creative resources. The entire process of rehearsal, taping, and editing was usually completed in approximately five hours, the script was in the hands of only one writer, and the director performed multiple tasks (directing, punching the cameras, and sometimes editing). Despite this simplified process, there were some technical problems. For example, at four of the seven taping sessions in which I was a participant observer, there were delays. On the first day, one of the booms (microphones) was not working well and created an echo. On the second day, one of the locations did not have enough light. On the third day, one of the camera stands was not functioning

properly. On the fourth day the sound cables were not properly connected and they had trouble with two booms. During all of the aforementioned inconveniences the director solved each problem. On two of those days, the taping sessions ended at 11:30 P.M., one hour later than scheduled. Unless an emergency occurred, no production meetings were held. All of the preliminary aspects were resolved over the telephone. In this way, everything was done with minimal cost. As a *Mi familia* production member observed, "we are not like the U.S. [television] market. We go ahead and do the best that is possible and then go in front of the cameras." Certainly, these limitations affected *Mi familia*'s potential, a factor of which all the interviewees were keenly aware.

26 *Mi familia* production member, interview by author, July 1997.

27 Carrasco, "Incesante fuga."

28 These portrayals coincide with the networks that are created and maintained by Puerto Ricans on the island and in the United States. The Puerto Rican immigrants, especially those belonging to the post-World War II group, visited their families regularly, something that encouraged those living on the mainland to sustain strong emotional ties to Puerto Rico's customs and traditions. See Duany, *The Puerto Rican Nation*; and Sánchez-Korrol, *From Colonia to Community*.

29 For an analysis of Puerto Ricans' perceptions of Nuyoricans, see Duany, *The Puerto Rican Nation*; Morris, *Puerto Rico*; and Ramos-Zayas, *National Performances*.

30 Morris, *Puerto Rico*, 125.

31 See Duany, *The Puerto Rican Nation*.

32 The topic of Puerto Rican communities in the United States and the issue of Puerto Rican assimilation into U.S. culture have been recurrent themes in locally produced comedies. For example, as early as 1954, some of Ramón Rivero's *La taberna India* comedy segments included references to jíbaros/as who had migrated to the United States during the 1940s and who, regardless of the fact that Spanish was their first language, insisted on talking in English when visiting the island. One of the most famous Nuyorican characters in Puerto Rico's commercial television was Johnny el men. Since the 1970s, Johnny el men had appeared in various locally produced comedies. In addition, Johnny el men was one of the principal characters featured on the 1980s WAPA-TV (channel 4) noon segment, *La tiendita de la esquina* (conceptualized and for the most part written by Puerto Rican film director Jacobo Morales). Future research should explore the ways in which Nuyoricans have been constructed in Puerto Rico's commercial television and in movies (for example, Jacobo Morales's *Linda Sara* and Frances Negrón-Muntaner's *Brincando el charco*). In addition, these media depictions should be compared with literary representations of the Puerto Rican diaspora. See Juan Flores, *La venganza de Cortijo y otros ensayos* (Río Piedras: Huracán, 1997); and Lisa Sánchez-González, *Boricua Literature: A Literary History of the Puerto Rican Diaspora* (New York: New York University Press, 2001).

33 As Nancy Morris contends, pro-statehood individuals do not question their Puerto Rican "identity," even though they support statehood for the island. See Morris, *Puerto Rico*, 103–26.

34 William Agosto, interview by author, July 1997. Agosto is the actor who created the character Pichón.

35 bell hooks, *Black Looks: Race and Representation* (Boston: South End Press, 1992), 92. See also Fanon, *Black Skin*.

36 See Richard Dyer, *White* (London: Routledge, 1994).

37 hooks, *Black Looks*.

38 Also see chapter 2's section on *El hijo de Angela María* and Chianita's character.

39 According to *Mi familia*'s production members, the incorporation of sex into the narratives was designed to irritate Morality in Media and the Catholic Church. On occasions when the station criticized the characters' behavior, *Mi familia*'s production staff immediately stated that it was morally permissible since sexuality was performed within the institution of matrimony.

40 Fanon, *Black Skin*.

41 Kobena Mercer, *Welcome to the Jungle: New Positions in Black Cultural Studies* (New York: Routledge, 1994).

42 Arcadio Díaz-Quiñones, *La memoria rota* (Río Piedras: Huracán, 1993).

43 Rafael Lama Bonilla, "Metamorfosis en Telemundo de Puerto Rico," *El Nuevo Día*, May 10, 1999.

44 See Dávila, *Latinos, Inc.*

45 According to a Telemundo media professional, *Mi familia* did not do well in the U.S. Spanish-language market. The U.S. rating numbers were not available.

46 "Encuesta Mediafax," *Primera Hora*, October 16, 2002.

47 Firuzeh Shokooh Valle, Karol Joselyn Sepúlveda, and Aixa Sepúlveda Morales, "Supremacía de 'Gata salvaje' provoca reclamo de productores," *Primera Hora*, October 16, 2002.

48 Ibid.

49 Ibid.

50 Ibid.

51 Milly Cangiano, "Primera fila," *Primera Hora*, October 28, 2002.

52 Rosalina Marrero-Rodríguez, "Los Seijo Díaz queda fuera de la programación de Telemundo," *Primera Hora*, October 30, 2002; and Damarys Quiñones-Torres, "Cero lágrimas," *Vea*, July 13, 2003.

53 Sinclair, "The Hollywood," 218.

54 Darryl Fears, "Race Divides Hispanics, Report Says; Integration and Income Vary with Skin Color," *Washington Post*, July 14, 2003.

55 "What's New Around the Union This Week," *Communication Workers of America*, January 28, 2004.

56 Ibid.
57 Marcelo Ballvé, "The Battle for Latino Media," *NACLA* 37, no. 4 (2004): 25.
58 See Streeter, *Selling the Air*, 132–48.
59 "What's New."
60 "UPAGRA Protests Outsourcing Effort," *Newspaper Guild*, February 27, 2004.

5. TRANSLATING AND REPRESENTING BLACKNESS

1 Rosalina Marrero-Rodríguez, "Diversidad de físicos en Miss Puerto Rico Universe 2004," *Primera Hora*, September 2, 2003.
2 Araújo, *A negação*, 89–95.
3 Appadurai, "Disjuncture and Difference."
4 Duany, *The Puerto Rican Nation*.
5 Lawrence Venuti, "Translation, Community, and Utopia," in *The Translation Studies Reader*, ed. Venuti Lawrence (London: Routledge, 2000), 468.
6 Venuti, "Translation," 485.
7 Taylor, *The Archive and the Repertoire*, 12.
8 Venuti, "Translation," 485.
9 I am using Michael Omi and Howard Winant's interpretation of Gramsci's theories of "war of maneuver" and "war of position" as described in *Racial Formation*, 86.
10 Ibid.
11 Gray, *Watching Race*, 77.
12 Hanchard, *Orpheus and Power*, 14.
13 Newcomb and Hirsch, "Television as a Cultural Forum."
14 Ibid., 513.
15 Philip Schlesinger, " 'Identities: Traditions and New Communities': A Response," *Media, Culture, and Society* 24, no. 5 (2002): 643–48.
16 For information regarding the 2003 selection of a nonwhite woman as Miss Universe–Puerto Rico, see Melba Brugueras, "Confesiones en un recorrido real," *El Vocero*, October 4, 2003; Jorge Luis Burgos, "Alba Reyes Santos emocionada con su coronación," *El Vocero*, October 4, 2003; Rosalina Marrero-Rodríguez, "Alba Reyes se sorprendió al ganar la corona," *Primera Hora*, October 4, 2003; Rosalina Marrero-Rodríguez, "Un evento de cuatro reinas," *Primera Hora*, October 4, 2004; and Vargas, "Primer encuentro con la soberana."
17 Brugueras, "Confesiones en un recorrido real"; Ana Enid López-Rodríguez, "Plagado de desaciertos el certamen de belleza," *El Nuevo Día*, October 4, 2003; and Marrero-Rodríguez, "Alba Reyes se sorprendió."
18 Marrero-Rodríguez, "Alba Reyes se sorprendió."
19 See the electronic postings "La nueva Miss Puerto Rico Universe . . . Miss Cidra, Alba Reyes"; "¿Si no la apoyamos nosotros, quién lo hará?"; and "La reina de nuestra cultura." Available at http://futuroe3.com/mpru/foros.htm, accessed October 15, 2003.

20 Stuart Hall, "What Is This 'Black' in Black Popular Culture," in *Black Popular Culture*, ed. Gina Dent (Seattle: Bay Press, 1992), 23.

21 L. S. Kim and Gilberto Blasini, "The Performance of Multicultural Identity in U.S. Network Television: Shiny, Happy Popstars (Holding Hands)," *Emergences* 11, no. 2 (2001), 291.

22 Licia Fiol-Mata, "Pop *Latinidad*: Puerto Ricans in the Latin Explosion, 1999," *Centro* 14, no. 1 (2002): 26–51. See also Dávila, *Latinos, Inc.*; and Flores, *From Bomba to Hip-Hop*.

23 Mary Beltrán, "The Hollywood Latina Body as Site of Social Struggle: Media Constructions of Stardom and Jennifer Lopez's Cross-over Butt," *The Quarterly Review of Film and Video* 19, no. 1 (January 2002): 71–86.

24 Lisa Lowe, *Immigrant Acts: On Asian American Cultural Politics* (Durham, N.C.: Duke University Press, 1996).

25 Paul Gilroy, *Against Race: Imagining Political Culture Beyond the Color Line* (Cambridge, Mass.: Harvard University Press, 2000); and Howard Winant, *The World Is a Ghetto: Race and Democracy Since World War II* (New York: Basic Books, 2001), 308.

26 Fanon, *Black Skin*.

27 Aixa Sepúlveda-Morales, "Miss Puerto Rico Universe borra sus marcas en 15 minutos," *Primera Hora*, February 25, 2004.

28 See the electronic postings "¿Qué es de la vida de Alba?" and "¿Crees que se le debe operar la nariz a Miss Universe Puerto Rico?" Available at http://futuroe3.com/mpru/foros.htm.

29 Ibid.

30 Hall, "What Is This 'Black.'"

Bibliography

Allen, Robert, ed. *To Be Continued: Soap Operas Around the World*. Chapel Hill: University of North Carolina Press, 1995.

Alvarez-Curbelo, Sylvia, and María Elena Rodríguez-Castro. *Del nacionalismo al populismo: Cultura y política en Puerto Rico*. Río Piedras, Puerto Rico: Huracán, 1993.

Alvarez-Nazario, Manuel. *El elemento afronegroide en el español de Puerto Rico*. San Juan, Puerto Rico: Instituto de Cultura Puertorriqueña, 1974.

Anderson, Benedict. *Imagined Communities: Reflections on the Origin and Spread of Nationalism*. London: Verso, 1991.

Aparicio, Frances. *Listening to Salsa: Gender, Latin Popular Music, and Puerto Rican Cultures*. London: Wesleyan University Press, 1998.

Appadurai, Arjun. "Disjuncture and Difference in the Global Cultural Economy." In *Global Culture: Nationalism, Globalization, and Modernity*, edited by Mike Featherstone, 295–310. London: Sage, 1990.

Araújo, Joel Zito. *A negação do Brasil: O negro na telenovela brasileira*. Sao Paolo, Brazil: Editora Senac, 2000.

Arogundade, Ben. *Black Beauty: A History and a Celebration*. New York: Thunder's Mouth Press, 2000.

Arroyo, Jossianna. "*Raíces* o la duplicidad de los imaginarios raciales en Puerto Rico." Paper presented at the Latin American Studies Association Conference, Houston, Texas, 2003.

Astroff, Roberta. "Communication and Contemporary Colonialism: Broadcast Television in Puerto Rico." *Studies in Latin American Popular Culture*, no. 11 (1987): 11–24.

Ballvé, Marcelo. "The Battle for Latino Media." *NACLA* 37, no. 4 (2004): 20–27.

Banton, Michael. *Ethnic and Racial Consciousness*. New York: Longman, 1997.

Barrera, Aída. *Looking for Carrascolendas: From a Child's World to Award-Winning Television*. Austin: University of Texas Press, 2001.

Beltrán, Mary. "The Hollywood Latina Body as Site of Social Struggle: Media Constructions of Stardom and Jennifer Lopez's Cross-over Butt." *The Quarterly Review of Film and Video* 19, no.1 (January 2002): 71–86.

Benmayor, Rina. "La 'Nueva Trova': New Cuban Song." *Latin American Music Review* 2, no. 1 (spring 1981): 11–29.

Benson-Arias, Jaime E. "Puerto Rico: The Myth of the National Economy." In *Puerto Rican Jam: Essays on Culture and Politics*, edited by Frances Negrón-Muntaner and Ramón Grosfoguel, 77–96. Minneapolis: University of Minnesota Press, 1997.

Berrey, Stephen. " 'Bad Negroes,' 'Troublemakers,' and 'Outside Agitators': The Criminalization of Black Resistance and Civil Rights Activism." Chapter 4, Ph.D. dissertation, University of Texas, n.d.

Betances, Samuel. "The Prejudice of Having No Prejudice in Puerto Rico, Part I." *The Rican*, no. 2 (1972): 41–54.

———. "The Prejudice of Having No Prejudice in Puerto Rico, Part II." *The Rican*, no. 3 (1973): 22–37.

Bhabha, Homi K. *The Location of Culture*. London: Routledge, 1994.

Blanco, Tomás. *El prejuicio racial en Puerto Rico*. Edited by Arcadio Díaz-Quiñones. Río Piedras, Puerto Rico: Huracán, 1985.

Bogle, Donald. *Toms, Coons, Mulattoes, Mammies, and Bucks: An Interpretive History of Blacks in American Films*. 3d ed. New York: Continuum, 1995.

———. *Prime Time Blues: African Americans on Network Television*. New York: Farrar, Straus and Giroux, 2001.

Bourdieu, Pierre. *The Field of Cultural Production*. Translated by Randal Johnson. New York: Columbia University Press, 1993.

Brent Zook, Kristal. *Color by Fox: The Fox Network and the Revolution in Black Television*. New York: Oxford University Press, 1999.

Brook, Vincent. *Something Ain't Kosher Here: The Rise of the "Jewish" Sitcom*. New Brunswick, N.J.: Rutgers University Press, 2003.

Buonanno, Milly. "The Paradigm of Indigenization: Television between Global Supply and Local Consumption." Paper presented at the Radio-TV-Film Department, University of Texas at Austin, 1998.

———. *El drama televisivo: Identidad y contenidos sociales*. Barcelona: Gedisa, 1999.

Butler, Judith. "Performative Acts and Gender Constitution: An Essay in Phenomenology and Feminist Theory." In *Performing Feminism: Feminist Critical Theory and Theatre*, edited by Sue-Ellen Case, 270–82. Baltimore: Johns Hopkins University Press, 1990.

Cardona, Javier. "You Don't Look Like." *Conjunto*, no. 106 (1997): 48–49.

Cobas, José A., and Jorge Duany. *Cubans in Puerto Rico: Ethnic Economy and Cultural Identity*. Gainesville: University Press of Florida, 1997.

Cohen Colleen, Ballerino, Richard Wilk, and Beverly Stoeltje. *Beauty Queen on the Global Stage: Gender, Contests, and Power*. New York: Routledge, 1996.

Colón-Zayas, Eliseo. "La hora del cuerpo: recepción y consumo de la comedia en Puerto Rico." *Diá·logos*, no. 30 (1991): 65–75.

Cue-Sierra, Mayra. "TV in Cuba: The Untold Story." In *Encyclopedia of Television*, 2d ed., edited by Horace Newcomb, 635–37. Chicago: Fitzroy Dearborn Publishers, 2004.

Dávila, Arlene. *Sponsored Identities: Cultural Politics in Puerto Rico*. Philadelphia: Temple University Press, 1997.

———. "El Kiosko Budweiser: The Making of a 'National' Television Show in Puerto Rico." *American Ethnologist* 25, no. 3 (1998): 452–71.

———. *Latinos, Inc.: The Marketing and Making of a People*. Berkeley: University of California Press, 2001.

Davis, Darien. "Criollo or Mulatto? Cultural Identity in Cuba, 1930–1960." In *Ethnicity, Race, and Nationalism in the Caribbean*, edited by Juan Manuel Carrión, 69–96. Río Piedras: University of Puerto Rico, 1997.

Davis, James F. *Who Is Black? Our Nation's Definition*. University Park: Pennsylvania State University Press, 1991.

De la Fuente, Alejandro. *A Nation for All: Race, Inequality, and Politics in Twentieth-Century Cuba*. Chapel Hill: University of North Carolina Press, 2001.

Díaz, Luis Felipe, and Marc Zimmerman, eds. *Globalización, nación, postmodernidad: Estudios culturales puertorriqueños*. San Juan, Puerto Rico: Ediciones LACASA, 2001.

Díaz-Quiñones, Arcadio. "Tomás Blanco: racismo, historia, esclavitud." In *El prejuicio racial en Puerto Rico*, edited by Arcadio Díaz-Quiñones, 13–91. Río Piedras, Puerto Rico: Huracán, 1985.

———. *La memoria rota*. Río Piedras, Puerto Rico: Huracán, 1993.

Downing, John. " 'The Cosby Show' and American Racial Discourse." In *Discourse and Discrimination*, edited by Geneva Smitherman-Donaldson and Teun Van Dijk, 46–73. Detroit: Wayne State University Press, 1988.

Duany, Jorge. "Popular Music in Puerto Rico: Toward an Anthropology of Salsa." *Latin American Music Review* 5, no. 2 (1984): 186–216.

———. "Ethnic Identity and Socioeconomic Adaptations: The Case of Cubans in Puerto Rico." *Journal of Ethnic Studies* 17, no. 1 (1989): 109–27.

———. *Los dominicanos en Puerto Rico: migración en la semi-periferia*. Río Piedras, Puerto Rico: Huracán, 1990.

———. "Caribbean Migration to Puerto Rico: A Comparison of Cubans and Dominicans." *International Migration Review* 26, no. 1 (1992): 46–66.

———. "Reconstructing Racial Identity: Ethnicity, Color, and Class among Dominicans in the United States and Puerto Rico." *Latin American Perspectives* 25, no. 100 (1998): 147–72.

———. "Two Wings of the Same Bird? Contemporary Puerto Rican Attitudes toward Cuban Immigrants." *Cuban Studies* 30 (1999): 26–51.

———. *The Puerto Rican Nation on the Move: Identities on the Island and in the United States*. Chapel Hill: University of North Carolina Press, 2002.

Duany, Jorge, Luisa Hernández-Angueira, and César Rey. *Economía subterránea y migración indocumentada en Puerto Rico*. Caracas, Venezuela: Nueva Sociedad, 1995.

Dyer, Richard. *White*. London: Routledge, 1994.

Early, James. "An African American-Puerto Rican Connection: An Auto-Bio-Memory Sketch of Political Development and Activism." In *The Puerto Rican Movement: Voices from the Diaspora*, edited by Andrés Torres and José A. Velázquez, 316–28. Philadelphia: Temple University Press, 1998.

Fanon, Frantz. *Black Skin, White Masks*. Translated by Charles Lam Markmann. New York: Grove Weidenfeld, 1967.

Feng, Peter X. *Identities in Motion: Asian American Film and Video*. Durham, N.C.: Duke University Press, 2002.

Fernández, Fátima. "Algo más sobre los orígenes de la televisión latinoamericana." *Diá·Logos*, 18 (1987): 33–45.

Ferrer, Ada. *Insurgent Cuba: Race, Nation, and Revolution, 1868–1898*. Chapel Hill: University of North Carolina Press, 1999.

Fiol-Mata, Licia. "Pop *Latinidad*: Puerto Ricans in the Latin Explosion, 1999." *Centro* 14, no. 1 (2002): 26–51.

Fiske, John. *Media Matters: Race and Gender in U.S. Politics*. Minneapolis: University of Minnesota Press, 1996.

Flores, Juan. *Divided Borders: Essays on Puerto Rican Identity*. Houston: Arte Público Press, 1993.

———. *La venganza de Cortijo y otros ensayos*. Río Piedras, Puerto Rico: Huracán, 1997.

———. *From Bomba to Hip-Hop: Puerto Rican Culture and Latino Identity*. New York: Columbia University Press, 2000.

Flores-Caraballo, Eliut D. "The Politics of Culture in Puerto Rican Television: A Macro/Micro Study of English vs. Spanish Language Television." Ph.D. dissertation, University of Texas, 1991.

Fox, Elizabeth, and Silvio Waisbord, eds. *Latin Politics, Global Media*. Austin: University of Texas Press, 2002.

Frederik, Laurie Aleen. "The Contestation of Cuba's Public Sphere in National Theatre and the Transformation from Teatro Bufo to Teatro Nuevo." *Gestos* 31 (2001): 65–98.

Freire, Paulo. *Pedagogy of the Opressed*. Translated by Myra Bergman Ramos. Rev. ed. New York: Continuum, 1993.

García Ramis, Magali. *Happy Days, Uncle Sergio*. Translated by Carmen C. Esteves. Fredonia, N.Y.: White Pine Press, 1995.

Gelpi, Juan G. *Literatura y paternalismo en Puerto Rico*. Río Piedras, Puerto Rico: Editorial de la Universidad de Puerto Rico, 1993.

Gilroy, Paul. *The Black Atlantic: Modernity and Double Consciousness*. Cambridge, Mass.: Harvard University Press, 1993.

———. *Against Race: Imagining Political Culture Beyond the Color Line*. Cambridge, Mass.: Harvard University Press, 2000.

Godreau, Isar. "Peinando diferencias, bregas de pertenencia: El alisado y el llamado 'pelo malo.' " *Caribbean Studies* 30, no. 1 (2002): 82–133.

González, José Luis. *El país de cuatro pisos y otros ensayos*. Río Piedras, Puerto Rico: Huracán, 1980.

Gordon, Edmund T. *Disparate Diasporas: Identity and Politics in an African Nicaraguan Community*. Austin: University of Texas Press, 1998.

Gosse, Van. *Where the Boys Are: Cuba, Cold War America, and the Making of a New Left*. London: Verso, 1993.

Gray, Herman. *Watching Race: Television and the Struggle for "Blackness."* Minneapolis: University of Minnesota Press, 1995.

———. "Remembering Civil Rights: Television, Memory, and the 1960s." In *The Revolution Wasn't Televised*, edited by Michael Curtin and Lynn Spigel, 349–58. London: Routledge, 1997.

———. "Black Representation in the Post Network, Post Civil Rights World of Global Media." In *Ethnic Minorities and the Media*, edited by Simon Cottle, 118–29. London: Open University Press, 2000.

Gripsrud, Jostein. *The Dynasty Years: Hollywood Television and Critical Media Studies*. London: Routledge, 1995.

Grosfoguel, Ramón. "The Divorce of Nationalist Discourses from the Puerto Rican People: A Sociohistorical Perspective." In *Puerto Rican Jam: Essays on Culture and Politics*, edited by Frances Negrón-Muntaner and Ramón Grosfoguel, 39–56. Minneapolis: University of Minnesota Press, 1997.

Grosfoguel, Ramón, and Chloé S. Georas. "Latino Caribbean Diasporas in New York." In *Mambo Montage: The Latinization of New York*, edited by Agustín Laó-Montes and Arlene Dávila, 97–118. New York: Columbia University Press, 2001.

Guerra, Lillian. *Popular Expression and National Identity in Puerto Rico: The Struggle for Self, Community, and Nation*. Gainesville: University of Florida Press, 1998.

Guisti-Cordero, Juan. "Afropuerto Rican Cultural Studies: Beyond Cultural Negroide and Antillanismo." *Centro* 8, nos. 1 and 2 (1996): 56–77.

Haggins, Bambi L. "Why 'Beulah' and 'Andy' Still Play Today: Minstrelsy in the New Millennium." *Emergences* 11, no. 2 (2001): 249–67.

Hall, Stuart. "The Whites of Their Eyes: Racist Ideologies and the Media." In *Silver Linings: Some Strategies for the Eighties: Contributions to the Communist University of London*, edited by Georges Bridges and Rosalind Brunt, 28–52. London: Lawrence and Wishart, 1981.

———. "What Is This 'Black' in Black Popular Culture." In *Black Popular Culture*, edited by Gina Dent, 21–36. Seattle: Bay Press, 1992.

Hamamoto, Darrell Y. *Nervous Laughter: Television Situation Comedy and Liberal Democratic Ideology*. New York: Praeger, 1989.

Hanchard, Michael George. "Black Cinderella?: Race and the Public Sphere in Brazil." *Public Culture*, no. 7 (1994): 165–85.

———. *Orpheus and Power: The Movimiento Negro of Rio De Janeiro and Sao Paulo, Brazil, 1945–1988*. Princeton, N.J.: Princeton University Press, 1994.

Helg, Aline. *Our Rightful Share: The Afro-Cuban Struggle for Equality, 1886–1912*. Chapel Hill: University of North Carolina Press, 1995.

Hernández, Claudia, and Andrew Paxman. *El Tigre: Emilio Azcárraga y su imperio Televisa*. Mexico City: Grijalbo, 2000.

Hernández, Luis Alberto. "The Origins of the Consumer Culture in Puerto Rico: The Pre-Television Years (1898–1954)." *Centro* 3, no. 1 (winter 1990–1991): 38–54.

Hilmes, Michele. *Radio Voices: American Broadcasting, 1922–1952*. Minneapolis: University of Minnesota Press, 1997.

hooks, bell. *Black Looks: Race and Representation*. Boston: South End Press, 1992.

Ibarra, Jorge. *Prologue to a Revolution: Cuba, 1898–1958*. Translated by Marjorie Moore. London: Lynne Rienner, 1998.

James, Winston. *Holding Aloft the Banner of Ethiopia: Caribbean Radicalism in Early Twentieth-Century America*. London: Verso, 1998.

Jiménez, Lillian. "From the Margin to the Center: Puerto Rican Cinema in New York." In *Latin Looks: Images of Latinas and Latinos in the U.S. Media*, edited by Clara Rodríguez, 188–99. Boulder, Colo.: Westview Press, 1997.

Jiménez-Muñoz, Gladys M. "Siomara mi hejmana: Diplo y el travestismo racial en el Puerto Rico de los años cincuenta." *Bordes* 2 (1995): 15–27.

Jiménez-Román, Miriam. "Un Hombre (Negro) Del Pueblo: José Celso Barbosa and the Puerto Rican 'Race' toward Whiteness." *Centro* 8, nos. 1 and 2 (1996): 8–29.

Kelley, Robin D. G. "Nap Time: Historicizing the Afro." *Fashion Theory* 1, no. 4 (1997): 339–52.

———. *Yo' Mama's Disfunktional!: Fighting the Culture Wars in Urban America*. Boston: Beacon Press, 1997.

Kim, L. S., and Gilberto Blasini. "The Performance of Multicultural Identity in U.S. Network Television: Shiny, Happy Popstars (Holding Hands)." *Emergences* 11, no. 2 (2001): 287–307.

Knight, Alden. "Tackling Racism in Performing Arts and the Media." In *Afro-Cuban Voices: On Race and Identity in Contemporary Cuba*, edited by Pedro Pérez Sarduy and Jean Stubbs, 108–17. Gainesville: University Press of Florida, 2000.

Kutzinski, Vera M. *Sugar's Secrets: Race and the Erotics of Cuban Nationalism*. Charlottesville: University Press of Virginia, 1993.

La Fountain-Stokes, Lawrence. "1898 and the History of a Queer Puerto Rican Century: Gay Lives, Island Debates, and Diasporic Experience." *Centro* 11, no. 1 (1999): 91–109.

Lane, Jill. "Blackface Nationalism, Cuba 1840–1868." *Theatre Journal* 50, no. 1 (1998): 21–28.

Laó-Montes, Agustín. "Niuyol: Urban Regime, Latino Social Movements, Ideologies of Latinidad." In *Mambo Montage: The Latinization of New York*, edited by Agustín Laó-Montes and Arlene Dávila, 119–58. New York: Columbia University Press, 2001.

Leal, Rine, ed. *Teatro mambí.* Havana: Editorial Letras Cubanas, 1978.

———. *Breve historia del teatro cubano.* Havana: Editorial Letras Cubanas, 1980.

———. *La selva oscura: de los Bufos de la neocolonia.* Havana: Editorial Arte y Literatura, 1982.

———. "Marginalismo y escena nacional." *Revista Tablas* 1 (January–May 1982): 13–22.

———. *Teatro del siglo XIX.* Vol. 1. Havana: Editorial letras cubanas, 1986.

Leeds Craig, Maxine. *Ain't I a Beauty Queen?: Black Women, Beauty, and the Politics of Race.* New York: Oxford University Press, 2002.

López, Ana. "Our Welcomed Guests: Telenovelas in Latin America." In *To Be Continued: Soap Operas Around the World*, edited by Robert Allen, 256–75. London: Routledge, 1995.

———. "Greater Cuba." In *The Ethnic Eye: Latino Media Arts*, edited by Chon Noriega and Ana López, 3–21. Minneapolis: University of Minnesota Press, 1996.

Lott, Eric. *Love and Theft: Blackface Minstrelsy and the American Working Class.* New York: Oxford University Press, 1993.

Lowe, Lisa. *Immigrant Acts: On Asian American Cultural Politics.* Durham, N.C.: Duke University Press, 1996.

Lumsden, Ian. *Machos, Maricones, and Gays: Cuba and Homosexuality.* Philadelphia: Temple University Press, 1996.

Marc, David. *Comic Visions: Television Comedy and American Culture.* Oxford: Blackwell Publishers, 1997.

Martín-Barbero, Jesús. *Communication, Culture, and Hegemony, from the Media to Mediations.* Translated by Elizabeth Fox and Robert A. White. London: Sage, 1993.

———. "Memory and Form in the Latin American Soap Opera." In *To Be Continued: Soap Operas around the World*, edited by Robert Allen, 276–84. London: Routledge, 1995.

Martín-Barbero, Jesús, and Sonia Muñoz, eds. *Televisión y melodrama: Género y lecturas de la telenovela en Colombia.* Bogotá, Colombia: Tercer Mundo, 1992.

Martínez-San Miguel, Yolanda. *Caribe Two Ways: Cultura de la migración en el Caribe insular hispánico.* San Juan, Puerto Rico: Ediciones Callejón, 2003.

Martorell, Antonio. "Ensayo de una mirada: La estética caribeña." *Plástica, órgano cultural de la Liga de Estudiantes de Arte de San Juan* (1981): 14–17.

Mazziotti, Nora, ed. *El espectáculo de la pasión: Las telenovelas latinoamericanas.* Buenos Aires: Ediciones Colihue, 1995.

———. *La industria de la telenovela: La producción de ficción en América Latina.* Buenos Aires: Paidós, 1996.

Mendoza, María Inés. "La telenovela venezolana: De artesanal a industrial." *Diá•logos*, no. 44 (1996): 23–42.

Mercer, Kobena. *Welcome to the Jungle: New Positions in Black Cultural Studies.* New York: Routledge, 1994.

Mirabal, Nancy Raquel. " 'No Country But the One We Must Fight For': The Emergence of an Antillean Nation and Community in New York City." In *Mambo Montage: The Latinization of New York*, edited by Agustín Laó-Montes and Arlene Dávila, 57–72. New York: Columbia University Press, 2001.

Moore, Robin D. *Nationalizing Blackness: Afrocubanismo and Artistic Revolution in Havana, 1920–1940.* Pittsburgh: University of Pittsburgh Press, 1997.

Morales, Iris. "Palante, Siempre Palante: The Young Lords." In *The Puerto Rican Movement: Voices from the Diaspora*, edited by Andrés Torres and José A. Velázquez, 210–27. Philadelphia: Temple University Press, 1998.

Morfi, Angelina. *Historia crítica de un siglo de teatro puertorriqueño.* Madrid: Manuel Pareja, 1980.

Morris, Nancy. *Puerto Rico: Culture, Politics, and Identity.* Westport, Conn.: Praeger, 1995.

———. "The Myth of Unadulterated Culture Meets the Threat of Imported Media." *Media, Culture, and Society* 24, no. 2 (2002): 278–89.

Muguercia, Magaly. "El 'teatro de arte' en Cuba entre 1936 y 1950." *Revista Tablas* 4 (1984): 2–15.

Muñoz, José Esteban. *Disidentifications: Queers of Color and Performance of Politics.* Minneapolis: University of Minnesota Press, 1999.

Neal, Mark Anthony. *What the Music Said: Black Popular Music and Black Public Culture.* London: Routledge, 1999.

Negrón-Muntaner, Frances. "Echoing Stonewall and Other Dilemmas: The Organizational Beginnings of a Gay and Lesbian Agenda in Puerto Rico, 1972–1977." *Centro* 4, no. 1 (1991–1992): 77–95.

———. "English Only Jamás but Spanish Only Cuidado: Language and Nationalism in Contemporary Puerto Rico." In *Puerto Rican Jam: Essays on Culture and Politics*, edited by Frances Negrón-Muntaner and Ramón Grosfoguel, 257–85. Minneapolis: University of Minnesota Press, 1997.

Negrón-Muntaner, Frances, and Ramón Grosfoguel, eds. *Puerto Rican Jam: Essays on Culture and Politics.* Minneapolis: University of Minnesota Press, 1997.

Negrón-Portillo, Mariano. "Puerto Rico: Surviving Colonialism and Nationalism." In *Puerto Rican Jam: Essays on Culture and Politics*, edited by Frances Negrón-

Muntaner and Ramon Grosfoguel, 39–56. Minneapolis: University of Minnesota Press, 1997.

Nelson, Jennifer A. "Abortion under Community Control: Feminism, Nationalism, and the Politics of Reproduction among New York City's Young Lords." *Journal of Women's History* 13, no. 1 (2001): 157–80.

Newcomb, Horace. *TV: The Most Popular Art*. New York: Anchor Books, 1974.

Newcomb, Horace, and Paul Hirsch. "Television as a Cultural Forum." In *Television: The Critical View*, 5th ed., edited by Horace Newcomb, 503–15. New York: Oxford University Press, 1994.

Noriega, Chon. *Shot in America: Television, the State, and the Rise of Chicano Cinema*. Minneapolis: University of Minnesota Press, 2000.

Omi, Michael, and Howard Winant. *Racial Formation in the United States: From the 1960s to the 1990s*. 2d ed. London: Routledge, 1994.

Otero-Garabís, Juan. *Nación y ritmo: Descargas desde el caribe*. San Juan, Puerto Rico: Ediciones Callejón, 2000.

Palés-Matos, Luis. *Tuntún de pasa y grifería: Poemas afroantillanos*. San Juan, Puerto Rico: Biblioteca de autores puertorriqueños, 1937.

Pérez-Sarduy, Pedro, and Jean Stubbs. *Afro-Cuban Voices: On Race and Identity in Contemporary Cuba*. Gainesville: University Press of Florida, 2000.

Popelnik, Rodolfo B. "Puerto Rico." In *Encyclopedia of Television*, edited by Horace Newcomb, 1319–21. Chicago: Fitzroy Dearborn Publishers, 1997.

———. "Television in Puerto Rico." In *Encyclopedia of Television*, 2d ed., edited by Horace Newcomb, 1858–62. Chicago: Fitzroy Dearborn Publishers, 2004.

Quijano, Anibal. "The Colonial Nature of Power and Latin America's Cultural Experience." In *Sociology in Latin America*, edited by Roberto Briceño-León and Heinz Sonntag, 27–38. Colonia Tovar, Venezuela: ISA, 1997.

Quintero-Rivera, Angel. *Conflictos de clase y política en Puerto Rico*. Río Piedras, Puerto Rico: Huracán, 1986.

———. *Patricios y plebeyos: Burgueses, hacendados, artesanos y obreros: Las relaciones de clase en el Puerto Rico de cambio de siglo*. Río Piedras, Puerto Rico: Huracán, 1988.

———. *Salsa, sabor y control: Sociología de la música tropical*. Madrid: Siglo veintiuno, 1998.

Raheja, Michelle. "Screening Identity: Beads, Buckskin and Redface in Autobiography and Film." Ph.D. dissertation, University of Chicago, 2001.

Ramos-Rosado, Marie. *La mujer negra en la literatura puertorriqueña*. Río Piedras, Puerto Rico: Editorial de la Universidad de Puerto Rico, 1999.

Ramos-Zayas, Ana Yolanda. *National Performances: The Politics of Class, Race, and Space in Puerto Rican Chicago*. Chicago: University of Chicago Press, 2003.

Rivera, Raquel Z. *New York Ricans from the Hip Hop Zone*. New York: Palgrave Macmillan, 2003.

Rivera-Batiz, Francisco, and Carlos E. Santiago. *Island Paradox: Puerto Rico in the 1990s*. New York: Russell Sage Foundation, 1996.

Rivero, Ramón. *Por que se ríe la gente*. San Juan, Puerto Rico: Biblioteca de autores puertorriqueños, 1981.

Rivero, Yeidy. "The Performance and Reception of Televisual Ugliness in *Yo Soy Betty La Fea*." *Feminist Media Studies* 3, no. 1 (2003): 65–81.

Robertson, Roland. "Glocalization: Time-Space and Homogeneity-Heterogeneity." In *Global Modernities*, edited by Mike Featherstone, Scott Lash, and Roland Robertson, 25–44. Thousand Oaks, Calif.: Sage, 1995.

Robreno, Eduardo. *Historia del teatro popular cubano*. Vol. 74, *Cuadernos de historia habanera*. Havana: Oficina del Historiador de la Ciudad de la Habana, 1961.

Rodríguez, América. "Creating an Audience and Remapping a Nation: A Brief History of U.S. Spanish Language Broadcasting." *Quarterly Review of Film and Television* 16, nos. 3–4 (1999): 357–75.

Rodríguez, Clara, ed. *Latin Looks: Images of Latinas and Latinos in the U.S. Media*. Boulder, Colo.: Westview Press, 1997.

Rodríguez-Fraticelli, Carlos. "Pedro Albizu Campos: Strategies of Struggle and Strategic Struggles." *Centro* 4, no. 1 (1991–1992): 25–33.

Rodríguez-Morazzani, Roberto. "Puerto Rican Political Generations in New York: Pioneros, Young Turks, and Radicals." *Centro* 4, no. 1 (1992): 96–116.

———. "Beyond the Rainbow: Mapping the Discourse on Puerto Ricans and 'Race.'" *Centro* 8, nos. 1 and 2 (1996): 149–70.

Roediger, David R. *The Wages of Whiteness: Race and the Making of the American Working Class*. New York: Verso, 1991.

Rogin, Michael. *Blackface, White Noise: Jewish Immigrants in the Hollywood Melting Pot*. Los Angeles: University of California Press, 1996.

Rosa, William. "La 'Confederación de las antillas' y la novela caribeña del siglo XIX." *Caribbean Studies* 22, no. 3/4 (1989): 1–11.

Rose, Tricia. *Black Noise: Rap Music and Black Culture in Contemporary America*. London: Wesleyan University Press, 1994.

Salgado, Cesar. "Cubarican: efectos de la capilaridad colonial." Paper presented at the Second Cuban Research Institute Conference on Cuban and Cuban-American Studies, Miami, Florida, 1999.

Sánchez-González, Lisa. "Reclaiming Salsa." *Cultural Studies* 13, no. 2 (1999): 237–50.

———. *Boricua Literature: A Literary History of the Puerto Rican Diaspora*. New York: New York University Press, 2001.

Sánchez-Korrol, Virginia. *From Colonia to Community: The History of Puerto Ricans in New York City*. Los Angeles: University of California Press, 1994.

Santiago, Javier. *La nueva ola portoricensis*. San Juan, Puerto Rico: Editorial del patio, 1994.

Santiago-Valles, Kelvin. "Policing the Crisis in the Whitest of All the Antilles." *Centro* 8, nos. 1 and 2 (spring 1996): 42–57.

Schlesinger, Philip. "On National Identity: Some Conceptions and Misconceptions Criticized." *Social Science Information* 26, no. 2 (1987): 219–64.

———. " 'Identities: Traditions and New Communities': A Response." *Media, Culture, and Society* 24, no. 5 (2002): 643–48.

Scott, James C. *Domination and the Arts of Resistance: Hidden Transcripts*. New Haven: Yale University Press, 1991.

Serrano, Basilio. " 'Rifle, Cañón, y Escopeta': A Chronicle of the Puerto Rican Student Union." In *The Puerto Rican Movement: Voices from the Diaspora*, edited by Andrés Torres and José A. Velázquez, 125–43. Philadelphia: Temple University Press, 1998.

Shohat, Ella, and Robert Stam. *Unthinking Eurocentrism: Multiculturalism and the Media*. London: Routledge, 1994.

Silén, Juan Angel. *De la guerrilla cívica a la nación dividida*. Río Piedras, Puerto Rico: Ediciones Librería Internacional, 1972.

———. *Historia de la nación puertorriqueña*. Río Piedras, Puerto Rico: Editorial Edil, Inc., 1980.

Sinclair, John. *Latin American Television: A Global View*. Oxford: Oxford University Press, 1999.

———. "From Latin Americans to Latinos: Spanish-Language Television and Its Audiences." Paper presented at the Cultural Industries and Dialogue Between Civilizations in the Americas, Montreal, Canada, 2002.

———. " 'The Hollywood of Latin America': Miami as Regional Center in Television Trade." *Television and New Media* 4, no. 3 (2003): 211–29.

———. "The Globalization of Latin American Media." *NACLA* (March/April 2004): 1–6.

Smith-Shomade, Beretta E. *Shaded Lives: African American Women and Television*. New Brunswick, N.J.: Rutgers University Press, 2002.

Sollors, Werner. *Beyond Ethnicity: Consent and Descent in American Culture*. New York: Oxford University Press, 1986.

Sommer, Doris. *Foundational Fictions: The National Romances of Latin America*. Berkeley: University of California Press, 1991.

Spigel, Lynn. *Make Room for TV: Television and the Family Ideal in Postwar America*. Chicago: University of Chicago Press, 1992.

Stoke, Curtis. "Race and Revolution in Cuba." *Race and Reason* 3 (1996–1997): 55–61.

Straubhaar, Joseph. "Beyond Media Imperialism: Assymetrical Interdependence and Cultural Proximity." *Critical Studies in Mass Communication* 8 (1991): 39–59.

————. "Distinguishing the Global, Regional, and National Levels of World Television." In *Media in Global Context*, edited by Annabelle Sreberny-Mohammadi, Dwayne Winseck, Jim McKenna, and Oliver Boyd-Barrett, 284–98. London: Arnold, 1997.

————. "Cultural Capital, Media Choices, and Cultural Proximity in the Globalization of Television in Brazil." Paper presented at the Latin American Studies Association, Chicago, 1998.

Streeter, Thomas. *Selling the Air: A Critique of the Policy of Commercial Broadcasting in the United States*. Chicago: University of Chicago Press, 1996.

Subervi-Vélez, Federico, Charles Ramírez-Berg, Patricia Constantakis-Valdés, Chon Noriega, Diana Ríos, and Kenton T. Wilkinson. "Mass Communication and Hispanics." In *Handbook of Hispanic Cultures in the United States: Sociology*, edited by Félix Padilla, 304–57. Houston: Arte Público Press, 1994.

Subervi-Vélez, Federico, Nitza Hernández-López, and Arlene Frambes-Buxeda. "Mass Media in Puerto Rico." *Centro* 3, no. 1 (winter 1990–1991): 16–37.

Tajima, Renee. "Moving the Image: Asian American Independent Filmmaking, 1970–1990." In *Moving the Image: Asian Pacific American Media Arts*, edited by Russell Leong, 10–33. Los Angeles: UCLA Asian American Studies Center and Visual Communications, 1991.

Taylor, Diana. *The Archive and the Repertoire: Performing Cultural Memory in the Americas*. Durham, N.C.: Duke University Press, 2003.

Taylor, Ella. *Prime-Time Families: Television Culture in Postwar America*. Berkeley: University of California Press, 1989.

Tirado-Avilés, Amilcar. "La forja de un líder: Pedro Albizu Campos, 1924–1930." *Centro* 4, no. 1 (1991–1992): 13–23.

Torres, Arlene. "La Gran Familia Puertorriqueña 'Ej Prieta De Belda' (the Great Puerto Rican Family Is Really Black)." In *Blackness in Latin America and the Caribbean: Social Dynamics and Cultural Transformations*, edited by Arlene Torres and Norman E. Whitten, 285–306. Bloomington: Indiana University Press, 1998.

Torregrosa, José Luis. *Historia de la radio en Puerto Rico*. Hato Rey, Puerto Rico: Esmaco, 1993.

Torres-Saillant, Silvio. *Caribbean Poetics: Toward an Aesthetic of West Indian Literature*. Cambridge: Cambridge University Press, 1997.

Twine, France Winddance. *Racism in a Racial Democracy: The Maintenance of White Supremacy in Brazil*. New Brunswick, N.J.: Rutgers University Press, 1998.

Tyson, Timothy B. *Radio Free Dixie: Robert F. Williams and the Roots of Black Power*. Chapel Hill: University of North Carolina Press, 1999.

Venuti, Lawrence. "Translation, Community, and Utopia." In *The Translation Studies Reader*, edited by Venuti Lawrence, 468–509. London: Routledge, 2000.

Wade, Peter. "Race and Class: The Case of South American Blacks." *Ethnic and Racial Studies* 8, no. 2 (1985): 233–49.

———. *Race and Ethnicity in Latin America*. Chicago: Pluto Press, 1997.

———. *Music, Race, and Nation: Música Tropical in Colombia*. Chicago: University of Chicago Press, 2000.

Winant, Howard. *Racial Conditions: Politics, Theory, Comparisons*. Minneapolis: University of Minnesota Press, 1994.

———. *The World Is a Ghetto: Race and Democracy since World War II*. New York: Basic Books, 2001.

Woodard, Komozi. *A Nation within a Nation: Amiri Baraka (Leroi Jones) and Black Power Politics*. Chapel Hill: University of North Carolina Press, 1999.

Young Lords Party and Michael Abramson. *Palante: Young Lords Party*. New York: McGraw-Hill, 1971.

Yuval-Davis, Nira, and Floya Anthias. *Woman-Nation-State*. New York: St. Martin's Press, 1989.

Zenón-Cruz, Isabelo. *Narciso descubre su trasero*. Humacao, Puerto Rico: Furidi, 1975.

NEWSPAPERS AND OTHER MATERIALS

"100 Estrellas que iluminaron el siglo." *Teve Guía*, December 2000.

"Acabó de filmar la película 'Una gallega en la Habana.'" *El Mundo*, February 21, 1955.

"Actores cubanos no cruzan piquete." *Bohemia* (Cuba) 43, no. 45. November 18, 1951, 39.

"Agencia de publicidad entrena a sus expertos." *El Mundo*, March 26, 1954.

"A Gilda Haddock le gusta tanto el drama como la comedia." *Teve Guía*, November 3, 1973, 17–18.

"Alberto González trae malas intenciones." *Bohemia* (Puerto Rico), March 5–11, 1973, 20.

Alfaro, Annie. "Aquel tiempo del teatro Bufo." *El Nuevo Día*, July 2, 1989.

"Al llegar la televisión necesitará más asientos." *El Mundo*, March 26, 1954.

"Angela Meyer vs. Sylvia del Villard." *Teve Guía*, August 3, 1974, 14–16.

"Angela Meyer vs. Sylvia del Villard." *Teve Guía, Televita dice*, August 10, 1974, 27–28.

Aponte Gómez, Marjorie. "¿Y la risa tiene color?" *El Nuevo Día*, October 12, 2000.

Azizi, Enver. "Diplo." *El Mundo*, February 4, 1946.

Badillo, Samuel. "Miss Mundo y los tahúres." *El Nuevo Día*, November 26, 1975.

Barreto, Roberto. "Mamá Inés: The Next Generation." *Claridad*, January 9–15, 1998.

Beinin, Irving. "Students Strike in Puerto Rico." *Guardian*, May 4, 1968.

———. "Puerto Ricans Plan Centennial Action." *Guardian*, May 25, 1968.

———. "MPU Looks to Workers." *Guardian*, June 1, 1968.

Benítez, Luz Esther (Lucecita). Documents. Fundación Nacional para la Cultura Popular, San Juan, Puerto Rico.

" 'Black Power' ridiculiza los prejuicios raciales." *Vea*, November 25, 1973, 32–34.

Borges, Norma. "Diplo." *El Mundo*, May 18, 1985.

Braschi, Wilfredo. "Diplo filmará cinta con Catita en Cuba." *El Mundo*, December 4, 1954.

Brignoni, Bartolomé. "Cálido recibimiento para reina de belleza." *El Mundo*, November 27, 1975.

Brugueras, Melba. "TV Día." *El Nuevo Día*, November 15, 1998.

———. "Confesiones en un recorrido real." *El Vocero*, October 4, 2003.

Burgos, Jorge Luis. "Resucita 'Chianita.' " *El Vocero*, August 18, 2001.

———. "Alba Reyes Santos emocionada con su coronación." *El Vocero*, October 4, 2003.

Cangiano, Milly. "Primera Fila." *Primera Hora*, October 28, 2002.

"Captan en Cuba WKAQ Telemundo." *El Mundo*, September 13, 1954.

Carlo, Dario. "Diplo vuelve tras de filmar cinta." *El Mundo*, February 24, 1955.

"Carol Myles y Jay en Puerto Rico." *El Mundo*, July 29, 1973.

Carrasco, Olga. "Incesante fuga de talento boricua." *El Nuevo Día*, June 7, 1999.

Cervoni, Rubita. "Revista Jet y Ebony cubrirán 'El Flamboyán.' " *El Mundo*, October 14, 1973.

" 'Chianita' se casará con Hugo Leonel Vaccaro." *Vea*, July 9, 1973, 60–63.

Cintrón, Isabel. "El artista negro está muy limitado en Puerto Rico." *El Mundo*, November 9, 1975.

"Conciertos Roberta Flack, atractivos del Flamboyán." *El Mundo*, April 21, 1973.

"Confusion over the Puerto Rican Vote." *New York Times*, December 25, 1998.

Cordero, Sonia. "Televisión." *El Vocero*, September 11, 1994.

Cordero-Avila, Julio. "José Luis Torregrosa." *El Mundo*, May 6, 1973.

"Cuba y Puerto Rico Son . . ." *Bohemia* (Cuba) 43, no. 13, March 26, 1950, 54.

Cue-Sierra, Mayra. "Historias inéditas." *Cubarte*, September 11, 2003.

———. "Nace la telenovela de continuidad en América Latina." *Cubarte*, September 19, 2003.

———. "El derecho de nacer." *Cubarte*, September 25, 2003.

Cuevas, Clara. "Taller folklórico Afro-Boricua se inaugura en Viejo San Juan." *El Mundo*, May 14, 1968.

———. "Lucecita y Sammy en Telemundo." *El Mundo*, February 7, 1970.

Curet-Alonso, Tite. "¿Declaran la guerra a Lucecita Benítez?" *Vea*, October 15, 1972, 86–89.

———. "¿Qué cosa es ser cómico?" *Vea*, July 8, 1973, 28–31.

De Cardi, El Barón. "Mona Marti ejerce 'El derecho de nacer' de mamá Dolores." *El Mundo*, March 7, 1959.

De León, Hilario. "Buscan revivir personaje de Diplo." *El Nuevo Día*, January 17, 2000.

Del Villard, Sylvia. "Folklore afro-boricua." *El Mundo*, June 19, 1968.

"De nuevo a lo de antes." *El Nuevo Día*, October 23, 1972.

"Derrotan el 'Afro' de Lucecita." *Vea*, May 8, 1970, 46–47.

"Día de reyes por el canal 4." *El Mundo*, January 6, 1973.

Díaz-Alfaro, Abelardo. "Homenaje a Ramón Ortiz del Rivero." *El Reportero*,
August 24, 1981.

"Diplo y Pinito en la Habana." *El Mundo*, February 7, 1955.

"Ebony Fashion Fair Show en Puerto Rico." *El Nuevo Día*, December 13, 1977.

"El auge de la televisión sigue en marcha." *El Mundo*, November 15, 1954.

"El Gran Show Libby's irá al aire por radio y televisión." *El Mundo*, March 26, 1954.

"El hijo de Angela María." *Teve Guía*, August 25, 1973, 84–88.

"El personaje de Angela Meyer da nota pintoresca a El hijo de Angela María." *Teve
Guía*, May 26, 1973, 42–43.

"El prejuicio racial en el lenguaje popular." *El Nuevo Día*, October 8, 2000.

Elwood-Licha, Rissig. "Exhausta, mareada y feliz." *El Nuevo Día*, November 27, 1975.

"Encuesta Mediafax." *Primera Hora*, October 16, 2002.

"Escogen mulata entre dos mil bellezas para competir en Inglaterra." *Teve Guía*,
July 3, 1975, 11.

"Esther Palés se enamoró de El hijo de Angela María." *Teve Guía*, February 24, 1973,
72–75.

Fears, Darryl. "Race Divides Hispanics, Report Says; Integration and Income Vary
with Skin Color." *Washington Post*, July 14, 2003.

Fernández-Miralles, Elsa. "Mona Marti hará un papel de negra por tercera vez." *Vea*,
February 25, 1973, 74–76.

———. "Soul Train." *Vea*, April 21, 1974, 10–12.

———. "70 Millones de personas ven Soul Train." *Vea*, July 8, 1974, 78–81.

———. "Chianita vuelve con sus descargas." *El Nuevo Día*, February 10, 1981.

Felices, Jorge. "Homenaje esta noche a la farándula bohemia." *El Mundo*,
December 26, 1943.

Ferrer, Melba. "Emancipation Fails to Abolish Racism." *San Juan Star*, March 22, 1997.

Franco, Rafael. "A Baby's Factory?" *San Juan Star*, April 23, 1998.

Fried, Joseph P. "East Harlem Youths Explain Garbage-Dumping Demonstration."
New York Times, August 19, 1969.

Frontera, Iván. "Don Cornelius visita Soul Train en P.R." *Teve Guia*, April 27, 1974,
72–75.

García, C. J. "El regalo de Tito." *El Nuevo Día*, October 3, 1999.

García, Pepo. "Alerta contra el discrimen racial." *El Nuevo Día*, January 17, 2000.

García-Cuevas, Eugenio. "Opinan los letrados." *El Nuevo Día*, October 8, 2000.

García Ramis, Magali. "La transformación de Lucecita." *Avance*, August 6, 1973, 21–25.

Goyco-Carmoega, Rosario. "Afirman no hay discriminación racial en TV isla." *El Mundo*, August 5, 1971.

"Gran programa musical se inicia mañana en Telemundo." *El Mundo*, November 29, 1954.

Hull, Harold. "Cuba marcha al frente de América Latina en TV." *El Mundo*, February 12, 1954.

Huyke, Emilio. "El gobierno no atiende el folklore afroboricua." *Vea*, June 6, 1976, 32–35.

———. "Sorprenden a su maestro . . . después de 20 años." *Vea*, September 12, 1976, 66–68.

———. "Gladys Rodríguez crea una familia con Tommy Muñiz." *Vea*, September 19, 1976, 30–32.

"India presenta nuevo programa." *El Mundo*, August 2, 1954.

"Jackson 5 y Don Cornelius." *El Mundo*, March 7, 1975.

Jamison, Todd Michael. "Blacks Break P.R. Television Comedy Barrier." *San Juan Star*, September 19, 1994.

"La historia de Diplo, favorito de los soldados portorriqueños." *El Mundo*, October 10, 1944.

Lama Bonilla, Rafael. "Metamorfosis en Telemundo de Puerto Rico." *El Nuevo Día*, May 10, 1999.

———. "Racismo publicitario." *El Nuevo Día*, October 13, 2000.

"La taberna despide hoy a Calderón." *El Mundo*, January 17, 1955.

"La WKAQ-TV sigue los pasos de la WKAQ." *El Mundo*, March 26, 1954.

"Lo cubano en las ondas." *Bohemia* (Cuba) 43, no. 27, May 27, 1951, 52.

López-Llano, Jorge. "Hay discrimen en el hablar." *El Reportero*, June 16, 1982.

———. "Racismo a todos los niveles." *El Reportero*, June 17, 1982.

———. "Doloroso discrimen en novelas." *El Reportero*, July 2, 1982.

———. "Silvia arremete contra el prejuicio." *El Reportero*, July 6, 1982.

López-Rodríguez, Ana Enid. "Plagado de desaciertos el certamen de belleza." *El Nuevo Día*, October 4, 2003.

"Lucecita." *San Juan Weekly*, October 3, 1970.

"Lucecita explica por que estuvo retirada por un año." *Vea*, August 12, 1973, 48–49.

"Lucecita no quiere quitarse el afro." *Teve Guía*, June 13, 1970, 13–16.

"Machuchal regresa a la TV." *Teve Guía*, March 10, 1973, 85–86.

"Malín." *Angela Luisa*, February 1973, 87.

"Malín Falú." *Angela Luisa*, October 1973, 73.

"Mañana cantará guajiras el trovador Portabales." *El Mundo*, January 31, 1955.

"Mapy y Fernando Cortés actuarán por Telemundo." *El Mundo*, March 26, 1954.

Marrero, Rubén. "Hay que 'tirar' la cosa en broma." *Vea*, January 11, 1976, 38–39.

———. "Su error fue abrir los ojos demasiado." *Vea*, August 15, 1976, 66–68.

Marrero-Rodríguez, Rosalina. "Los Seijo Díaz queda fuera de la programación de Telemundo." *Primera Hora*, October 30, 2002.

———. "Diversidad de físicos en Miss Puerto Rico Universe 2004." *Primera Hora*, September 2, 2003.

———. "Alba Reyes se sorprendió al ganar la corona." *Primera Hora*, October 4, 2003.

———. "Un evento de cuatro reinas." *Primera Hora*, October 4, 2003.

Martínez, Belén M. "Angela Meyer lleva a Chanita al disco." *Teve Guía*, August 31, 1974, 10–12.

———. "Sylvia del Villard dice 'o comemos todos o no come nadie.'" *Teve Guía*, August 31, 1974, 14–16.

Mathews, J. B. "Communist Role in Assassination Plot." In J. B. Mathews Papers, n.d. Box 470. Duke University, Durham, North Carolina.

———. "Pueblos Hispanos." In J. B. Mathews Papers, 1943. Box 470. Duke University, Durham, North Carolina.

Matilla, Alfredo. "La buena risa." *El Mundo*, May 14, 1950.

Merino-Méndez, Ruth. "'Un hombre, un comediante y una época': Filman trayectoria artística de Diplo." *El Mundo*, July 21, 1975.

Meyners, José Arnaldo. "Diplo: una personalidad artística en ascenso." *El Mundo*, July 1, 1945.

"Mona Marti es negra Balbina en la novela Sierra Negra." *El Mundo*, July 16, 1950.

"Mona Marti retorna a El derecho de nacer." *Teve Guía*, June 9, 1973, 10–11.

Montero, Mayra. "Suizos." *El Nuevo Día*, May 6, 2001.

"Noticias." *El Mundo*, November 18, 1950.

"Nunca pensó que llegaría a interpretar a 'Diplo.'" *Vea*, November 3, 1974, 52–53.

Olán, María O. "Malín Falú: La música no tiene color." *El Mundo*, August 26, 1973.

———. "No estoy en contra de nada, ni de nadie . . . sino a favor de algo." *El Mundo*, September 9, 1973.

Piñero Vega, Nancy. "Dinga y mandinga televisiva." *El Nuevo Día*, October 13, 2000.

"PIP rinde homenaje póstumo actor Diplo." *El Imparcial*, August 28, 1956.

"Presentarán programa música Salsa en TV." *El Mundo*, October 7, 1973.

Previdi, Mario. "Lucecita impone el 'African Look.'" *Teve Guía*, June 13, 1970.

"Programa piloto." *El Nuevo Día*, March 26, 1973.

Quiñones-Torres, Damarys. "Cero lágrimas." *Vea*, July 13, 2003.

"Reconocen labor de Diplo." *El Mundo*, November 15, 1954.

Rexach, Victor R. "Chianita recarga para la carga." *El Reportero*, February 11, 1981.

Rey, Raquel. "Sylvia del Villard ataca a los 'negros pintados.'" *Teve Guía*, May 13, 1973, 74–76.

———. " 'Para una actriz verdadera no hay papeles secundarios' dice Angela Meyer."
    Teve Guía, May 26, 1973, 16–18.

Reyes-Vargas, Patricia. "Diplo, un gran actor y un gran corazón." *El Imparcial*,
    September 1, 1956.

Reyes-Vargas, Patricia, and Harold Lidin. "50,000 asisten a entierro de Diplo."
    El Imparcial, August 27, 1956.

———. "Estudiantes denuncian racismo en la UPR." *El Imparcial*, March 29, 1965.

Ríos, Belén. " 'Chianita' nació por casualidad." *Vea*, July 8, 1973, 67–69.

———. " 'Mamá Dolores' no se parece a 'Panchita.' " *Vea*, July 8, 1973, 70–72.

Rivas, Lillian. "Diplo y su risa en nuestra memoria." *El Mundo*, May 27, 1990.

Rivera, Manuel Ernesto. "Sin estadísticas para medir el discrimen racial." *El Nuevo
    Día*, December 18, 2001.

Rivera-Esquilín, Eileen. "Judith Pizarro . . . entre el drama y la comedia." *El Vocero*,
    December 17, 1997.

———. "Bizcocho decide no volver a Telemundo." *Primera Hora*, January 31, 2003.

Rodríguez, Kelvin. "¿Racismo en los certámenes?" *El Nuevo Día*, January 15, 1997.

Rodríguez, Nydita S. "Alrededor del mundo con Miss Mundo." *El Nuevo Día*,
    October 19, 1976.

Rodríguez-Burns, Francisco. "Afro que escondemos." *Primera Hora*, January 21, 2002.

Rojas-Daporta, Malén. "Diplo es productor de películas cortas." *El Mundo*,
    November 12, 1955.

Rojas-Daporta, Malén, and Juan Manuel-Ocasio. "Millares asisten al sepelio."
    El Mundo, August 27, 1956.

Rosell, Rosendo. *Diario las Américas*, May 24, 1973.

Routté-Gómez, Eneid. "El Negro: El blanco del racismo." *El Nuevo Día*, October 13,
    2000.

Saéz, Mike. "El Negrito Doroteo." *Teve Guía*, January 13, 1973, 74–75.

Santana, Mario. "Oculto en el clóset el prejuicio racial." *El Nuevo Día*, March 23, 1998.

———. "Racismo que se ve y se siente cada día." *El Nuevo Día*, March 24, 1998.

Santiago, Javier. "La historia detrás de un afro." *El Nuevo Día*, October 15, 2000.

Santiago-Vidal, Migdalia. "¿Qué esconde Angela Meyer detrás de Chianita?" *El
    Mundo*, March 10, 1985.

———. "Carmen Belén Richardson." *El Mundo*, August 4, 1985.

Santos-Febres, Mayra. "Por cientos contranatura." *El Nuevo Día*, May 6, 2001.

Sepúlveda-Morales, Aixa. "Miss Puerto Rico Universe borra sus marcas en 15
    minutos." *Primera Hora*, February 25, 2004.

Shokooh-Valle, Firuzeh, Karol Joselyn Sepúlveda, and Aixa Sepúlveda Morales.
    "Supremacía de 'Gata salvaje' provoca reclamo de productores." *Primera Hora*,
    October 16, 2002.

Silva-Casanova, Manuel. "Yo tengo un amigo negro." *Avance*, May 14, 1973, 55–58.

Silvestry de Basaldua, Lydia Mercedes. "Los apostadores vs. Wilnelia." *El Nuevo Día*, November 24, 1975.

"Stokely's Castroite Links." *Human Events*, March 18, 1967.

Tavárez, William. "Se define como ejemplo vivo de la liberación femenina." *El Caribe*, May 9, 1973.

"Televisión." *Bohemia* (Cuba) 42, no. 15, April 9, 1950, 56.

"Televisión en 1950." *Bohemia* (Cuba) 42, no. 21, May 21, 1950, 92.

"Televisión en octubre." *Bohemia* (Cuba) 42, no. 13, March 26, 1950, 53.

"Todos tenemos algún color: Mona Martí." *Bohemia* (Puerto Rico), June 18–24, 1973, 43.

Torregrosa, Angela Luisa. "Miss Mundo 1976." *Angela Luisa*, January 1976, 16–17.

———. "Teve cuñas." *El Nuevo Día*, September 11, 1994.

Torres-Torres, Jaime. "¿Dónde está el negrito bembón?" *El Nuevo Día*, October 8, 2000.

Ullman, Constance. "Puerto Ricans Mark 100-Years Fight for Freedom." *Guardian*, October 5, 1968.

"UPAGRA Protests Outsourcing Effort." *Newspaper Guild*, February 27, 2004.

Vargas, Patricia. "Majestad negra." *El Nuevo Día*, October 10, 2000.

———. "Primer encuentro con la soberana." *El Nuevo Día*, October 4, 2003.

Vásquez, Sucre. "De su pueblo con amor." *El Nuevo Día*, November 27, 1975.

Vega, Ana Lydia. "La felicidad, ja, ja, ja, ja y la universidad." *El Mundo*, September 23, 1990.

Vega, Brenda S. "Música 'Soul' tiene seguidores en la isla." *El Mundo*, July 20, 1973.

Vergara, Francisco. "Chianita es más boricua que el maví." *El Nuevo Día*, November 20, 1974.

Villar, Gloria. "'Diplo' debutará en Nueva York el día 21." *El Mundo*, November 9, 1947.

———. "Mano Meco el de las carcajadas y Rivera Pérez el serio." *El Mundo*, February 4, 1951.

———. "El hijo de Angela María." *Teve Guía*, August 25, 1973, 84–88.

"Vote por su candidato." *El Mundo*, February 5, 1951.

"WAPA-TV inauguró sus transmisiones." *El Mundo*, May 3, 1954.

"What's New Around the Union This Week." *Communication Workers of America*, January 28, 2004.

"WKAQ-TV comenzará transmisiones." *El Mundo*, February 12, 1954.

"Y amigos, esta es mamá Dolores." *El Mundo*, July 26, 1949.

Yglesias, José. "Right on with the Young Lords." *New York Times*, June 7, 1970.

Zervigón, Pedro. "Sylvia del Villard y la dignidad de su negritud." *El Nuevo Día*, February 9, 1990.

PLAYS, SCRIPTS, RECORDINGS, AND AUDIOVISUAL MATERIALS

Cabrera, Pablo. *La verdadera historia de Pedro Navaja*. Play. 1980.

Chianita de parranda. Produced by Tomás Figueroa and Quality Sound Inc., 1974. Record.

Diplo. Produced by WIPR, 1980. Television special.

Diplo y su tremendo hotel. Produced by Fundación Ramón Rivero, 2000. Compact disc.

El hijo de Angela María. Produced by Telemundo-WKAQ, 1973. Television show.

Los suegros. Produced by Producciones Ayax, 1984. Television show.

Lucecita Benítez en vivo desde el Carnegie Hall. Produced by BMG Entertainment, 2000. Compact disc.

Mi familia. Produced by Paquito Cordero Teleproducciones, 1994–1999. Television show.

Montero, Manuel. *Los suegros*. Television Scripts. 1981–1991.

———. *Los suegros y los nietos*. Television Scripts. 1983–1988.

———. *Altagracia, empleada doméstica*. Television Scripts. N.d.

Raza pura. Produced by Tomás Figueroa and Quality Sound Inc., 1973. Record.

Rivero, Ramón. *La vida en broma*. Radio Scripts. 1943–1945.

———. *Hay que defenderse*. Play. 1945.

———. *El tremendo hotel*. Radio Scripts. 1948–1956.

———. *El tremendo hotel*. Play. 1950.

———. *La taberna India*. Television Scripts. 1954–1955.

San Pedro, Felipe. *Mi familia*. Television Scripts. 1994–1999.

Telemundo: 40 años de recuerdos. Produced by Tony Mojena, 1994. Television special.

Index

Yeidy M. Rivero is an
assistant professor in the
Department of Communication
and Culture at Indiana University,
Bloomington.

Library of Congress
Cataloging-in-Publication Data
Rivero, Yeidy M.
Tuning out blackness : race and nation in the
history of Puerto Rican television / Yeidy M.
Rivero.
p. cm. — (Console-ing passions)
Includes bibliographical references and index.
ISBN 0-8223-3531-X (cloth : alk. paper) —
ISBN 0-8223-3543-3 (pbk. : alk. paper)
1. Television broadcasting—Puerto Rico—
History. 2. Blacks on television. I. Title.
II. Series.
PN1992.3.P9R58 2005
791.45′65289607295—dc22
2004029835